Available in Print & eBo
visit thetutorverse.co

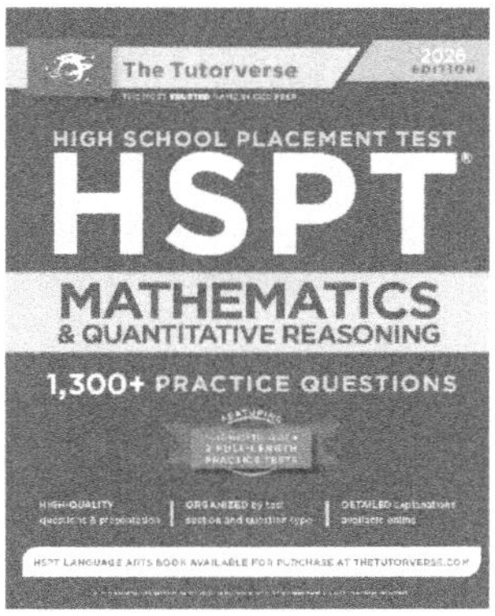

View or Download Answer Explanations
at thetutorverse.com/books

Table of Contents

Middle Level ISEE®
1000+ Practice Questions

Welcome

Dear Students, Parents, and Educators,

Like any other skill, proficiency in taking standardized tests – like the Middle Level ISEE – is learned through practice. Though test-taking tips and tricks are useful in their own way, they are no substitute for a strong foundation of core learning and an in-depth command of the subject-matter.

In order to help students achieve their very best, this workbook contains over 1,000 practice questions – more questions than 6 actual exams! We've identified core concepts that are critical for success and crafted questions to help build competency and confidence in these areas. The questions in this workbook have been refined in part based on the work our tutors have done preparing students for the Middle Level ISEE. They build on fundamentals and grow progressively more challenging to help even the most advanced students reach their potential. In addition, detailed answer explanations for every question are available for free online at www.thetutorverse.com/.

Online and computer-based testing is more prevalent than ever. Because of this, and due to the overwhelming demand for even more ISEE content, we've launched our ISEE Digital platform on https://thetutorverse.com/digital/. As of this book's publication, students, parents, and educators can access over thousands of additional practice questions from their internet-connected devices.

This year, we've added bonus mixed practice question sets covering each math topic area to help students lock in all the good learning they've gained while studying. Once you finish reviewing each topic (like Numbers & Operations or Measurements & Geometry), quiz yourself with the corresponding mixed practice question set before moving on to the next topic!

The goal of this workbook is to provide students with enough high-quality practice materials to supplement any study regimen. Whether students use this workbook for independent study or with a professional tutor or teacher, we believe that the practice will benefit students both on the Middle Level ISEE and beyond.

Best wishes, good luck, and welcome to The Tutorverse!

Regards,

The Team at The Tutorverse

How to Use This Book

Overview

The purpose of this workbook is to provide students, parents, and educators with plentiful and high-quality practice materials that are relevant to the Middle Level ISEE. Though this workbook includes information with respect to the test's structure and content – and includes tips, suggestions, and strategies, as well – the primary goal of this workbook is to provide copious practice and to introduce new words, concepts, and skills.

Organization

This workbook is organized into six main sections. Each section is designed to accomplish different objectives. These sections and objectives are as follows:

- Diagnostic Practice Test (Form A)
  This section is designed to help students identify topics requiring the most practice. The diagnostic test is the same length as the actual Middle Level ISEE. The diagnostic test covers many of the major topics that can be found on the Middle Level ISEE, and should be used as a gauge to estimate the amount of additional practice needed on each topic.

- Verbal Reasoning
  Verbal Reasoning is the first of four practice sections in this workbook. This section provides practice for synonym and sentence completion questions found on the first section of the Middle Level ISEE. Questions in this section are further divided by difficulty level.

- Reading Comprehension
  This section is the second of four practice sections in this workbook and includes passages and questions that assess many of the skills tested on the Middle Level ISEE. The reading passages cover a wide range of passage types and topics that might be encountered on the actual exam. Similarly, the questions included are designed to give students practice with each of the several question types on the exam.

- Quantitative Reasoning & Mathematics Achievement
  This is the third of four practice sections. There are many subject-matter topics in this section, which are organized as indicated in the table of contents, and progress in difficulty. We've also included mixed practice question sets to help you review each topic area prior to taking the final practice tests!

- The Essay
  The final practice section of this workbook, The Essay provides information about the writing prompts on the actual exam and includes several practice prompts.

- Final Practice Test (Form B)
  The final practice test helps to familiarize students with the format, organization, and time allotments on the Middle Level ISEE. This test should be taken once students have completed the diagnostic test and have spent sufficient time answering the appropriate questions in the practice sections.

At the beginning of each of the above listed sections are detailed instructions. Students should carefully review these instructions, as they contain important information about the actual exam and how best to practice.

Strategy

Every student has different strengths and abilities. We don't think there is any one strategy that will help every student ace the exam. Instead, we believe there are core principles to keep in mind when preparing for the Middle Level ISEE. These principles are interrelated and cyclical in nature.

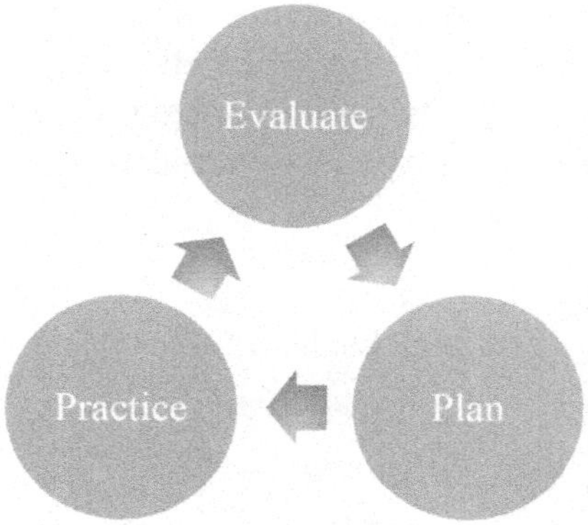

- Evaluate
  A critical step in developing a solid study plan is to have a clear idea of how to spend your time. What subjects are more difficult for you? Which types of questions do you frequently answer incorrectly? Why? These and many other questions should be answered before developing any study plan. The diagnostic test is just one way to help you evaluate your abilities.

- Plan
  Once you've taken stock of your strengths and abilities, focus on actions. How much time do you have before the test? How many areas do you need to work on during that time? Which areas do you need to work on? How many questions (and of which type) do you need to do each day, or each week? The answers to these and other questions will help you determine your study and practice plan.

- Practice
  Once you settle on a plan, try to stick with it as much as you can. To study successfully requires discipline, commitment, and focus. Try turning off your phone, TV, tablet, or other distractions. Not only will you learn more effectively when you're focused, but you may find that you finish your work more quickly, as well.

- Reevaluate
  Because learning and studying is an ongoing process, it is important to take stock of your improvements along the way. This will help you see how you are progressing and allow you to make adjustments to your plan. The practice test at the end of this workbook is designed to help you gauge your progress.

Help

Preparing for a standardized test such as the Middle Level ISEE can be a difficult and trying time. In addition to challenging material, preparing for a standardized test can often feel like an extra responsibility. For these reasons, it's important to recognize when students need extra help.

Because the Middle Level ISEE is administered to students across different grade levels, some students may find material in this workbook to be difficult or entirely new. This is normal and to be expected, as certain material included in this workbook may not yet have been taught to some students. For example, 6th graders may not yet have learned some of the concepts taught to 7th graders.

Though students will only be scored against other students in their grade (6th graders vs. other 6th graders; 7th graders vs. other 7th graders), mastering advanced materials can often provide a competitive advantage in achieving higher scores. This workbook includes such materials.

In addition to detailed answer explanations, which are available online at www.thetutorverse.com (be sure to ask an adult before going online), we encourage students to reach out to trusted educators to help prepare for the Middle Level ISEE. Strong tutors, teachers, mentors, and consultants can help students with many aspects of preparation – from evaluating and reevaluating needs, to creating an effective plan, to helping make the most of students' practice.

Diagnostic Practice Test (Form A)

Overview

The first step in an effective study plan is to know your strengths and areas for improvement.

This diagnostic test assesses your mastery of certain skills and concepts that you may see on the actual exam.

The primary difference between this diagnostic test and the actual exam is in the scoring. Students will receive a stanine score on the actual exam. This score is determined based on that student's performance as compared with all other students who have taken that particular exam (for a given grade level). This diagnostic test does not result in a stanine score, and is intended to be used to gauge your mastery over skills and concepts, *not* as a gauge of how you will score on the test.

Lastly, note that a number of questions on the actual test will not be scored, as they are included for research purposes only. However, students will not know which questions on the actual test will not be scored. For practice purposes, this diagnostic test includes the same number of questions as the actual test, including the number of questions that will not be scored. This gives students a more realistic experience in terms of test taking.

Format

The format of the diagnostic test is similar to that of the actual test. The diagnostic includes the following sections:

Diagnostic Test Section	Questions	Time Limit
Verbal Reasoning	40	20 minutes
Quantitative Reasoning	37	35 minutes
Break #1	N/A	5 minutes
Reading Comprehension	36	35 minutes
Mathematics Achievement	47	40 minutes
Break #2	N/A	5 minutes
Essay Prompt	1	30 minutes
Total	**161**	**170 minutes**

Answering

Use the answer sheet provided on the next several pages to record your answers. You may wish to tear these pages out of the workbook.

Diagnostic Test Answer Sheet

Section 1: Verbal Reasoning

1. Ⓐ Ⓑ Ⓒ Ⓓ
2. Ⓐ Ⓑ Ⓒ Ⓓ
3. Ⓐ Ⓑ Ⓒ Ⓓ
4. Ⓐ Ⓑ Ⓒ Ⓓ
5. Ⓐ Ⓑ Ⓒ Ⓓ
6. Ⓐ Ⓑ Ⓒ Ⓓ
7. Ⓐ Ⓑ Ⓒ Ⓓ
8. Ⓐ Ⓑ Ⓒ Ⓓ
9. Ⓐ Ⓑ Ⓒ Ⓓ
10. Ⓐ Ⓑ Ⓒ Ⓓ
11. Ⓐ Ⓑ Ⓒ Ⓓ
12. Ⓐ Ⓑ Ⓒ Ⓓ
13. Ⓐ Ⓑ Ⓒ Ⓓ
14. Ⓐ Ⓑ Ⓒ Ⓓ
15. Ⓐ Ⓑ Ⓒ Ⓓ
16. Ⓐ Ⓑ Ⓒ Ⓓ
17. Ⓐ Ⓑ Ⓒ Ⓓ
18. Ⓐ Ⓑ Ⓒ Ⓓ
19. Ⓐ Ⓑ Ⓒ Ⓓ
20. Ⓐ Ⓑ Ⓒ Ⓓ
21. Ⓐ Ⓑ Ⓒ Ⓓ
22. Ⓐ Ⓑ Ⓒ Ⓓ
23. Ⓐ Ⓑ Ⓒ Ⓓ
24. Ⓐ Ⓑ Ⓒ Ⓓ
25. Ⓐ Ⓑ Ⓒ Ⓓ
26. Ⓐ Ⓑ Ⓒ Ⓓ
27. Ⓐ Ⓑ Ⓒ Ⓓ
28. Ⓐ Ⓑ Ⓒ Ⓓ
29. Ⓐ Ⓑ Ⓒ Ⓓ
30. Ⓐ Ⓑ Ⓒ Ⓓ
31. Ⓐ Ⓑ Ⓒ Ⓓ
32. Ⓐ Ⓑ Ⓒ Ⓓ
33. Ⓐ Ⓑ Ⓒ Ⓓ
34. Ⓐ Ⓑ Ⓒ Ⓓ
35. Ⓐ Ⓑ Ⓒ Ⓓ
36. Ⓐ Ⓑ Ⓒ Ⓓ
37. Ⓐ Ⓑ Ⓒ Ⓓ
38. Ⓐ Ⓑ Ⓒ Ⓓ
39. Ⓐ Ⓑ Ⓒ Ⓓ
40. Ⓐ Ⓑ Ⓒ Ⓓ

Section 2: Quantitative Reasoning

1. Ⓐ Ⓑ Ⓒ Ⓓ
2. Ⓐ Ⓑ Ⓒ Ⓓ
3. Ⓐ Ⓑ Ⓒ Ⓓ
4. Ⓐ Ⓑ Ⓒ Ⓓ
5. Ⓐ Ⓑ Ⓒ Ⓓ
6. Ⓐ Ⓑ Ⓒ Ⓓ
7. Ⓐ Ⓑ Ⓒ Ⓓ
8. Ⓐ Ⓑ Ⓒ Ⓓ
9. Ⓐ Ⓑ Ⓒ Ⓓ
10. Ⓐ Ⓑ Ⓒ Ⓓ
11. Ⓐ Ⓑ Ⓒ Ⓓ
12. Ⓐ Ⓑ Ⓒ Ⓓ
13. Ⓐ Ⓑ Ⓒ Ⓓ
14. Ⓐ Ⓑ Ⓒ Ⓓ
15. Ⓐ Ⓑ Ⓒ Ⓓ
16. Ⓐ Ⓑ Ⓒ Ⓓ
17. Ⓐ Ⓑ Ⓒ Ⓓ
18. Ⓐ Ⓑ Ⓒ Ⓓ
19. Ⓐ Ⓑ Ⓒ Ⓓ
20. Ⓐ Ⓑ Ⓒ Ⓓ
21. Ⓐ Ⓑ Ⓒ Ⓓ
22. Ⓐ Ⓑ Ⓒ Ⓓ
23. Ⓐ Ⓑ Ⓒ Ⓓ
24. Ⓐ Ⓑ Ⓒ Ⓓ
25. Ⓐ Ⓑ Ⓒ Ⓓ
26. Ⓐ Ⓑ Ⓒ Ⓓ
27. Ⓐ Ⓑ Ⓒ Ⓓ
28. Ⓐ Ⓑ Ⓒ Ⓓ
29. Ⓐ Ⓑ Ⓒ Ⓓ
30. Ⓐ Ⓑ Ⓒ Ⓓ
31. Ⓐ Ⓑ Ⓒ Ⓓ
32. Ⓐ Ⓑ Ⓒ Ⓓ
33. Ⓐ Ⓑ Ⓒ Ⓓ
34. Ⓐ Ⓑ Ⓒ Ⓓ
35. Ⓐ Ⓑ Ⓒ Ⓓ
36. Ⓐ Ⓑ Ⓒ Ⓓ
37. Ⓐ Ⓑ Ⓒ Ⓓ

Section 3: Reading Comprehension

1. Ⓐ Ⓑ Ⓒ Ⓓ
2. Ⓐ Ⓑ Ⓒ Ⓓ
3. Ⓐ Ⓑ Ⓒ Ⓓ
4. Ⓐ Ⓑ Ⓒ Ⓓ
5. Ⓐ Ⓑ Ⓒ Ⓓ
6. Ⓐ Ⓑ Ⓒ Ⓓ
7. Ⓐ Ⓑ Ⓒ Ⓓ
8. Ⓐ Ⓑ Ⓒ Ⓓ
9. Ⓐ Ⓑ Ⓒ Ⓓ
10. Ⓐ Ⓑ Ⓒ Ⓓ
11. Ⓐ Ⓑ Ⓒ Ⓓ
12. Ⓐ Ⓑ Ⓒ Ⓓ
13. Ⓐ Ⓑ Ⓒ Ⓓ
14. Ⓐ Ⓑ Ⓒ Ⓓ
15. Ⓐ Ⓑ Ⓒ Ⓓ
16. Ⓐ Ⓑ Ⓒ Ⓓ
17. Ⓐ Ⓑ Ⓒ Ⓓ
18. Ⓐ Ⓑ Ⓒ Ⓓ
19. Ⓐ Ⓑ Ⓒ Ⓓ
20. Ⓐ Ⓑ Ⓒ Ⓓ
21. Ⓐ Ⓑ Ⓒ Ⓓ
22. Ⓐ Ⓑ Ⓒ Ⓓ
23. Ⓐ Ⓑ Ⓒ Ⓓ
24. Ⓐ Ⓑ Ⓒ Ⓓ
25. Ⓐ Ⓑ Ⓒ Ⓓ
26. Ⓐ Ⓑ Ⓒ Ⓓ
27. Ⓐ Ⓑ Ⓒ Ⓓ
28. Ⓐ Ⓑ Ⓒ Ⓓ
29. Ⓐ Ⓑ Ⓒ Ⓓ
30. Ⓐ Ⓑ Ⓒ Ⓓ
31. Ⓐ Ⓑ Ⓒ Ⓓ
32. Ⓐ Ⓑ Ⓒ Ⓓ
33. Ⓐ Ⓑ Ⓒ Ⓓ
34. Ⓐ Ⓑ Ⓒ Ⓓ
35. Ⓐ Ⓑ Ⓒ Ⓓ
36. Ⓐ Ⓑ Ⓒ Ⓓ

Section 4: Mathematics Achievement

1. Ⓐ Ⓑ Ⓒ Ⓓ
2. Ⓐ Ⓑ Ⓒ Ⓓ
3. Ⓐ Ⓑ Ⓒ Ⓓ
4. Ⓐ Ⓑ Ⓒ Ⓓ
5. Ⓐ Ⓑ Ⓒ Ⓓ
6. Ⓐ Ⓑ Ⓒ Ⓓ
7. Ⓐ Ⓑ Ⓒ Ⓓ
8. Ⓐ Ⓑ Ⓒ Ⓓ
9. Ⓐ Ⓑ Ⓒ Ⓓ
10. Ⓐ Ⓑ Ⓒ Ⓓ
11. Ⓐ Ⓑ Ⓒ Ⓓ
12. Ⓐ Ⓑ Ⓒ Ⓓ
13. Ⓐ Ⓑ Ⓒ Ⓓ
14. Ⓐ Ⓑ Ⓒ Ⓓ
15. Ⓐ Ⓑ Ⓒ Ⓓ
16. Ⓐ Ⓑ Ⓒ Ⓓ
17. Ⓐ Ⓑ Ⓒ Ⓓ
18. Ⓐ Ⓑ Ⓒ Ⓓ
19. Ⓐ Ⓑ Ⓒ Ⓓ
20. Ⓐ Ⓑ Ⓒ Ⓓ
21. Ⓐ Ⓑ Ⓒ Ⓓ
22. Ⓐ Ⓑ Ⓒ Ⓓ
23. Ⓐ Ⓑ Ⓒ Ⓓ
24. Ⓐ Ⓑ Ⓒ Ⓓ
25. Ⓐ Ⓑ Ⓒ Ⓓ
26. Ⓐ Ⓑ Ⓒ Ⓓ
27. Ⓐ Ⓑ Ⓒ Ⓓ
28. Ⓐ Ⓑ Ⓒ Ⓓ
29. Ⓐ Ⓑ Ⓒ Ⓓ
30. Ⓐ Ⓑ Ⓒ Ⓓ
31. Ⓐ Ⓑ Ⓒ Ⓓ
32. Ⓐ Ⓑ Ⓒ Ⓓ
33. Ⓐ Ⓑ Ⓒ Ⓓ
34. Ⓐ Ⓑ Ⓒ Ⓓ
35. Ⓐ Ⓑ Ⓒ Ⓓ
36. Ⓐ Ⓑ Ⓒ Ⓓ
37. Ⓐ Ⓑ Ⓒ Ⓓ
38. Ⓐ Ⓑ Ⓒ Ⓓ
39. Ⓐ Ⓑ Ⓒ Ⓓ
40. Ⓐ Ⓑ Ⓒ Ⓓ
41. Ⓐ Ⓑ Ⓒ Ⓓ
42. Ⓐ Ⓑ Ⓒ Ⓓ
43. Ⓐ Ⓑ Ⓒ Ⓓ
44. Ⓐ Ⓑ Ⓒ Ⓓ
45. Ⓐ Ⓑ Ⓒ Ⓓ
46. Ⓐ Ⓑ Ⓒ Ⓓ
47. Ⓐ Ⓑ Ⓒ Ⓓ

Section 5: Essay

Section One: Verbal Reasoning (Part One – Synonyms)

Questions: 40

Time Limit: 20 minutes

Directions: Select the word that is most nearly the same in meaning as the word in capital letters. You have 20 minutes to complete part one AND part two.

1. PRIMARY:

(A) eventful
(B) main
(C) minor
(D) petty

2. LOFTY:

(A) basic
(B) grand
(C) heavy
(D) independent

3. SOLITARY:

(A) enjoyable
(B) firm
(C) isolated
(D) weak

4. ACCUMULATE:

(A) adjust
(B) explain
(C) gather
(D) tolerate

5. CONDEMN:

(A) beg
(B) denounce
(C) imprison
(D) reduce

6. ADEQUATE:

(A) contradictory
(B) enough
(C) loath
(D) probable

7. TENTATIVE:

(A) committed
(B) confident
(C) experimental
(D) reliable

8. NECESSITY:

(A) concern
(B) luxury
(C) option
(D) requirement

9. CONSULT:

(A) appoint
(B) argue
(C) complain
(D) discuss

10. PREDICTION:

(A) estimate
(B) memory
(C) pronunciation
(D) speech

11. VIE:

(A) color
(B) feud
(C) finesse
(D) surrender

12. PLAUSIBLE:

(A) delayed
(B) realistic
(C) stupendous
(D) susceptible

Go on to the next page. ➡

13. DISPUTE:

(A) drone
(B) murmur
(C) quarrel
(D) shame

14. SPECULATE:

(A) disagree
(B) guess
(C) hoard
(D) validate

15. IMPEDE:

(A) different
(B) hinder
(C) scatter
(D) stampede

16. FLAGRANT:

(A) aromatic
(B) conventional
(C) shameless
(D) vagrant

17. INTRICATE:

(A) bare
(B) elite
(C) ornate
(D) proficient

18. LANGUISH:

(A) decipher
(B) deteriorate
(C) grieve
(D) prosper

19. EXUBERANT:

(A) contemptuous
(B) enthusiastic
(C) grim
(D) mellow

20. RENOUNCE:

(A) abandon
(B) defer
(C) proclaim
(D) shriek

Go on to the next page. ➡

Section One: Verbal Reasoning (Part Two – Sentence Completion)

Directions: Select the word that best completes the meaning of the sentence.

21. In a famous experiment, most people – even professional athletes – were not able to ------- the difference between expensive sneakers and inexpensive sneakers.

    (A) detect
    (B) disregard
    (C) refuse
    (D) trace

22. Unless I use an ice cube to ------- the itching, I will often scratch a mosquito bite until my skin is red and painful.

    (A) exploit
    (B) intensify
    (C) preserve
    (D) soothe

23. Because Abby did not ------- having more than a few guests, she did not purchase enough utensils for everyone to use.

    (A) anticipate
    (B) mention
    (C) remember
    (D) risk

24. The store's ------- and half-hearted attempt at correcting their mistake only served to make the customer more angry.

    (A) courageous
    (B) feeble
    (C) numerous
    (D) vivid

25. The massive, unexpected earthquake in rural Kamchatka would have resulted in ------- had it struck in a more heavily populated area.

    (A) catastrophe
    (B) controversy
    (C) disgrace
    (D) siege

26. Because outside food and beverages were forbidden in the movie theater, the usher had no choice but to ------- Quincy's candy and throw it away.

    (A) authorize
    (B) confiscate
    (C) extract
    (D) smuggle

27. When on a safari, it is best not to ------- the animals, for even seemingly gentle creatures like giraffes and gazelles can injure people and damage property when provoked.

    (A) admire
    (B) antagonize
    (C) gratify
    (D) raise

28. No matter how much Lois tried, she could not convince her daughter to ------- her possession of the lollipop even though it was time for dinner.

    (A) compromise
    (B) covet
    (C) relinquish
    (D) reveal

29. Because travelers may run into unexpected situations, such as construction or heavy traffic, it is important to consider ------- routes before setting out on a road trip.

    (A) alternative
    (B) balmy
    (C) panoramic
    (D) usual

30. Because Larry played frequently and studied tips in his spare time, many considered him to be a(n) ------- golfer.

    (A) avid
    (B) dire
    (C) disgruntled
    (D) noncommittal

Go on to the next page. ➡

31. Many Americans questioned the ------- of the British Empire, not believing that they should be governed by a country so far away.

(A) anthology
(B) authority
(C) availability
(D) crusade

32. Sam's strength of will would ------- every time he saw pasta, making it very difficult for him to adhere to his diet.

(A) conspire
(B) falter
(C) swelter
(D) teem

33. Her advisers counseled against such a(n) ------- plan, for they believed the plan to be unnecessarily risky.

(A) brazen
(B) despicable
(C) historic
(D) visible

34. The author, who had always lived modestly, was suddenly propelled to fortune with the signing of a(n) ------- book deal.

(A) abhorrent
(B) lucrative
(C) rudimentary
(D) unsatisfactory

35. Though Hilda could not understand the words being sung, she lost herself in the opera's ------- music – music that was the most beautiful she had ever heard.

(A) conservative
(B) focal
(C) sublime
(D) vigorous

36. Despite the fact that Valery did not prefer ------- decorations, she knew that the room would have looked boring if decorated simply and plainly.

(A) abrasive
(B) conceivable
(C) desolate
(D) extravagant

37. Efrain could tell with certainty that there was a skunk nearby due to the ------- smell.

(A) characteristic
(B) congested
(C) prospective
(D) tampered

38. Except for the ------- at the end of her routine, the judges found the gymnast's routine to be uninteresting.

(A) ambition
(B) flourish
(C) repetition
(D) talisman

39. Before electronic calculators, performing complex calculations must have been relatively -------, as such operations were performed manually and often took a long time to complete.

(A) influential
(B) liberal
(C) quick
(D) tedious

40. Each year, as new tree saplings sprout around the edge of the field, the forest ------- on the boundaries of the field.

(A) assembles
(B) encroaches
(C) improves
(D) rebels

STOP. Do not go on until instructed to do so.

STOP

Section Two: Quantitative Reasoning (Part One – Word Problems)

Questions: 37

Time Limit: 35 minutes

Directions – Choose the best of the four possible answers. You have 35 minutes to complete parts one AND two.

1. The figure shows the first three elements of a pattern.

What is the fifth element of this pattern?

(A)

(B)

(C)

(D)

2. The Cooperville replica of the Washington Monument is built at a scale factor of $\frac{1}{15}$ of the actual monument. If the replica stands 37 ft. high, how tall is the actual Washington Monument?

(A) 22 ft.
(B) 52 ft.
(C) 222 ft.
(D) 555 ft.

3. The grid shows three vertices of a rhombus.

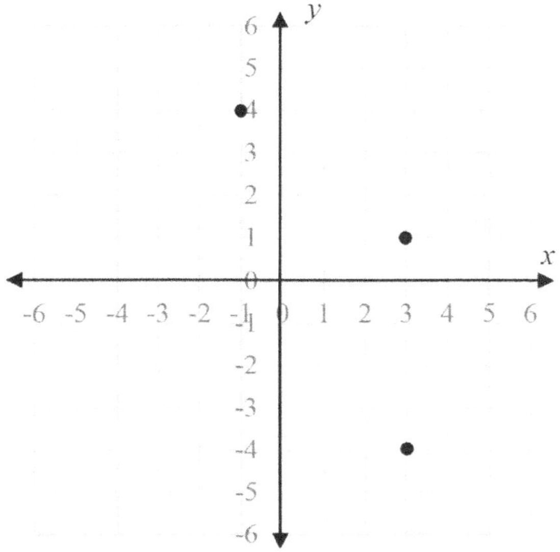

Which could be the coordinates of the fourth vertex of the rhombus?

(A) (0,0)
(B) (0,–1)
(C) (–1,0)
(D) (–1,–1)

4. The stem-and-leaf plot below shows the grade each student in a class earned on a science test.

Stem	Leaf
7	2 6 8 9
8	1 3 4 6 7 7 8 9
9	2 3 7 8 9

All of the following are grades scored by at least one student EXCEPT

(A) 72
(B) 85
(C) 88
(D) 93

Go on to the next page.

5. A bowling ball weighing 7.257 kilograms is placed on a balancing scale. A cube of sugar weighs 1 gram. How many cubes of sugar need to be added to the opposite side of the scale in order to balance the scale?

(A) 7,257
(B) 725.7
(C) 72.57
(D) 7.257

6. Each square in the grid shown has an area of 4 in^2.

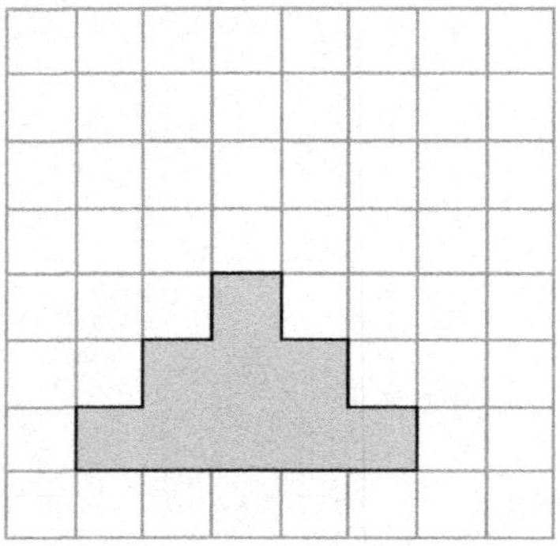

What is the perimeter of the shaded region, in inches?

(A) 16 in.
(B) 32 in.
(C) 36 in.
(D) 64 in.

7. Which of the following is the closest estimate of $58 \div 3(3^2 - 3)$?

(A) 2
(B) 3
(C) 40
(D) 120

8. The circle graph shows the number of animals on a farm.

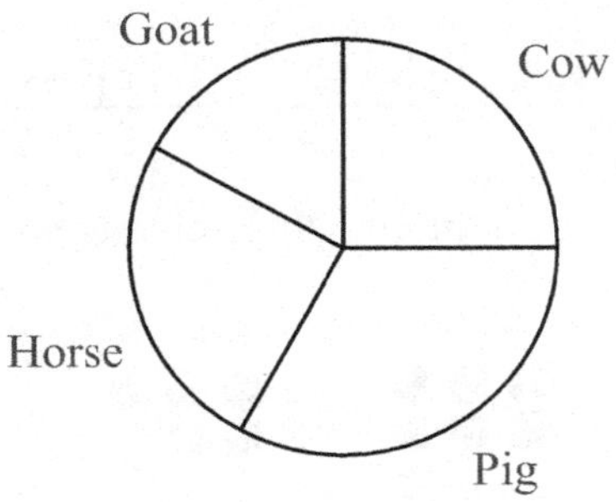

Which table could show the same data?

(A)

ANIMALS ON A FARM

Animal	Quantity
Cow	15
Goat	15
Horse	25
Pig	45

(B)

ANIMALS ON A FARM

Animal	Quantity
Cow	20
Goat	10
Horse	10
Pig	60

(C)

ANIMALS ON A FARM

Animal	Quantity
Cow	25
Goat	25
Horse	25
Pig	25

(D)

ANIMALS ON A FARM

Animal	Quantity
Cow	25
Goat	15
Horse	25
Pig	35

Go on to the next page.

9. The pattern shown below can be folded along the dotted lines into a prism.

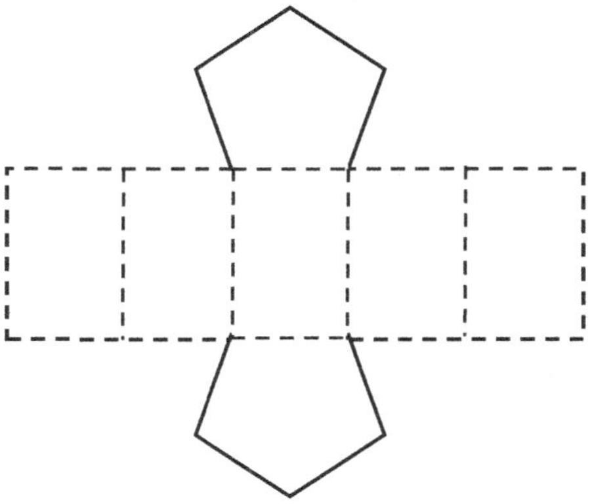

Which of the following would result from folding the above pattern?

(A)

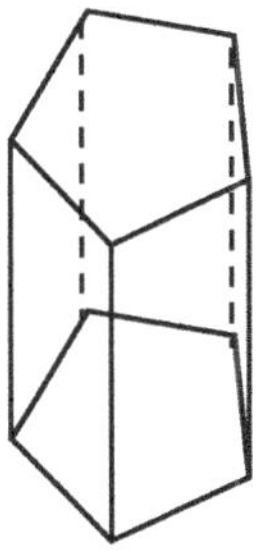

(B)

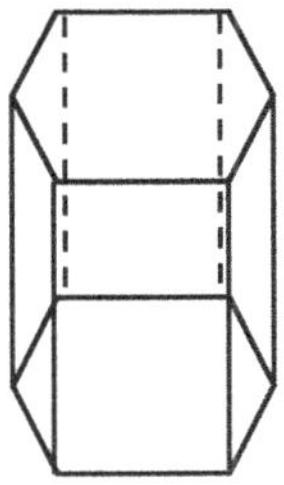

(C)

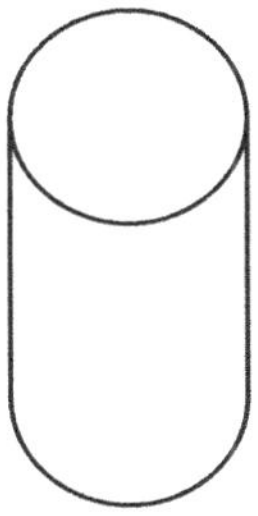

(D)

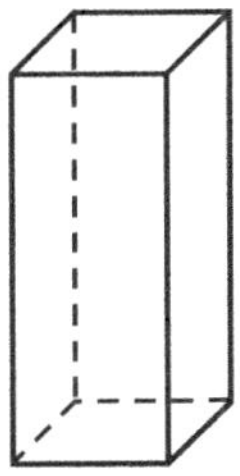

10. If $7x = bx$, what is the value of b?

(A) $\frac{1}{7}$
(B) 1
(C) 7
(D) 14

11. Wallace usually runs 8 miles in 2 hours. If he only has 30 minutes to run today, how many miles can he run?

(A) 1
(B) 2
(C) 4
(D) 6

12. ABCD is a square that touches the circle at points A, B, C, and D.

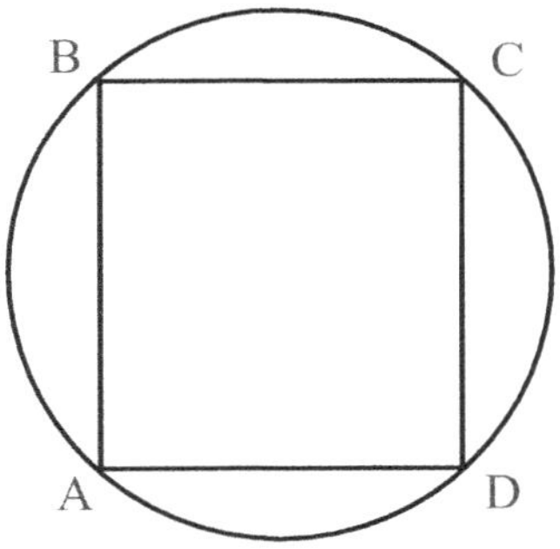

BD (not shown) has a length of 8 mm. What is the area of the circle?

(A) 4π sq. mm.
(B) 8π sq. mm.
(C) 16π sq. mm.
(D) 64π sq. mm.

Go on to the next page. ➡

13. Triangle A is shown below.

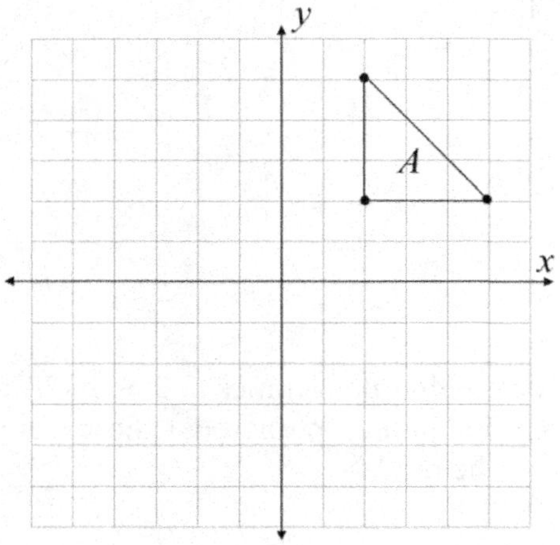

Which diagram shows Triangle A after a reflection over the x-axis?

(A)

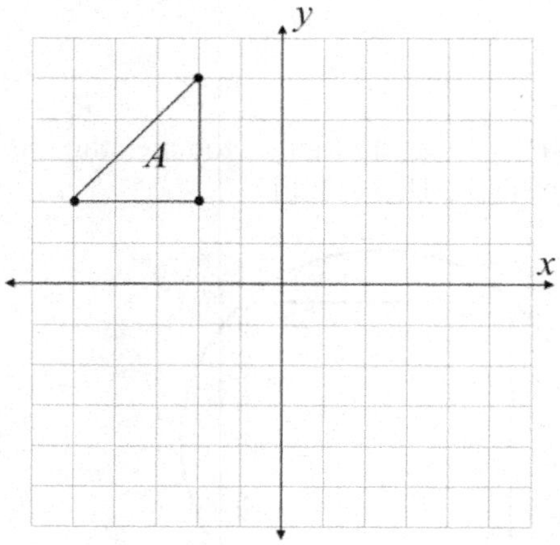

(C)

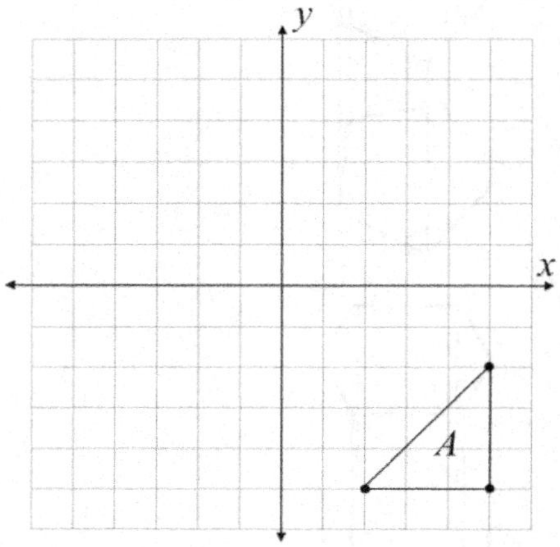

(B)

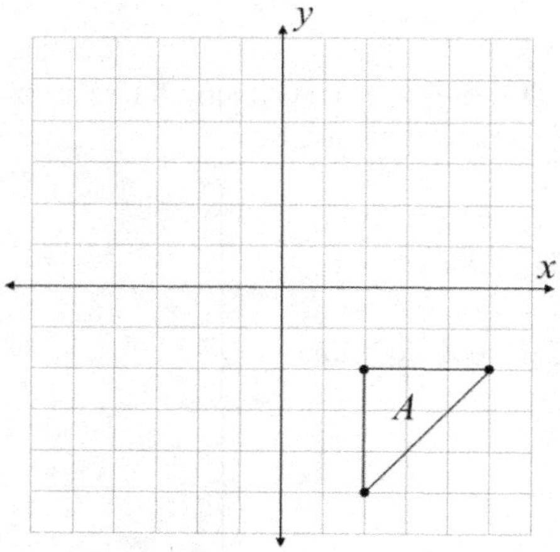

(D)

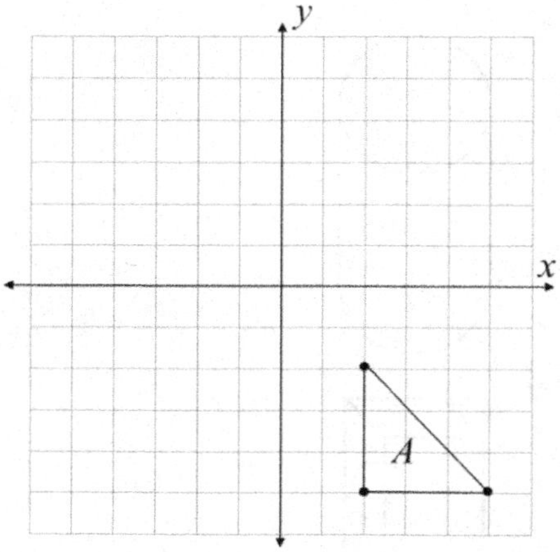

Go on to the next page.

14. A certain snail crawls at a speed of 10 km per year. Earth has a circumference of 40×10^6 meters. How many years would it take this snail to crawl around Earth?

(A) 400
(B) 4,000
(C) 40,000
(D) 400,000

15. Triangle *ABC* is similar to Triangle *DEF*.

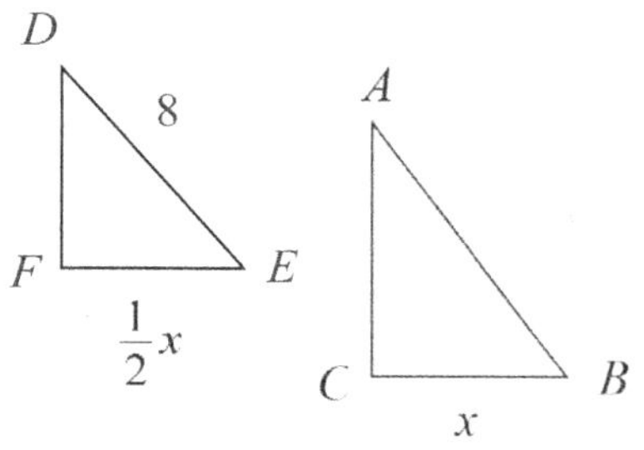

What is the length of side *AB*?

(A) 4
(B) 6
(C) 12
(D) 16

16. The graph below shows the temperature of 4 cars that were parked in the sun one afternoon.

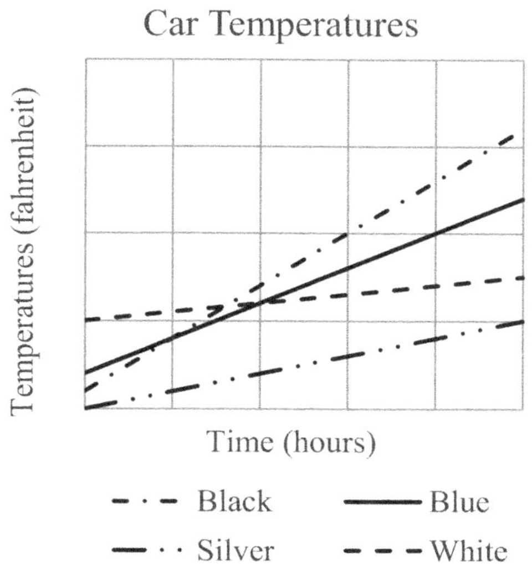

Which car had the greatest hourly increase in temperature?

(A) the blue car
(B) the black car
(C) the silver car
(D) the white car

17. Which expression results in a value between the integers 9 and 10?

(A) $\sqrt{36} + \sqrt{49}$
(B) $\sqrt{36 + 49}$
(C) $\sqrt{36 + 49^2}$
(D) $\sqrt{36^2 + 49^2}$

Go on to the next page. ➡

18. The graph shows Yancy's elevation above sea level while he was hiking up a mountain trail from a beach at sea level.

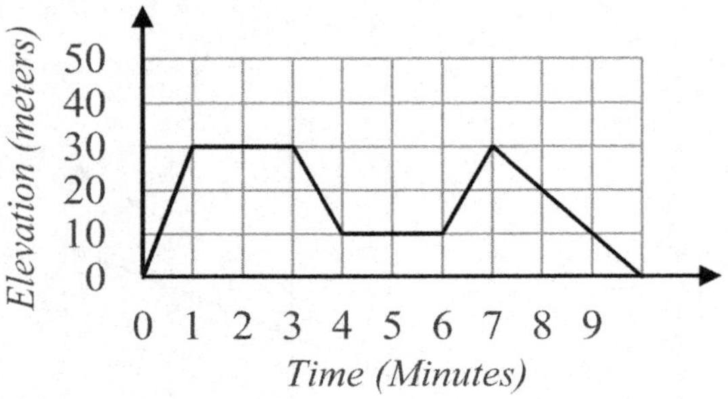

Which of the following most likely happened between minutes 4 and 6?

(A) Yancy slowed down but didn't stop hiking.
(B) Yancy was hiking on a flat part of the trail.
(C) Yancy hiked back down to the beach, then back up the mountain.
(D) Yancy hiked downhill, paused for two minutes, then hiked back up the same hill.

19. A certain bucket can hold 1,500 milliliters of water when it is filled to the top. At the moment, the bucket is only $\frac{1}{3}$ full of water.

Approximately how many **liters** (L) of water **must** be added to fill the bucket to the top?

(A) 0.5 L
(B) 1.0 L
(C) 1.5 L
(D) 15.0 L

20. At Gary's Goofy Game shop, Gary sells giant dice. The surface areas of these dice range from 400-800 square millimeters. If Gary has 50 dice, approximately how much space, in cubic millimeters, will these dice take up?

(A) 20,000
(B) 30,000
(C) 40,000
(D) 50,000

21. One perfect square is subtracted from another. Which difference is never possible?

(A) 7
(B) 8
(C) 9
(D) 10

22. On an *xy*-plane, the center of a certain circle is located at the origin. A line segment is drawn from the origin to point (3,4), and represents the circle's radius. What is the circumference of the circle?

(A) 5π units
(B) 9π units
(C) 10π units
(D) 16π units

Go on to the next page.

Section Two: Quantitative Reasoning (Part Two – Quantitative Comparisons)

Directions – Compare the amount in Column A to the amount in Column B using the information provided in each question. All questions in this part have the following answer choices:

(A) The amount in column A is greater.
(B) The amount in column B is greater.
(C) The two amounts are equal.
(D) The relationship cannot be determined from the information provided.

	Column A	Column B
23.	The smallest positive integer x, if $\frac{1}{x}$ is a repeating decimal	The number of values of n for which $\frac{1}{n} > 0.25$, if n is an integer

Orly took four tests. The mean of her tests was 85.

	Column A	Column B
24.	Orly's median test score	90

Every night, Joe spends 8 hours sleeping. For every hour Joe spends sleeping, he works for 1 hour and 15 minutes.

	Column A	Column B
25.	In 9 days, the number of hours Joe spends sleeping	In a 7-day week, the number of hours Joe spends working

	Column A	Column B
26.	x, if $x^2 = 121$	$\sqrt{121}$

Susan the stamp collector wants to give a copy of her favorite stamp to her friend, Dave. The unusual stamp is a square with sides of 2 cm. long. Susan makes a first copy of the stamp at a scale factor of $\frac{5}{2}$, and gives it to Dave. Dave then makes another copy of the stamp at a scale factor of $\frac{1}{5}$.

	Column A	Column B
27.	The area of Susan's original stamp	The area of Dave's final copy of the stamp

	Column A	Column B
28.	In a coordinate plane, the sum of the x-coordinate and y-coordinate of a point in the second quadrant	In a coordinate plane, the sum of the x-coordinate and y-coordinate of a point in the fourth quadrant

Go on to the next page. ➡

The scatter-plot below shows the results of a survey where people were asked about how much time they spend reading per week, and how tall they were.

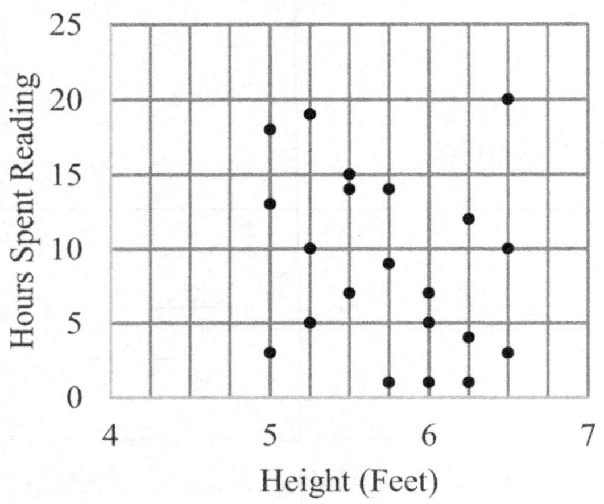

	Column A	Column B
29.	The height, in feet, of the person who spends the most time reading per week	For people 6.5 ft. tall, the average number of hours spent reading per week

In a colony of bees, there are 30 males and 50 females. Two females are queens and do not sting. All the other females sting, but none of the males do. Matt the beekeeper picks up a bee at random.

	Column A	Column B
30.	60%	The probability that Matt picks up a bee that can sting

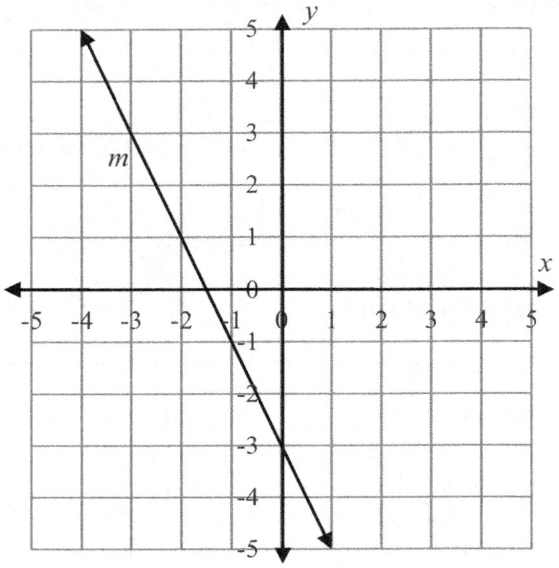

	Column A	Column B
31.	The slope of line m	The slope of line $y = \frac{1}{2}x + 3$

	Column A	Column B
32.	A prime number	The greatest common factor of 27 and 32

In a standard 52-card deck, there are 4 different suits, each of which contains 13 different cards. One card is chosen at random from the deck. It is then put back into the deck, and a second card is chosen at random from the deck.

	Column A	Column B
33.	The probability of getting two jacks	The probability of getting one jack and one queen

Go on to the next page.

In Mrs. Rooks' history class, there are 8 boys and 12 girls.

	Column A	Column B
34.	If four more girls enter the class, the percentage of girls in the class	If two boys leave the class, the percentage of girls in the class

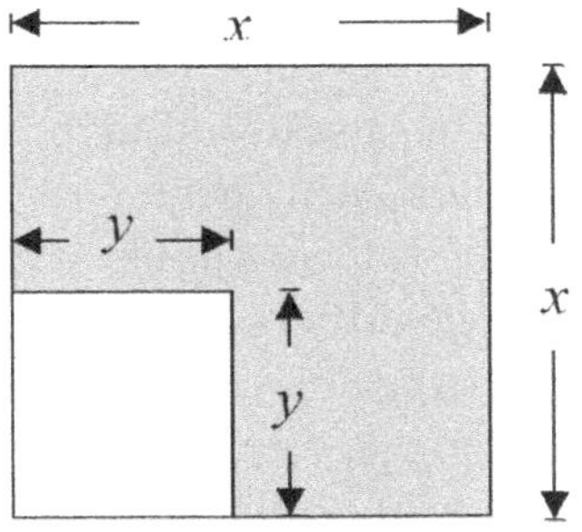

Note: Figures are not drawn to scale.

	Column A	Column B
35.	The area of the shaded region	$(x - y)^2$

If $14x + 12y = -2y$, then

	Column A	Column B
36.	the value of the expression $7x + 7y$.	the value of the expression $28x + 28y$.

	Column A	Column B
37.	$\sqrt{64} - \sqrt{49}$	$\sqrt{6.4} - \sqrt{4.9}$

STOP. Do not go on until instructed to do so.

STOP

Section Three: Reading Comprehension

Questions: 36

Time Limit: 35 minutes

Directions – Answer the questions following each passage based on what is either stated or implied in the passage. You have 35 minutes to complete 36 questions.

Questions 1-6

Most schools in the United States follow a similar calendar. Schools are usually in session from the end of summer to the beginning of summer. For parents and students alike, this schedule has become a fact of life. This timing has become so ingrained within American life that we even have names for the different parts of the school calendar: "back to school" represents the last few weeks of "summer vacation," when parents and students alike get ready for "the school year." Though this routine is now the norm, there are many reasons why we should consider alternative school calendars.

One such reason relates to the length of "summer vacation." Many believe that the traditional three-month break from schooling is too long and is harmful to students' education. Over time, educators and parents have observed that students often forget what they have learned during a long, three-month vacation. In fact, many teachers claim that they must often spend time at the beginning of a school year to remind students of concepts that had already been taught the year before. This means students learn less than they could each year. By changing the school calendar, students may be able to learn and remember more.

Another such reason relates to the fact that student schedules are not aligned with parent schedules. Such differences can result in a lack of necessary adult supervision. Though students have nearly three months off in the form of summer vacation, many parents do not. For these parents, finding safe, engaging, and fun summer programs can be difficult, time-consuming, and expensive. By aligning vacations with those given to working parents, families may be able to spend more time together. For example, instead of spending money to send children to camp, families would be able to go on vacation together.

Though there are certainly many benefits to the current school calendar, there are also many reasons to change it. Our society is constantly changing. It only makes sense that we take time to think about how our daily lives should change with it.

Go on to the next page. ➡

1. One of the main points of the passage is to

   (A) describe the benefits of changing a tradition.
   (B) explain why traditions should be followed strictly.
   (C) improve the ability of families to vacation together.
   (D) discuss how to increase the amount of material learned by students.

2. The phrases "back to school," "summer vacation," and "the school year" (lines 8-11)

   (A) highlight the importance of routine to learning.
   (B) describe the best way to organize the calendar year.
   (C) describe how confusing the school calendar has become.
   (D) emphasize how much the school calendar influences American culture.

3. In line 34, "engaging" most nearly means

   (A) boring.
   (B) costly.
   (C) interesting.
   (D) ordinary.

4. The author would support which of the following statements about education?

   (A) Long vacations are as important as learning.
   (B) It is not necessary to adapt to changes in society.
   (C) Coordinating with parent schedules is not difficult.
   (D) School calendars should be beneficial to student learning.

5. The passage's style is most similar to the style of a

   (A) short story.
   (B) newspaper editorial.
   (C) reference book.
   (D) set of instructions.

6. Which of the following best describes the organization of the passage?

   (A) A theory is explored in general.
   (B) An opinion is supported by observations.
   (C) Facts are presented in chronological order.
   (D) A specific event is described in great detail.

Go on to the next page. ➡

Questions 7-12

Almost 300 feet long and over 100 feet wide, the Main Concourse of Grand Central Station in New York City is very impressive. Serving as a train station, a marketplace, a meeting place, a dining venue, and even a gym, Grand Central is a wonder of design and engineering. Steeped in history, the station is home to some of America's most famous heirlooms: the four-faced clock standing at the heart of the Main Concourse; the vaulted ceilings of the whispering gallery; the original mechanical flap-board destination sign. In the rush to get from one part of the station to another, it's possible to miss one of the most beautiful features of the station: the ceiling of the Main Concourse.

The ceiling soars over a hundred feet above the heads of thousands upon thousands of travelers. It is painted in a turquoise blue-green, and depicts constellations visible from October through March. These are rendered in gold paint. The constellations are comprised of over 2,000 individual stars. Two golden arches stretch from east to west. One represents the earth's orbit around the sun. The other represents the earth's equator. Even the Milky Way is visible as a cloud of tiny stars, which stretches from the southwest to northeast corners of the ceiling.

Great care was taken during the planning and creation of the ceiling. However, a mistake was still made in the depiction of the constellations. Though the correct constellations are shown, the orientation and placement of several patterns are inconsistent with what we see in the actual night sky. All of the stars on the ceiling are rendered as they would appear from Earth, except for Taurus and Gemini. These constellations are reversed. They are instead depicted as they would be seen looking down at Earth from above. Though Gemini should be near Orion's elevated arm, the ceiling of the concourse displays Taurus in this position. The most likely explanation is that an error occurred when transposing an astronomical sketch onto the ceiling. Despite the inconsistency in its design, the ceiling is nonetheless a beautiful and impressive work of art.

Go on to the next page. ➡

7. Which of the following sentences best expresses the main idea of the passage?

(A) Train stations are very busy.
(B) Works of art must be error-free.
(C) The ceiling of a train station can be a work of art.
(D) Train stations can sometimes have more than one function.

8. The passage suggests that the ceiling of the Main Concourse is

(A) not painted an appropriate color.
(B) not as beautiful as the four-faced clock.
(C) not as well-known as other parts of Grand Central.
(D) ruined because of the mistake in the constellations.

9. The main purpose of the second paragraph (lines 17-28) is to

(A) show how practical Grand Central can be.
(B) discuss the mistakes in the Main Concourse's decor.
(C) describe the appearance of the Main Concourse ceiling.
(D) compare the Main Concourse ceiling with other parts of the train station.

10. The phrase "several patterns" (line 34) refers to

(A) constellations.
(B) the Milky Way.
(C) Earth's orbit.
(D) the flap-board sign.

11. In line 44, the word "transposing" most nearly means

(A) cleaning.
(B) painting.
(C) removing.
(D) transferring.

12. According to the author, all of the following were intentionally included in the ceiling of the Main Concourse ceiling EXCEPT

(A) the paint color.
(B) the golden arches.
(C) the golden constellations.
(D) the Gemini and Taurus' reversal.

Go on to the next page. ➡

Questions 13-18

The weekend that I received my driver's license was a particularly busy one.

My father was running around the house doing chores. The kitchen sink was leaking, the gutters on the roof needed to be cleaned, and the yard outside needed to be raked clean of the fallen autumn leaves. My mother needed to take my younger sister to soccer practice, then to piano lessons, and then to the school bake sale.

I, too, had big plans. I was excited to drive around town with my friends. We planned to drive to the nearby lake to skip stones. The last thing I wanted now that I had the keys to my freedom was to do chores.

As I threw on a sweater and headed for the front door, my mother's voice followed me down the hallway.

"Where do you think you're going, mister?" she asked.

"Out. With Jordan," I replied impatiently.

"Not so fast," she snapped. "I need you to help out around here."

Through experience, I knew that there was no arguing with her when she spoke like that. Grudgingly, I turned to face my mother and listened to her instructions.

That's how I found myself staring at an endless wall of peanut butter. My mother had asked me to pick up groceries before I went out with my friends. She had given me a piece of paper. On it was a neatly written grocery list, and part of that list was peanut butter. Though I had been shopping with my mother before, I had never really paid attention to what she bought and how she decided to buy what she did.

The entire aisle was filled with jars of peanut butter – shelf after shelf, row after row of every kind of peanut butter imaginable: smooth, simple, creamy, crunchy, chunky, extra chunky, natural. To make matters even more complicated, there were at least five different brands on display, each of which made several types of peanut butter. As I stood there wondering about the difference between "just right" and "smooth natural" peanut butter, I grew frustrated that I needed to go grocery shopping at all. Why did my mother ask me to do this, and why were her instructions so unspecific?

It dawned on me, as I stared at the fifth jar of extra-crunchy peanut butter, that my new-found freedom wasn't exactly free. It naturally came with additional responsibilities. For a moment, my mind wandered away from the impossible task of buying peanut butter. I thought about the morning's events. My mother hadn't forbid me to spending time with my friends. Instead, she had only asked that I use my new privileges to help the family, too. On top of that, I needed to make my own decisions about what to buy. She was treating me, I realized, as an adult.

Pride swelled up within me. I found myself smiling as I grabbed a jar of chunky, all-natural peanut butter and headed for the cashier.

Go on to the next page. ➡

13. The author would most likely agree with which statement?

    (A) Grocery shopping is something only parents should do.
    (B) The freedom of adulthood is accompanied by responsibilities.
    (C) Chores are boring and should be avoided no matter the cost.
    (D) Obtaining a driver's license is more important than studying or helping around the house.

14. The phrase "keys to my freedom" (lines 13-14) can best be interpreted as the author's

    (A) 18th birthday.
    (B) new sports car.
    (C) driver's license.
    (D) lack of responsibilities.

15. According to the passage, the author knew not to argue with his mother because

    (A) his father told him to help his mother with chores.
    (B) he does not win arguments when his mother speaks in a certain way.
    (C) she does not approve of spending time by the lake skipping stones.
    (D) she is very particular about the type of peanut butter that she likes to eat.

16. The author's tone when describing the experience of buying peanut butter (lines 36-48) can best be described as

    (A) annoyed.
    (B) depressed.
    (C) excited.
    (D) satisfied.

17. In line 49, "dawned on" most nearly means

    (A) rose up.
    (B) brightened for.
    (C) occurred to.
    (D) demanded of.

18. The passage implies that the author feels proud of being treated as an adult because

    (A) he can follow instructions very well.
    (B) he does not need to help with chores.
    (C) he realizes that his mother trusts him to make his own decisions.
    (D) he is free to drive around town whenever he likes and with whomever he chooses.

Go on to the next page. ➡

Questions 19-24

The changing of water into different physical states is described as the water cycle. Water can take on liquid, gaseous, and solid states. The transformation of water into these different states involves different chemical and physical reactions and processes. Each form and each process has different effects on the environment.

On Earth, the sun powers the water cycle. The heat from the sun causes liquid water found in oceans, lakes, and rivers – even in plants – to evaporate. Evaporation transforms liquid water into water vapor, which rises high into the air. Some estimates suggest that almost 90% of global evaporation takes place over the oceans.

The higher the water vapor rises, the colder it becomes. As a result of the lower temperature, water vapor begins to condense into water droplets, much like it does on the outside of a glass of ice-water on a hot day. As it condenses, during a phenomenon known as precipitation, the droplets start to fall out of the sky in the form of liquid water. Many scientists estimate that 80% of global precipitation takes place over the oceans. The form of the precipitation itself – rain, snow, hail, etc. – depends on local climate conditions.

Much of this precipitation falls back into bodies of water or onto land, where it continues the water cycle. Some precipitation falls as frozen water, like snow and ice, which can stay frozen basically forever. Frozen water is, therefore, effectively removed from the water cycle until it melts. Ice in Antarctica and Greenland, for example, have been dated to be approximately 800,000 years old.

Though it may seem as if frozen water can do little once removed from the water cycle, snow and ice have actually shaped much of present-day Earth. As global temperatures change, mountains of ice known as glaciers advance and retreat. Glaciers grind valleys into the earth and leave mountains in their wake. This process can take thousands of years. Conversely, the frequency and intensity of liquid rain precipitation can lead to soil erosion and even violent landslides in a matter of minutes. Rain chisels away at stones, helping to pulverize even the mightiest mountain or boulder. Over time, rain even helps to gouge rivers and canyons into the land.

Water also plays a large role in shaping environmental temperatures as it evaporates and subsequently condenses. The process of evaporation uses up energy from the surrounding environment, thus generating a cooling effect. The process of condensation gives off energy into the surrounding environment, thus generating a warming effect.

The water cycle is an integral part of the global environment. It influences everything from climates and ecosystems to the geological features of the earth itself.

Go on to the next page.

19. Which sentence best expresses the passage's main idea?

(A) The water cycle is unique to Earth.
(B) Without water, there would be no life on Earth.
(C) Water influences many aspects of the environment.
(D) There is no need to understand the different physical states of water.

20. In line 32, the phrase "basically forever" most nearly means

(A) indefinitely.
(B) purposefully.
(C) stubbornly.
(D) temporarily.

21. According to lines 37-51, though water can be frozen for long periods of time, it continues to have an impact on the environment by

(A) creating various geological features.
(B) contributing to landslides and soil erosion.
(C) causing earthquakes that result in tsunamis.
(D) grinding boulders into smaller stones and eventually into sand.

22. The passage's organization is most similar to that of a

(A) novel.
(B) personal letter.
(C) scholarly paper.
(D) persuasive essay.

23. According to the passage, temperatures are influenced by

(A) landslides.
(B) condensation.
(C) mountains of ice.
(D) frozen precipitation.

24. It can be inferred from the passage that the author would agree with which of the following statements?

(A) Atmospheric pressure hinders the water cycle.
(B) The water cycle is more efficient today than it was in the past.
(C) Once water freezes, it no longer has an influence on the environment.
(D) Invisible processes that control the water cycle have visible effects on Earth.

Go on to the next page.

Questions 25-30

We turned off of the paved road at the sign that announced "Pick Your Own" in bold red letters. The car kicked up a cloud of dust as we bounced up and down the uneven dirt road. Trees stood all around us, as far as we could see. Though the trees were planted in orderly rows, it was impossible to see all the way to the end of each row, for at some point the path between trees would wind up or around a gentle hill. It did not seem unreasonable, at the time, to think that the trees might go on forever.

The smell grew stronger with each bump or hole in the road. The unmistakably sweet, earthly smell of decaying fruit was sharp in our nostrils. By the time we reached the clearing in the woods, where we were to park our car, we were intoxicated by the juicy, syrupy aroma that danced on the wind.

We paid the entrance fee, picked up the bright-red, five-gallon buckets, and started to walk between the trees. Each of the hundreds – or thousands – of trees was dotted with a hundred or more plump peaches. Each peach, round and smiling, had its own unique color. Some peaches were light pink, barely kissed by the sun, while others were a deep garnet, a bolder red than any ruby. Yet others were a combination of the two, one side being light red and the other, having spent weeks soaking in the warm light of the sun, displaying a red so deep that it could have been mistaken for an apple.

After a short while, we stopped to better savor the experience. Looking back the way we came, we expected to see the parking lot and our car. Instead, all we could see was the grass path and the peach trees on either side. It felt as if we had wandered into a fairytale – there were no voices and no sounds besides a gentle breeze in the trees and the soft droning of insect wings. The heavily perfumed and warm, humid air hung heavily between the trees, having a strangely drowsy effect on our group.

Someone suggested that we try a peach, and the idea woke us from our thoughts – but which tree to choose? We each instinctively headed for a different tree – but now, which peach to choose? Each peach looked better than the last, and each person developed his own criteria: choose only the most red; choose only the largest; choose only the softest; or else, choose some combination of those factors.

The first, the last, and every bite in between was bliss. In little trickles, the nectar – the very essence of peach itself – leaked from the corner of our mouths and ran down our chins, dripping onto the ground. Smiling and laughing at each other and ourselves, we forgot our good manners and our upbringing. Still chewing, mouths full of the freshest peaches any of us had ever enjoyed, we each motioned for the others to come to our respective tree, for surely it had the best peaches in the entire orchard.

After each of our third, fourth, or maybe even fifth peaches, silence once again settled over us. We had eaten our fill, and had in the meantime filled our buckets with choice fruit. Nothing more needed to be said. It was difficult to imagine life getting any better than this.

Go on to the next page. ➡

25. One of the main points of the passage is to

(A) compare peaches with other fruit.
(B) describe the layout of an orchard.
(C) provide facts and tips for growing fruit.
(D) share a powerful and beautiful experience.

26. According to the first paragraph (lines 1-11), it seemed that the trees were endless because

(A) the land was flat and unchanging.
(B) trees were planted in orderly rows.
(C) they extend beyond what can be seen nearby.
(D) the author's friends had read about the orchard in a newspaper.

27. The passage implies that the "syrupy aroma that danced on the wind" (lines 17-18) is caused by

(A) rotting peaches.
(B) farm animals on the orchard.
(C) overly-ripe apples that are decaying on the ground.
(D) the large number of insects flying around the orchard.

28. The phrase "kissed by the sun" (lines 25-26), refers to

(A) the temperature outside.
(B) the brightness of the sun.
(C) how the peaches turn red from sunlight.
(D) getting sunburned while picking peaches

29. According to the author, all of the following factors were used to select peaches EXCEPT

(A) color.
(B) hardness.
(C) size.
(D) smell.

30. In line 60, the word "motioned" most nearly means

(A) agreed.
(B) beckon.
(C) proposed.
(D) raced.

Go on to the next page. ➡

Questions 31-36

Throughout history, many people have aspired to conquer the world. Yet few have come close to that lofty dream. Those that strive for and come close to this dream are immortalized in history. In this endeavor, there are few people in history more famous than Alexander III of Macedon and Genghis Khan of Mongolia. But which of these titans of conquest was the greatest?

More commonly known as Alexander the Great, Alexander III of Macedon was a king of Macdeon, which was a powerful kingdom in ancient Greece. Alexander the Great was undefeated in battle and commanded a large, experienced army. He attacked and defeated the nearby kingdom of Persia, led by King Darius III, in a number of now-legendary battles. Not satisfied by this victory or by any subsequent victory, Alexander the Great continued to push east in the hopes of reaching the very end of the world itself. At its peak, in the 4th century BC, Alexander the Great's kingdom was one of the largest in the ancient world, stretching eastward from Greece through Egypt and across to present-day India.

Ultimately, Alexander the Great was forced to stop his eastward expansion. However, the result of his ambitions remain evident even today. Though his empire began to crumble soon after his death, his efforts resulted in the expansion of Greek culture across much of Asia Minor and Central Asia. Great cities, such as Alexandria in Egypt, were named after him, and still stand today. Military leaders for generations would go on to study his strategies and methods.

Unlike Alexander the Great, who inherited his sovereignty and army from his father, Genghis Khan consolidated power by uniting many different and nomadic tribes in Northeast Asia. Born as Temüjin and later known as the Great Khan, Genghis Khan would go on to found one of the largest empires in history.

After founding the Mongol Empire, Genghis Khan went on to conquer most of Eurasia and eventually came to control much of 13th century Central Asia and China. Unlike Alexander the Great, whose empire began to fail shortly after his death, Genghis Khan's leadership and vision facilitated the ongoing expansion of his empire by his descendants. His offspring would go on to conquer much of present-day China, Korea, Russia, Eastern Europe, and Southwest Asia.

Genghis Khan not only unified a disparate people, but also created a single writing system. The Great Khan was also tolerant of different religions and sought to learn from Buddhists, Muslims, Christians, and Taoists alike. Under his rule, the famous Silk Road flourished, as did the exchange of ideas between the East and the West.

The actions, vision, and leadership of Alexander the Great and Genghis Khan have had an immeasurably great impact on the course of human history. While everyone's actions create a ripple in history, these two conquerors made waves. Ultimately, it is impossible to determine who had a greater impact on the world. Though separated by over a thousand years, Alexander the Great and the Great Khan both left a legacy that we can never fully comprehend.

Go on to the next page. ➡

31. The author would most likely agree with which statement about famous historical figures?

(A) Every person has an equally large impact on human history.
(B) It is difficult to determine which historical figures had the greatest impact on the world.
(C) The most important factor in ranking the greatness of historical figures is their tolerance for other cultures.
(D) By focusing on a few criteria, it is possible to determine that some historical figures are greater than others.

32. In line 2, the word "aspired" most nearly means

(A) helped.
(B) needed.
(C) remembered.
(D) wanted.

33. The passage suggests that great people possess all of the following traits EXCEPT

(A) ambition
(B) leadership.
(C) luck.
(D) vision.

34. According to the passage, all of the following are examples of Alexander the Great's legacy EXCEPT

(A) cities were named after Alexander.
(B) people studied Alexander's actions.
(C) Alexander's face was carved onto coins.
(D) Greek culture was spread beyond Greece.

35. According to the passage, Genghis Khan's tolerance resulted in

(A) his control over Eurasia.
(B) a sharing of religious ideas.
(C) the naming of cities after the Great Khan.
(D) the wise rule and command of his descendants.

36. The sentence "While everyone's actions create a ripple in history, these two conquerors made waves" (lines 64-66) suggests that

(A) having a big impact on the world is mostly a matter of luck.
(B) neither Alexander the Great nor Genghis Khan could conquer the seas.
(C) Alexander the Great and Genghis Khan had an above-average impact on the world.
(D) it is unclear whether or not Alexander the Great or Genghis Khan had a greater impact on the world.

STOP. Do not go on until instructed to do so.

STOP

Section Four: Mathematics Achievement

Questions: 47

Time Limit: 40 minutes

Directions – Select the best answer from the four answer choices. You have 40 minutes to complete 47 questions.

1. Which expression is equal to 250?

(A) $2^1 \times 5^1$
(B) $2^2 \times 5^2$
(C) $2^3 \times 5^2$
(D) $2^1 \times 5^3$

2. Mason baked 3 times as many cookies as Devon. If they baked 36 cookies altogether, which equation can be used to find out how many cookies Devon baked?

(A) $36 = 3x$
(B) $36 = 4x$
(C) $36 = 3x + 1$
(D) $36 = 4x + 1$

3. Ichiro is preparing for a hotdog eating contest. On Monday, he ate 24 hotdogs. On Tuesday, he ate 25% more hotdogs than on Monday. How many hotdogs did Ichiro eat on Tuesday?

(A) 6
(B) 12
(C) 30
(D) 49

4. $1.3 \div \frac{1}{4} =$

(A) 0.325
(B) 1.05
(C) 1.55
(D) 5.2

5. The bar graph shows the monthly high temperature for a certain town in Pennsylvania in 2013.

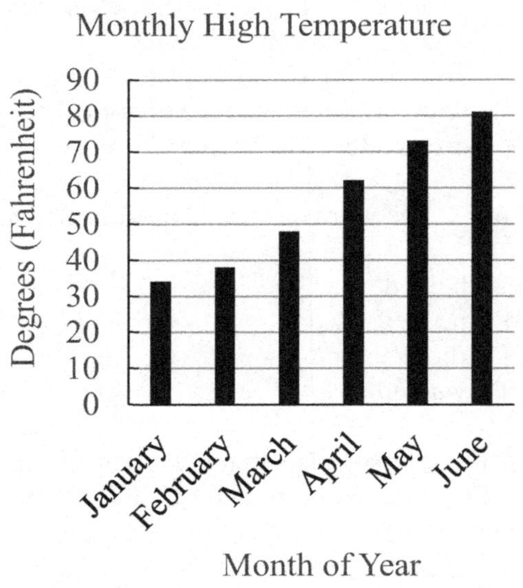

According to the graph, for all months shown, how much greater is the median than the mean temperature?

(A) 0°F
(B) 5°F
(C) 10°F
(D) 55°F

6. A parallelogram is shown below.

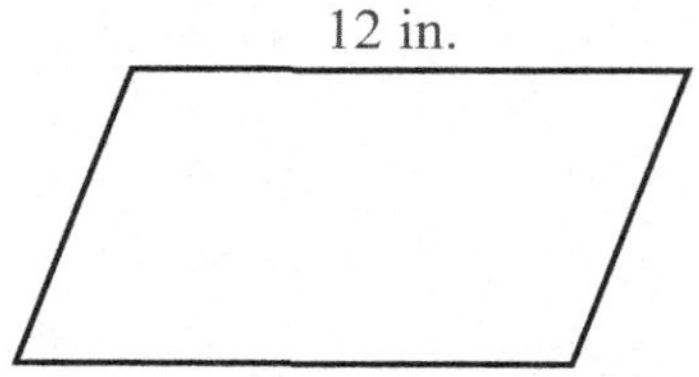

Note: Area of a parallelogram = $b \times h$.

If the area of the above parallelogram is 144 in^2, what is the height, h, of the parallelogram?

(A) 12 in.
(B) 24 in.
(C) 48 in.
(D) 132 in.

Go on to the next page.

7. What is the value of a in the equation $\frac{a}{5} - 3 = 9$?

(A) 9
(B) 12
(C) 48
(D) 60

8. The probability of picking a bruised apple out of a barrel is $\frac{3}{4}$. Which of the following could NOT be the number of apples in the barrel?

(A) 4
(B) 6
(C) 8
(D) 12

9. What is the value of the numerical expression 429 – 602?

(A) –227
(B) –173
(C) 173
(D) 227

10. The squares ABGF and BCHG are congruent, and together form rectangle ACHF.

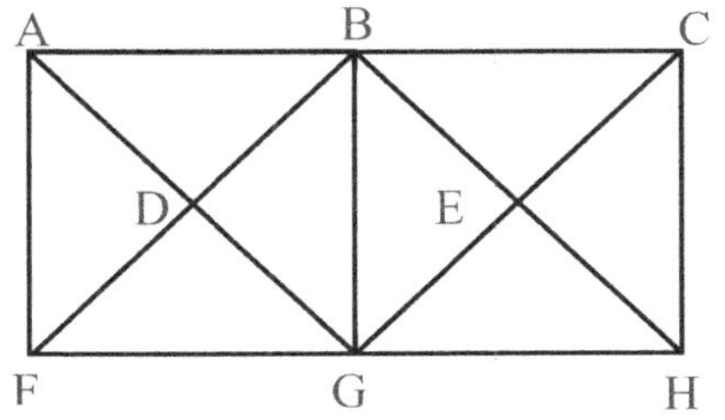

Square BEGD represents what fraction of rectangle ACHF?

(A) $\frac{1}{4}$
(B) $\frac{1}{3}$
(C) $\frac{1}{2}$
(D) $\frac{3}{4}$

11. If $3^x = 81$, then $3x =$

(A) 4
(B) 12
(C) 27
(D) 81

12. Dan took 7 math tests this semester, and he got grades of 72, 86, 89, 96, 98, 100, and x. If 89 is his median score, what is the highest possible integer value for x?

(A) 88
(B) 89
(C) 90
(D) 91

13. A rectangular fish pond is 10 feet long and 18 feet wide, and every point on the floor is of equal depth. If the pond is filled to a depth of 6 inches, what is the volume of the water in the pond?

(A) 34 ft^3
(B) 90 ft^3
(C) 180 ft^3
(D) 1,080 ft^3

14. To win a free lunch at school, Kalvin must do two things. First, Kalvin must roll a standard, six-sided die. Second, Kalvin must spin a spinner on a board with four equally-sized spaces, which are colored green, blue, red, and black. Kalvin wins the lunch if he rolls a 6 and the spinner lands on green. What is Kalvin's chance of winning the free lunch?

(A) $\frac{1}{24}$
(B) $\frac{1}{10}$
(C) $\frac{1}{6}$
(D) $\frac{1}{4}$

Go on to the next page. ➡

15. At basketball practice, Jack made x free throws on Monday. He made $1.25x$ free throws on Tuesday. On Wednesday, he made 1.75 times more free throws than he did on Tuesday. If he made 16 free throws on Monday, how many did he make over the course of the three days?

(A) 116
(B) 71
(C) 59
(D) 35

16. A rectangle has a width of 10 ft. and a length of 10 ft. If the length is decreased by 10% and the width is increased by 10%, what is the area of the new shape?

(A) 90 ft^2
(B) 99 ft^2
(C) 100 ft^2
(D) 110 ft^2

17. What is the value of x in the equation $2\frac{1}{6} \div 4\frac{2}{5} = x$?

(A) $-9\frac{8}{15}$
(B) $-2\frac{1}{2}$
(C) $\frac{65}{132}$
(D) $9\frac{8}{15}$

18. A swimming pool that has 500 liters of water in it is being drained of water at a rate of 17 liters per minute. Which of the following equations could represent the amount of water in the swimming pool, y, after a certain amount of time, x?

(A) $y = -17x + 500$
(B) $y = -17x - 500$
(C) $y = 17x - 500$
(D) $y = 17x + 500$

19. If $1{,}212 = 12(y + 1)$, then $y =$

(A) 10
(B) 11
(C) 100
(D) 101

20. The thermometer shown below displays the temperature when Frank went to sleep one night.

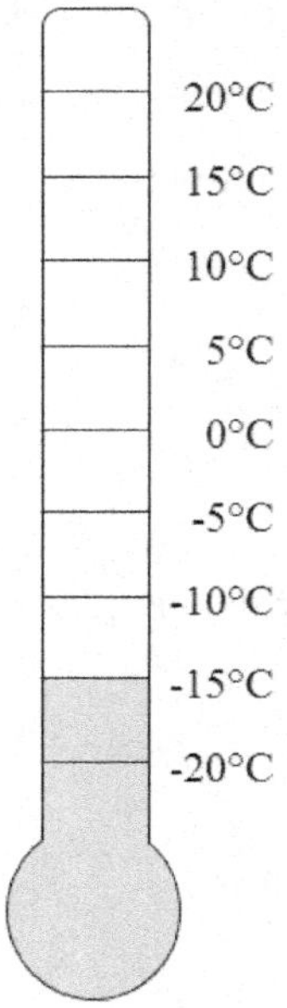

If the temperature was 12°C when he woke up the next morning, by how many degrees did the temperature increase overnight?

(A) 3
(B) 12
(C) 15
(D) 27

21. If $x! = x(x-1)(x-2)(x-3)(x-4)$, and $5! = 120$, how many distinct prime factors does 120 have?

(A) 3
(B) 4
(C) 5
(D) 16

Go on to the next page.

22. The surface area of a cube is 150 cm^2. What is its volume?

(A) 25 cm^3
(B) 125 cm^3
(C) 15,625 cm^3
(D) 125,000 cm^3

23. Erica has a monthly budget of $300 to spend on all of her expenses. She used $\frac{2}{3}$ on rent, and $\frac{1}{4}$ on food. How much money remains for her other expenses?

(A) $25
(B) $100
(C) $250
(D) $275

24. The table shows the favorite fruit of all the students in a school's 6th grade class. The data for orange is missing.

FAVORITE FRUIT

Fruit	Number of Students
Apple	25
Banana	20
Orange	
Peach	40
Mango	10

A circle graph is made from the data. If the central angle of the portion of the graph representing apple is 90°, how many people chose orange?

(A) 5
(B) 95
(C) 100
(D) 105

25. Moore has 4 more quarters than nickels. The total amount of quarters and nickels that he has is $3.10. Which equation represents the amount of money, in dollars, that Moore has?

(A) $0.3x = 4.1$
(B) $0.3x + 1 = 3.1$
(C) $0.05x + 0.25x + 4 = 3.1$
(D) $0.05x + 4x + 0.25 = 3.1$

26. What is the slope of the line $5y - 2x = -12$?

(A) -2
(B) $-\frac{2}{5}$
(C) $\frac{2}{5}$
(D) 2

27. 20 boys and 12 girls were born in Hospital A. Compared with Hospital A, there were 25% fewer boys and 50% more girls born in Hospital B. How many babies were born in both hospitals combined?

(A) 21
(B) 33
(C) 43
(D) 65

28. The following qualities apply to a certain quadrilateral:

1) Each of the four angles are right angles.
2) Opposite sides are parallel.

Based only on the information described above, which of the following **must** be the name of the quadrilateral described above?

(A) square
(B) rhombus
(C) rectangle
(D) trapezoid

Go on to the next page. ➡

29. Which of the following choices is closest to $\frac{9}{37}$?

(A) 0.1
(B) 0.2
(C) 0.3
(D) 0.4

30. A right triangle has a hypotenuse of 10 cm and one leg of 8 cm. How long is the second leg? *Note: the lengths of a right triangle's sides are* $c^2 = a^2 + b^2$.

(A) 2 cm
(B) 4 cm
(C) 6 cm
(D) 12 cm

31. In a video game tournament, the number of participants in each round is given by the table below.

Round	Number of Participants
1	160
2	80
3	40

If the pattern continues, how many participants will remain in the 5th round?

(A) 0
(B) 5
(C) 10
(D) 20

32. Gary can wash a car in an hour. It takes his brother, Barry, half as long to wash a car. How long would it take the two brothers to wash the car together?

(A) 20 minutes
(B) 40 minutes
(C) 45 minutes
(D) 90 minutes

33. During lunch, students are trading snacks. 4 fruit snacks are worth 9 pretzels. 2 fruit snacks are worth 12 graham crackers. How many graham crackers are needed to trade for a dozen pretzels?

(A) 8
(B) 12
(C) 16
(D) 32

34. A circle with radius 4 is inscribed inside a square, as shown below.

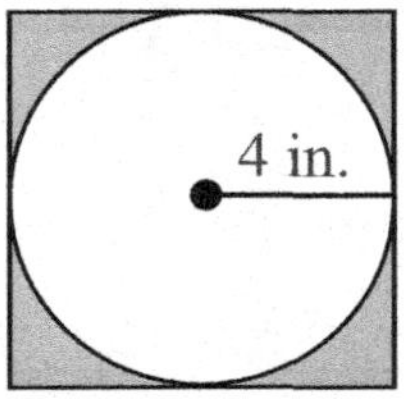

What is the probability that a random point inside the square is also inside the circle? *Note: area of a circle* $= \pi r^2$.

(A) $\frac{1}{4}$
(B) $\frac{3}{4}$
(C) $\frac{\pi}{4}$
(D) $\frac{3\pi}{4}$

Go on to the next page. ➡

35. The chart below shows the high temperatures in Milwaukee during a 30-day period.

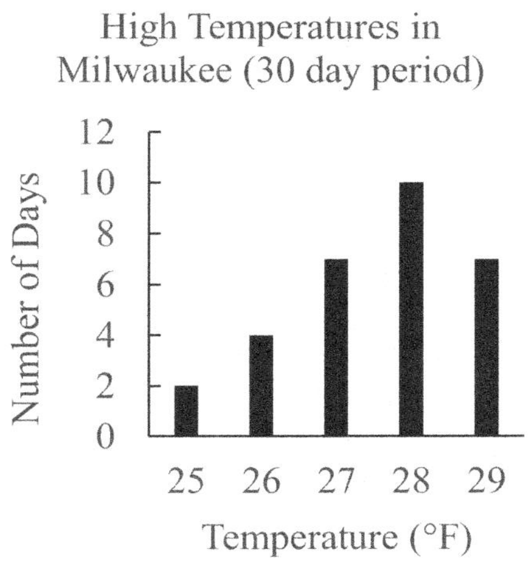

Which two quantities are equal?

(A) the median of temperatures and the range of temperatures
(B) the range of temperatures and the mode of temperatures
(C) the median of temperatures and the mode of temperatures
(D) the mean of temperatures and the range of temperatures

36. The club president needs to order cookies for their annual fundraiser. A package of cookies costs \$5.00 each, plus a 10% sales tax. There is also a shipping fee that is charged based on the number of packages per order. The table gives the total cost of the four different order sizes.

COST OF COOKIES

Packages of Cookies per Order	Total Order Cost
5	\$32.50
10	\$65.00
15	\$97.50
20	\$130.00

What is the shipping fee charged per package?

(A) \$1
(B) \$2
(C) \$3
(D) \$4

37. A toy store sells a red-colored cube with a volume of 27 cm^3. A similar, blue-colored cube is also available, at a scale factor of $\frac{2}{3}$. What is the volume of the blue-colored cube?

(A) 8 cm^3
(B) 9 cm^3
(C) 10 cm^3
(D) 18 cm^3

38. Which of the following choices is equivalent to the equation $x = \frac{3}{y} + y$?

(A) $x + y = \frac{1}{3}y$
(B) $x - y = \frac{1}{3}y$
(C) $\frac{x}{3} = \frac{y}{3} + y$
(D) $xy = 3 + y^2$

39. Customers at a marble shop are allowed to play with the marbles in a certain box. The shopkeeper finds that 0.25 times the total number of marbles in the box are lost by the end of any given day. If there were 128 marbles in the box on Monday morning, how many marbles are in the box on Wednesday morning?

(A) 96
(B) 72
(C) 36
(D) 8

40. If $x = 4(y + 4)$, what is the value of $x - 2$?

(A) $4y - 2$
(B) $4y + 2$
(C) $4y + 14$
(D) $4y + 16$

Go on to the next page. ➡

41. In the circular wheel pictured below, all sections have the same area.

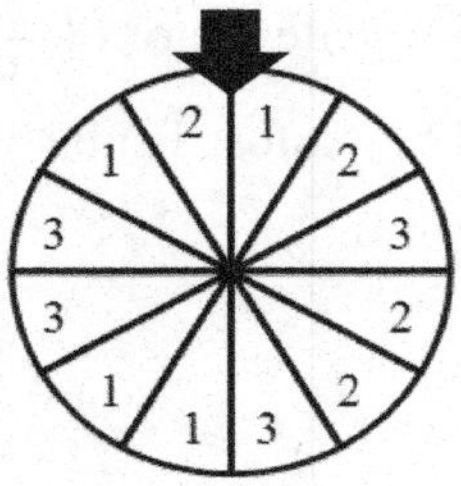

The above wheel is spun, and a number is determined by the black arrow. What is the probability that the number determined by the black arrow is prime?

(A) $\frac{1}{12}$
(B) $\frac{1}{3}$
(C) $\frac{2}{3}$
(D) 1

42. A right circular cylinder has a radius of 3 and a height of 8. Which of the following is closest to the surface area of the cylinder? *Note: surface area of a cylinder* $= 2\pi r^2 + 2\pi r \times h$

(A) 54π in^2
(B) 66π in^2
(C) 96π in^2
(D) 192π in^2

43. School is in session for 180 days at Dunwood Prep. At Donovan Prep, school is in session for 160 days. It rained on 72 of the days both schools were in session. What is the difference in the percentage of rainy days there were at Dunwood Prep compared with Donovan Prep?

(A) 5%
(B) 20%
(C) 40%
(D) 45%

44. Torval must deliver 90 newspapers by bicycle on Sunday. It took him 6 minutes to deliver the first 20 newspapers. At this rate, how much time will it take him to deliver the remaining papers?

(A) 21 minutes
(B) 27 minutes
(C) 30 minutes
(D) 33 minutes

45. A set of six numbers has a mean of 20. What additional number **must** be included in this set to create a new set with a mean that is four more than the mean of the original set?

(A) 24
(B) 48
(C) 120
(D) 168

46. A rectangular outdoor patio measures 6 feet long by 8 feet wide. Abigail plans to cover the patio in square tiles measuring 6 inches on each side. How many square tiles must she use to cover the entire patio with a single layer of tile? *Note: 1 foot = 12 inches.*

(A) 16
(B) 96
(C) 192
(D) 228

47. Which of the following choices is equivalent to the expression $\left(\sqrt{\frac{x}{3}}\right)^2$?

(A) $3x$
(B) $\sqrt{\frac{x}{3}}$
(C) $\frac{x^2}{3^2}$
(D) $\sqrt{\frac{x^2}{3^2}}$

STOP. Do not go on until instructed to do so.

STOP

Section Five: Essay Prompt

Time Limit: 30 minutes

Directions – You have 30 minutes to plan and write an essay on the topic printed below. Do not write on another topic. How well you write is more important than how much you write. You may only write in the appropriate section of the answer sheet. Write neatly so that someone else can read your handwriting. You may take notes in the section below. Write only in blue or black pen.

TOPIC:

If you could interview anyone, living or dead, who would it be? J.K Rowling.

NOTES:

Scoring the Diagnostic Practice Test (Form A)

Using your answer sheet and referring to the answer key at the back of the book, calculate the percentage of questions you answered correctly in each section by taking the number of questions you answered correctly in that section and dividing it by the number of questions in that section. Multiply this number by 100 to determine your percentage score. The higher the percentage, the stronger your performance in that section. The lower the percentage, the more time you should spend practicing that section.

Note that the actual test will not evaluate your score based on percentage correct or incorrect. Instead, it will evaluate your performance relative to all other students in your grade who took the test, and report a stanine score.

Record your results here:

Section	Questions Correct	Total Questions	Percent Questions Correct
Verbal Reasoning	_____	40	_____%
Quantitative Reasoning	_____	37	_____%
Reading Comprehension	_____	36	_____%
Mathematics Achievement	_____	47	_____%

Carefully consider the results from your diagnostic test when coming up with your study plan. Remember, the Middle Level ISEE is given to students in grades 6-7. Unless you've finished 7th grade, chances are that there is material on this test that you have not yet been taught. If this is the case, and you would like to improve your score beyond what is expected of your grade, consider outside help – such as a tutor or teacher – who can help you learn more about the topics that are new to you.

Answer Key

The answer key to this diagnostic test can be found at the back of the book in the Answer Key section. The keys are organized by section, and each question has an answer associated with it. Visit www.thetutorverse.com for detailed answer explanations.

The answer explanations for the diagnostic test also describe the content area tested by each question. Use this information to help identify which sections of the book to prioritize. Students should ask a parent or guardian's permission before going online. Note that there are no answers provided to the essay sections. Instead, consider having a tutor, teacher, or other educator review your writing and give you constructive feedback.

Get a Scaled Score Report @ thetutorverse.com/digital

Looking for an estimated Scaled Score Report? First, save your printed bubble sheet!

Then, navigate to thetutorverse.com/digital. Scroll to the "Get a Score Report" feature and follow the on-screen instructions. You'll be prompted to create or log in to your account on thetutorverse.com.

More Practice Tests Available Online

Need to take more practice tests? Want to work through more practice sections? Check out our computer-based practice on thetutorverse.com/digital. Take a fully-timed, automated practice test. Or, work through thousands of additional practice questions. Get this workbook for FREE using the code at the front of this workbook.

Verbal Reasoning

On the Actual Test

In the Verbal Reasoning section of the Middle Level ISEE, you will encounter two types of questions:

- *Synonyms* – This section assesses your ability to recognize words and reason through different relationships and subtle differences among words.
- *Sentence Completion* – Sentence completion questions consist of a sentence with one word missing from the sentence. Your task is to select the missing word that most appropriately completes the sentence.

Both Synonyms and Sentence Completion questions are designed to test your vocabulary and reasoning skills.

There will be 40 questions on the actual Verbal Reasoning section, which you will have 20 minutes to complete. In the Verbal Reasoning section, there will be five questions that will not be scored. These questions are included for trial and research purposes only. You will not know which questions are trial questions.

In This Practice Book

This section contains many exams' worth of materials to help you practice. The questions within each of the following sections grow progressively more difficult, as they do on the actual exam. For example, question 20 will be more difficult than question 2, and so on.

Verbal Reasoning practice consists of the following sections:

- Synonyms
    - Introductory
    - Intermediate
    - Advanced
- Sentence Completion
    - Introductory
    - Intermediate
    - Advanced

There are additional instructions and recommendations at the beginning of each of the Synonyms and Sentence Completion pages which you should review before starting.

Synonyms

Overview

Each synonym question consists of a word written in capital letters followed by four answer choice words written in lower-case letters. Your task is to select one of the four listed answer choices that is most nearly the same in meaning as the word in capital letters. Not every question word will necessarily have an answer choice with the exact same meaning!

How to Use This Section

How much time you spend on this section should be based on your diagnostic test results as well as your study plan. For most students, even those who score very well on the diagnostic test, we recommend that you practice at least 10-15 questions per week in preparing for the exam. Those who score well on the diagnostic test and have an expansive vocabulary may wish to focus more on intermediate and advanced questions, while other students may wish to focus on introductory and intermediate questions.

The purpose of this section is to introduce you to new words. You may find many of the words in this section to be challenging. Don't be surprised if you need to look up many of the words that you encounter in this section! We encourage you to make a list of words that give you trouble, whether they appear in questions or answer choices. Write down the definition of each word as well as a sentence using the word. You might also want to consider writing down positive or negative associations, any root words that can help you remember the word, or any words that are commonly encountered with that word.

Tutorverse Tips!

Answer choices in this section are always listed in alphabetical order. As you read the question words in capital letters, think of a word that you might use instead of the question word.

Sometimes, words can have more than one meaning. Don't let this confuse you! Look at the answer choices to make an educated guess as to which meaning is being used in the question. Then, use your reasoning skills to select the word that most nearly means the same as the word in capital letters.

If you don't know what a word means, try using it in a sentence. This will often help you see which word can be used to replace the question word. If this doesn't help, see if you can figure out whether or not the word has any positive or negative associations that match those of answer choices.

Remember that on the Middle Level ISEE, there is no penalty for guessing. If you don't know the answer to a question, take your best guess.

Finally, there is no better preparation for the Synonym section than spending time reading. The practice of reading, whether for school or for pleasure, will help you build up your vocabulary. It will give you practice in utilizing context clues and figuring out what unknown words might mean. Reading at or above your current grade level will help you make better sense of more complicated words and sentences.

Introductory

Directions – Choose the word that is most nearly the same in meaning as the word in capital letters.

1. ANXIOUS:

(A) calm
(B) nervous
(C) patient
(D) sad

2. OBNOXIOUS:

(A) critical
(B) deadly
(C) flammable
(D) unpleasant

3. PRIOR:

(A) brief
(B) cumulative
(C) original
(D) previous

4. DEVOUR:

(A) consume
(B) deposit
(C) expel
(D) recall

5. EVALUATE:

(A) appreciate
(B) assess
(C) criticize
(D) praise

6. DEBATE:

(A) agreement
(B) argument
(C) election
(D) poll

7. BENEFIT:

(A) advantage
(B) kindness
(C) luxury
(D) obstacle

8. ACCOMPLISH:

(A) accommodate
(B) accustom
(C) assist
(D) complete

9. ACKNOWLEDGE:

(A) accept
(B) avoid
(C) contemplate
(D) object

10. ABOLISH:

(A) adorn
(B) deceive
(C) start
(D) stop

11. CONTEXT:

(A) background
(B) likeness
(C) logic
(D) writing

12. COMPOSE:

(A) associate
(B) campaign
(C) decay
(D) write

13. OPTIMISTIC:

(A) friendly
(B) gloomy
(C) hopeful
(D) terrified

14. STRATEGY:

(A) discipline
(B) method
(C) question
(D) security

15. ADAPT:

(A) change
(B) pity
(C) qualify
(D) remove

16. EXHIBIT:

(A) display
(B) donate
(C) observe
(D) prohibit

17. CONSECUTIVE:

(A) alternating
(B) changing
(C) similar
(D) uninterrupted

18. COLLIDE:

(A) adhere
(B) avalanche
(C) slide
(D) strike

19. EXCEL:

(A) free
(B) spread
(C) suffer
(D) surpass

20. ENCOUNTER:

(A) meet
(B) oppose
(C) resist
(D) wait

21. ABNORMAL:

(A) average
(B) plain
(C) shrewd
(D) strange

22. REMORSE:

(A) appreciation
(B) code
(C) grief
(D) peace

23. PORTABLE:

(A) awkward
(B) clean
(C) convenient
(D) exposed

24. SPONTANEOUS:

(A) intended
(B) simultaneous
(C) specific
(D) unprompted

25. TOXIC:

(A) functional
(B) harmful
(C) nauseating
(D) splendid

26. DATA:

(A) assumption
(B) information
(C) reason
(D) machine

27. OVERWHELM:

(A) deflect
(B) engulf
(C) punish
(D) upset

28. MERELY:

(A) appropriately
(B) eventually
(C) only
(D) recently

29. DISMAL:

(A) beautiful
(B) bleak
(C) cheery
(D) ridiculous

30. THRIVE:

(A) baffle
(B) coax
(C) mesmerize
(D) prosper

31. IGNITE:

(A) darken
(B) maintain
(C) reduce
(D) spark

32. OMIT:

(A) ignore
(B) risk
(C) send
(D) submit

33. HOAX:

(A) cut
(B) hope
(C) prank
(D) truth

Intermediate

Directions – Choose the word that is most nearly the same in meaning as the word in capital letters.

1. DWELL:

(A) improve
(B) inhabit
(C) sleep
(D) vacate

2. APPEAL:

(A) cancel
(B) request
(C) settle
(D) unwrap

3. REINFORCE:

(A) boost
(B) expect
(C) impose
(D) rule

4. INEVITABLE:

(A) certain
(B) late
(C) lively
(D) restrained

5. CHRONOLOGICAL:

(A) consequential
(B) reasonable
(C) sensible
(D) sequential

6. BARREN:

(A) empty
(B) lush
(C) remote
(D) rural

7. BOYCOTT:

(A) approve
(B) believe
(C) claim
(D) reject

8. CONCISE:

(A) brief
(B) festive
(C) guilty
(D) unbelievable

9. EMPLOY:

(A) confuse
(B) disregard
(C) trick
(D) utilize

10. CORRESPOND:

(A) bore
(B) direct
(C) feature
(D) match

11. AGITATE:

(A) distress
(B) enjoy
(C) make
(D) relax

12. COMPEL:

(A) avoid
(B) coerce
(C) endorse
(D) request

13. ADJACENT:

(A) eroded
(B) involved
(C) neighboring
(D) still

14. PERSIST:

(A) annoy
(B) emerge
(C) endure
(D) obey

15. NOTORIOUS:

(A) deadly
(B) legendary
(C) obscure
(D) ordinary

16. INDIFFERENT:

(A) altered
(B) neutral
(C) opinionated
(D) similar

17. GRUESOME:

(A) appalling
(B) handsome
(C) hilarious
(D) scarlet

18. TREACHEROUS:

(A) deceptive
(B) educational
(C) loyal
(D) rowdy

19. PASTURE:

(A) barn
(B) field
(C) home
(D) wheat

20. OBLIVIOUS:

(A) empty
(B) furious
(C) tardy
(D) unaware

21. NIMBLE:

(A) angry
(B) exhausted
(C) ignorant
(D) spry

22. BRAWL:

(A) accept
(B) befriend
(C) fight
(D) ignore

23. ABRASIVE:

(A) considerate
(B) indecisive
(C) kind
(D) rough

24. COPIOUS:

(A) abundant
(B) imitation
(C) modest
(D) wicked

25. AVERT:

(A) advertise
(B) avoid
(C) negotiate
(D) signal

26. ASPIRE:

(A) criticize
(B) descend
(C) generate
(D) hope

27. BENIGN:

(A) affectionate
(B) dangerous
(C) fragile
(D) unbelievable

28. BESTOW:

(A) award
(B) conceal
(C) remove
(D) tarnish

29. CONTROVERSY:

(A) disagreement
(B) proof
(C) refutation
(D) truth

30. DEFECT:

(A) error
(B) intention
(C) result
(D) virtue

31. SUBJECTIVE:

(A) enjoyable
(B) horrible
(C) impartial
(D) personal

32. BELLIGERENT:

(A) aggressive
(B) consistent
(C) despairing
(D) intelligent

33. PINNACLE:

(A) barricade
(B) conjecture
(C) summit
(D) vase

Advanced

Directions – Choose the word that is most nearly the same in meaning as the word in capital letters.

1. PERSPECTIVE:

(A) dread
(B) excerpt
(C) outlook
(D) perspiration

2. REBUKE:

(A) admire
(B) devote
(C) instill
(D) scold

3. CITE:

(A) evoke
(B) locate
(C) plagiarize
(D) quote

4. ENDEAVOR:

(A) attempt
(B) encourage
(C) fail
(D) waver

5. ARTICULATE:

(A) imagine
(B) model
(C) understand
(D) vocalize

6. GULLIBLE:

(A) adventurous
(B) experienced
(C) impressionable
(D) stubborn

7. COMPREHEND:

(A) detain
(B) realize
(C) release
(D) support

8. DEJECTED:

(A) discovered
(B) improved
(C) forlorn
(D) removed

9. BARTER:

(A) banter
(B) exchange
(C) foster
(D) pioneer

10. COMPONENT:

(A) bastion
(B) computer
(C) ingredient
(D) relic

11. INTEGRATE:

(A) apply
(B) begin
(C) mingle
(D) testify

12. CAPRICIOUS:

(A) enormous
(B) royal
(C) stable
(D) unpredictable

13. FORTIFY:

(A) depend
(B) disperse
(C) strengthen
(D) terminate

14. CHARACTERIZE:

(A) compare
(B) forge
(C) objectify
(D) represent

15. SLEEK:

(A) eccentric
(B) lonely
(C) modest
(D) smooth

16. CALAMITY:

(A) catastrophe
(B) cliché
(C) nervousness
(D) uncertainty

17. ANARCHY:

(A) chaos
(B) control
(C) dictatorship
(D) regime

18. COMMEMORATE:

(A) desecrate
(B) honor
(C) impersonate
(D) memorize

19. DERIVE:

(A) insult
(B) motivate
(C) obtain
(D) propel

20. INCENSE:

(A) anger
(B) joke
(C) motivate
(D) wonder

21. PROPRIETOR:

(A) accomplice
(B) asset
(C) owner
(D) tradition

22. ALLOT:

(A) deter
(B) distribute
(C) numerous
(D) surpass

23. SUCCUMB:

(A) entice
(B) lure
(C) resist
(D) yield

24. LEEWAY:

(A) flexibility
(B) inexperience
(C) renown
(D) trickery

25. ABDICATE:

(A) quit
(B) remember
(C) satisfy
(D) understand

26. PRONE:

(A) luminous
(B) pretty
(C) susceptible
(D) upright

27. INCREDULOUS:

(A) doubtful
(B) fraudulent
(C) genuine
(D) substantial

28. ADMONISH:

(A) criticize
(B) praise
(C) prophesize
(D) remind

29. FAMISHED:

(A) charitable
(B) hungry
(C) intelligent
(D) popular

30. IRATE:

(A) furious
(B) gentle
(C) lordly
(D) vindictive

31. VOCATION:

(A) announcement
(B) holiday
(C) meeting
(D) mission

32. OBSTINATE:

(A) tired
(B) immune
(C) stubborn
(D) wary

33. RETICENT:

(A) guarded
(B) plentiful
(C) rewarding
(D) verbose

Sentence Completion

Overview

Sentence completion questions assess your ability to understand the meaning of words and how they are used in sentences. Each question consists of a sentence with one missing word. Your task is to choose the word that best completes the sentence based on the context and logic of the sentence as well as the meaning of the word.

How to Use This Section

How much time you spend on this section should be based on your diagnostic test results as well as your study plan. For most students, even those who score very well on the diagnostic test, we recommend that you practice at least 5-10 questions per week in preparing for the exam. Those who score well on the diagnostic test and have an expansive vocabulary or otherwise feel confident in verbal reasoning skills may wish to focus more on intermediate and advanced questions, while other students may wish to focus on introductory and intermediate questions.

The purpose of this section is to introduce you to new words. You may find many of the words in this section to be challenging. Don't be surprised if you need to look up many of the words that you encounter in this section! We encourage you to make a list of words that give you trouble, whether they appear in sentence questions or answer choices. Write down the definition of each word as well as a sentence using the word. You might also want to consider writing down positive or negative associations, any root words that can help you remember the word, or any words that are commonly encountered with that word.

Tutorverse Tips!

Context clues are very important. Read the sentence in its entirety in order to understand the overall meaning.

Then, focus on key words and clues that might help you determine the correct answer. For example, words such as "though" and "despite" can signal that the correct answer choice might be one that implies the opposite of what is given in the sentence. Similarly, words such as "because" and "since" can signal that the correct answer choice might be one that implies the same meaning as what is given in the sentence. Pay special attention to the meaning or connotation of adjectives, as the description of subjects they modify will give you a clue as to the right answer choice.

Once you've decided on an answer choice, reread the sentence including your answer choice in the sentence to make sure the sentence makes sense with the overall meaning.

Remember that on the Middle Level ISEE, there is no penalty for guessing. If you don't know the answer to a question, take your best guess.

Finally, there is no better preparation for the Sentence Completion section than spending time reading. Reading introduces you to different ways that sentences can be put together. By spending time reading, you will start to see all of the different ways that ideas can be expressed in a sentence. Reading at or above your current grade level will help you make better sense of more complicated words and sentences.

Introductory

Directions – Choose the word that best completes the sentence.

1. The scientist's job was to ------- the samples in order to determine whether or not the water was safe for drinking.

(A) analyze
(B) copy
(C) improve
(D) reject

2. When I called the library to renew my book, the librarian informed me that I could no longer ------- the lending period, for my book was already long overdue.

(A) elude
(B) extend
(C) identify
(D) reduce

3. As a(n) ------- of his prank, the student was required to report to school on Saturday for detention.

(A) ailment
(B) artifact
(C) cause
(D) consequence

4. When travelling by bus, it is sometimes necessary to ------- from one route to another.

(A) leap
(B) linger
(C) migrate
(D) transfer

5. Whereas Xena was one to ------- her enemies, her brother Yardley preferred to avoid conflict.

(A) appease
(B) commend
(C) confront
(D) skirt

6. Considering Greg had never formally trained for a marathon before, the fact that he finished the race at all was -------.

(A) expected
(B) impressive
(C) negative
(D) realistic

7. Because Ms. Kaban had been focusing on multiplication for the last several weeks, a(n) ------- portion of the upcoming test was going to be on multiplication.

(A) irrelevant
(B) luxurious
(C) peculiar
(D) significant

8. Because the sugar would not -------, and instead sat in clumps at the bottom of the pitcher, Hillary had a difficult time making lemonade.

(A) dissolve
(B) erupt
(C) harden
(D) perish

9. The little girl ignored her mother's warning and continued to blow into the balloon, causing it to ------- until it exploded.

(A) contract
(B) expand
(C) plummet
(D) withdraw

10. Though many people laughed at Thomas' invention, believing it to be useless and -------, it would go on to become one of the most important creations in the world.

(A) absurd
(B) beneficial
(C) practical
(D) rigid

11. It was unlike Darren to -------, as he was usually very proactive and preferred to arrive at appointments early.

(A) approach
(B) commit
(C) delay
(D) hurry

12. Famous for remaining as still as statues, the guards at Buckingham Palace remain ------- in the face of nearly all distractions.

(A) exhausted
(B) marvelous
(C) stationary
(D) thrifty

13. Despite rest, water, and medication, Russel's headache would not -------, making it impossible for him to focus on his work.

(A) abate
(B) intensify
(C) progress
(D) worsen

14. Harriet's mother scolded her for ------- the pigeons that had been resting peacefully on the park bench until a moment ago.

(A) feeding
(B) harassing
(C) praising
(D) questioning

15. The flashing lights and wailing siren let other drivers know that there was an emergency and that there was a(n) ------- need for them to make way for the ambulance.

(A) futile
(B) leisurely
(C) precise
(D) urgent

16. Usually calm and patient, Charlotte's father surprised everyone when he grew ------- as a result of the waiter's simple and honest mistake.

(A) distant
(B) infuriated
(C) relaxed
(D) satisfied

17. Wildlife preserves, a(n) ------- for animals, are lands set aside by the government that are protected from hunting and human development.

(A) drawback
(B) illusion
(C) myth
(D) sanctuary

18. With pleading eyes, Florence ------- her father to let her stay up past her bed time to watch the ice-skating finale.

(A) begged
(B) detained
(C) fought
(D) permitted

19. Hiking out of Yosemite Valley took every ounce of Victor's strength and, after nearly six hours of hiking, he was ------- from his effort.

(A) disappointed
(B) doubtful
(C) fragile
(D) weary

20. Some televisions allow the viewer to watch different channels at the same time, though how anyone can watch two or three shows ------- is beyond my understanding.

(A) assertively
(B) comparably
(C) consecutively
(D) simultaneously

21. Between homework, basketball, and newspaper club, Edward had so much going on that he found it difficult to ------- his time and energy.

(A) predict
(B) prioritize
(C) retire
(D) sift

22. The valley's settlers were rewarded with a harvest so ------- that they had enough food to last two winters.

(A) bountiful
(B) durable
(C) prevalent
(D) variable

23. Old Faithful geyser erupts more regularly and more predictably than many other geysers, whose eruptions are more ------- in nature.

(A) coordinated
(B) hesitant
(C) irregular
(D) unsurprising

24. Xavier had been working on a single math problem for weeks and was convinced that the ------- was unsolvable.

(A) enigma
(B) innovation
(C) novel
(D) translation

25. As the robbery later proved, though the bank seemed -------, it was in fact powerless to stop thieves.

(A) forgiving
(B) influential
(C) secure
(D) vulnerable

26. Though she wanted to ------- her good fortune to skill, Jenny knew that winning the jackpot had more to do with luck than skill.

(A) credit
(B) dedicate
(C) infer
(D) reference

27. Because he used a permanent pen, Maurice was unable to ------- his response to the questionnaire even though he had made a mistake.

(A) dispatch
(B) highlight
(C) modify
(D) simulate

28. All of the firefighters emerged ------- from the fire, which was a relief given the ferocity of the blaze.

(A) equivalent
(B) injured
(C) pampered
(D) unscathed

29. In order to move the huge dinner table through the narrow hallway, the family needed to ------- it first and hope that they could reassemble it later.

(A) assume
(B) compile
(C) dismantle
(D) export

30. Because she was certain that she had done poorly on the quiz, Evelyn was ------- when she received her score and saw that she had done extremely well.

(A) anguished
(B) bewildered
(C) justified
(D) pacified

31. Kristen felt that there was something ------- about her desk; though nothing was missing, things seemed slightly out of place.

(A) amiss
(B) cheerful
(C) distant
(D) filthy

32. Despite Cassian's best efforts to soothe and calm his baby boy, his son could not be quieted and remained -------.

(A) drowsy
(B) legendary
(C) perturbed
(D) senseless

33. Over time, lack of physical activity has been shown to be ------- to a person's health, often leading to serious medical conditions.

(A) advantageous
(B) contagious
(C) detrimental
(D) routine

Intermediate

Directions – Choose the word that best completes the sentence.

1. Since people have turned to more convenient options, such as the cellphone, public payphones have become -------.

   (A) abstract
   (B) obsolete
   (C) popular
   (D) troublesome

2. If we continue to ------- our natural resources, eventually nothing will remain.

   (A) deplete
   (B) preserve
   (C) supplement
   (D) value

3. Because of the ------- in the cafeteria, recess for all students was cancelled for the day.

   (A) abundance
   (B) clamber
   (C) incident
   (D) opportunity

4. Larry's favorite pastime was to ------- his older sister's anger, which he accomplished by running around her room while yelling.

   (A) deprive
   (B) provoke
   (C) restrain
   (D) thwart

5. The donors who had established the school had chosen to remain -------, as they did not need public recognition.

   (A) anonymous
   (B) candid
   (C) consistent
   (D) patient

6. Contrary to popular belief, many researchers agree that working more than forty hours a week actually makes people less -------, not more so.

   (A) elegant
   (B) languid
   (C) productive
   (D) suspicious

7. In response to the vicious claims made against him, the politician decided to ------- with his own equally hurtful claims.

   (A) celebrate
   (B) collaborate
   (C) improvise
   (D) retaliate

8. The octopus is known not only for its intelligence, but for its ability to ------- its surroundings in order to disguise itself from its predators.

   (A) dissect
   (B) mimic
   (C) restrict
   (D) understand

9. The owner of the restaurant did not like to ------- anyone, but the group of friends was so loud and disruptive that he had no choice but to deny them admittance.

   (A) abandon
   (B) accommodate
   (C) exclude
   (D) intimidate

10. Due to its unchanging location near the north celestial pole, Polaris, the North Star, is famous for maintaining a(n) ------- position in the night sky.

   (A) appropriate
   (B) approximate
   (C) constant
   (D) massive

11. Charities request donations during the holiday season because they know that people are typically more likely to ------- then than at other times of the year.

(A) compete
(B) contribute
(C) offend
(D) reject

12. Though Fran tried her best to ------- her mother to allow her to attend the concert, her mother could not be convinced.

(A) permit
(B) persuade
(C) reassure
(D) tempt

13. For three unbroken weeks, the clouds were so dark and ------- that the citizens of Pleasantville could barely tell the difference between day and night.

(A) dense
(B) drowsy
(C) omniscient
(D) ruthless

14. Though many supported increasing the speed limit on highways, the government feared that higher speeds would ------- the public's safety.

(A) appease
(B) endanger
(C) enhance
(D) overthrow

15. Though there were many qualities that attracted the buyers to the home, the deciding ------- was the location.

(A) factor
(B) genre
(C) occasion
(D) verdict

16. Although Milton was generally regarded as a(n) ------- worker, his failure to master the new equipment after several years left his managers wondering about his abilities.

(A) competent
(B) credible
(C) inept
(D) poised

17. The socialite hoped to use her family name and financial resources to achieve celebrity and increase the ranking of her social -------.

(A) jeopardy
(B) policy
(C) refuge
(D) status

18. Zion National Park is home to many strange stone formations that, though -------, are still beautiful.

(A) bizarre
(B) drastic
(C) extensive
(D) monotonous

19. Jordan could not argue with the professor's -------, for the idea itself made logical sense and seemed to be consistent with many people's experiences.

(A) blunder
(B) connotation
(C) esteem
(D) viewpoint

20. Whereas the previous manager had made many mistakes and was ------- in carrying out his duties, the new manager was detail-oriented and focused.

(A) attentive
(B) blunt
(C) rude
(D) negligent

21. More ------- than the average investigator, the detective was able to draw conclusions that her peers could not.

    (A) apprehensive
    (B) astute
    (C) ferocious
    (D) formal

22. Because different ways of thinking can often lead to new ideas, ------- is often valued by schools and businesses.

    (A) appearance
    (B) conformity
    (C) diversity
    (D) honesty

23. Rather than supporting her ideas with facts, Dana frequently chooses to ------- her opinions only with exclamation marks.

    (A) correlate
    (B) emphasize
    (C) nurture
    (D) paraphrase

24. Though the athlete had suffered many setbacks and encountered many obstacles, she was nevertheless ------- in her pursuit of the Olympic gold medal.

    (A) deceitful
    (B) irate
    (C) resolute
    (D) vicious

25. Sage had such a yearning for knowledge that no amount of intellectual stimulation could ------- her thirst for understanding.

    (A) conserve
    (B) fathom
    (C) quench
    (D) rupture

26. A witty ------- may seem like a good idea at the time, but responding negatively to an insult can often result in further trouble.

    (A) promise
    (B) retort
    (C) vow
    (D) whim

27. As the party drew to a close, the departing guests, having had their fun and eaten their fill, spoke among themselves of the host's gracious and ------- disposition.

    (A) desperate
    (B) hospitable
    (C) loathsome
    (D) stodgy

28. Many fans believed the referees to be -------, for there was evidence that the referees had accepted bribes from the winning team.

    (A) corrupt
    (B) oblivious
    (C) primitive
    (D) rudimentary

29. The young child, ignorant of the word's negative meaning and connotation, did not realize that it was ------- and hurtful to certain groups of people.

    (A) customary
    (B) derogatory
    (C) gaudy
    (D) predatory

30. Staring at the flying pig, Torval found that he was ------- and could neither move nor make a noise.

    (A) exonerated
    (B) flabbergasted
    (C) naïve
    (D) peevish

31. Though some ------- handbags are easy to identify as such, many more escape detection and are bought and sold as legitimate and original products.

(A) authentic
(B) casual
(C) counterfeit
(D) trivial

32. The sickness had spread so quickly and quietly that the government was suddenly faced with a(n) -------.

(A) election
(B) epidemic
(C) parody
(D) void

33. Whereas Zephyr displayed a great desire to learn, the teacher could tell that when it came to education, Andreas possessed nothing but -------.

(A) apathy
(B) bias
(C) curiosity
(D) prowess

Advanced

Directions – Choose the word that best completes the sentence.

1. The -------, who controlled the country with absolute power, desired that the largest diamonds be set in her royal jewels.

(A) actor
(B) monarch
(C) musician
(D) servant

2. The fact that the politicians were ------- in their decision to raise taxes was surprising, as they rarely agreed on anything.

(A) divided
(B) fatigued
(C) inexperienced
(D) unanimous

3. The Rocky Mountains forms a(n) -------, unbroken wall from New Mexico all the way north to British Columbia.

(A) continuous
(B) disjointed
(C) efficient
(D) narrow

4. The powerful woman was ------- in business, political, and social circles, holding many highly visible positions.

(A) inconspicuous
(B) nonchalant
(C) prominent
(D) reserved

5. Kolya, the foreign exchange student who only had a(n) ------- understanding of American words and phrases, had a difficult time understanding jokes and sarcasm.

(A) admirable
(B) complex
(C) figurative
(D) literal

6. Because a small group of people control all of the oil in the world, they are able to easily ------- the price of oil to reflect their own wishes.

(A) assemble
(B) document
(C) eclipse
(D) manipulate

7. Afraid of water, the dirty cat was at first ------- to take a bath but later found the experience to be tolerable.

(A) eager
(B) reluctant
(C) resolved
(D) yearning

8. Jackie is thinking about keeping a diary in which she would ------- all of the things that had happened to her each day.

(A) access
(B) captivate
(C) possess
(D) recount

9. Ben intended to ask the professor to ------- further on a concept he found confusing, but Professor Doe had already moved on to the next topic.

(A) declare
(B) elaborate
(C) generate
(D) propel

10. Ms. Smith was quick to ------- basic rules governing behavior in her class so that the students would not be confused about her expectations.

(A) establish
(B) exaggerate
(C) pursue
(D) reflect

11. A lion rearing up on its hind legs clawing at the air was the ------- of the Lancaster family for nearly a century, flying on the family's flags and banners.

(A) criteria
(B) emblem
(C) rant
(D) tragedy

12. Because their names are well-known, some famous people choose to adopt a -------, which helps them to maintain privacy.

(A) grudge
(B) perception
(C) pseudonym
(D) warrant

13. The students elected Gerry as student council president because they knew that she would ------- their needs and represent their interests well.

(A) advocate
(B) embargo
(C) interrogate
(D) wrangle

14. Knowing how difficult it is to draw well, Fabian has a ------- respect for artists, even saying how drawing is the highest form of art.

(A) blasé
(B) disdainful
(C) profound
(D) superficial

15. The Nile River Delta was extremely -------; the land produced so much food that farmers had plenty to spare.

    (A) fertile
    (B) formidable
    (C) pungent
    (D) resilient

16. Without enough information, Lara was unable to ------- one possibility against the other, leaving her unable to make an informed decision.

    (A) contrast
    (B) deploy
    (C) evolve
    (D) fend

17. Without the support of powerful friends, which was ------- to the success of the plan, Yanez knew that he had no hope of overcoming the opposition.

    (A) crucial
    (B) marginal
    (C) recurring
    (D) sovereign

18. Rather than keep the error a secret, Will knew that a(n) ------- admission of guilt would be the best way to move past his mistake.

    (A) disingenuous
    (B) haggard
    (C) overt
    (D) sedative

19. When Lisa casually mentioned that she only owned one pair of shoes, Sharon ------- replied that she had at least twenty pairs of only the most expensive shoes.

    (A) capably
    (B) consistently
    (C) gingerly
    (D) haughtily

20. Looking out at the open water and seeing nothing but endless waves, it is easy to understand how people used to believe that the ocean was -------.

    (A) belligerent
    (B) exotic
    (C) infinite
    (D) proud

21. Forced into an impossible situation and with no other option but to admit defeat, Irene had no choice but to -------.

    (A) chastise
    (B) forfeit
    (C) inaugurate
    (D) operate

22. By the time archaeologists arrive, important historical sites are often already -------, having been robbed of important and valuable artifacts.

    (A) coherent
    (B) deceptive
    (C) plundered
    (D) pristine

23. Many people search for peace and ------- in the mountains of the world, for such places are often removed from the distractions and cares of modern life.

    (A) evidence
    (B) serenity
    (C) suspense
    (D) transition

24. Outraged at what she perceived to be unfair treatment, Gina took ------- with the clerk and vowed never to return to the store.

    (A) acclaim
    (B) candor
    (C) mirth
    (D) umbrage

25. The mistaken belief that lightning can never strike the same place twice is a ------- believed by many.

(A) decree
(B) fallacy
(C) procedure
(D) prophecy

26. As the company generated a significant portion of its ------- from Bob, the company knew that it could not afford to lose the income associated with him.

(A) complexity
(B) expense
(C) revenue
(D) rubble

27. The discovery, production, and widespread use of electricity marked a new ------- in human history – a period of time unlike any other before it.

(A) arena
(B) burden
(C) epoch
(D) semester

28. The attack on Pearl Harbor is considered by many to be a(n) ------- moment in American history, as the events of that day helped spur the otherwise neutral United States to join the world war.

(A) carefree
(B) insightful
(C) pivotal
(D) virtuous

29. Unaccustomed to such noises, smells, and sights, Oscar felt as though his senses had been ------- by his new and unfamiliar surroundings.

(A) assailed
(B) comforted
(C) elapsed
(D) instituted

30. The protestors hoped to ------- their numbers by recruiting new people to join their cause.

(A) augment
(B) caption
(C) encompass
(D) minimize

31. Filled with a deep sense of -------, the boy scout decided not to approach the house at the top of the hill because it was abandoned and looked haunted.

(A) anticipation
(B) contempt
(C) determination
(D) foreboding

32. A revolutionary new creation, the ------- machine would go on to change the lives of billions.

(A) eventful
(B) hackneyed
(C) impractical
(D) inventive

33. Many people noticed and liked Perry, for he had a winning personality and a ------- laugh that was as genuine as it was contagious.

(A) greedy
(B) hearty
(C) mutinous
(D) wry

Reading Comprehension

Overview

In the Reading Comprehension section, students are asked to read passages and answer questions that pertain to those passages. The reading passages cover a variety of subject areas including the sciences, arts, history, and modern life. Questions are one to two sentences in length and ask students to respond to questions related to a number of different topics.

On the Actual Test

In the Reading Comprehension section of the Middle Level ISEE, you will encounter six reading passages, each between 300-600 words long. There will be 36 questions on the actual Reading Comprehension section, which you have 35 minutes to complete. The questions you will see relate to:

- *Main Idea* – What is the general message, premise, or idea in a section or passage? What is the author trying to tell the reader?
- *Supporting Ideas* – What are specific ideas supporting the important messages, premises, or ideas? How does the author expand on his or her main idea?
- *Inference* – What are some conclusions that can be drawn from the passage? What should a reader be able to infer based on the passage?
- *Vocabulary* – What do certain words or phrases mean?
- *Logic & Organization* – How is the passage structured? What type of writing does the author use?
- *Mood, Tone, Style, & Figurative Language* – What feeling is the author trying to convey? How does the author use figurative language such as metaphors and similes to establish a mood or set a tone?

Of the 36 questions, six questions in the Reading Comprehension section will not be scored. These questions are included for trial and research purposes only. You will not know which questions are trial questions.

In This Practice Book

All passages in this book are between 300-600 words in length, and all lines in a passage are numbered. The passages cover a wide range of topics and styles. Questions are presented based on the order in which the subject-matter appears in the passage. This is unlike questions in other sections of the exam, which are ordered by difficulty.

The passages and questions in this section are designed to be similar to the actual Middle Level ISEE. Each passage has six questions. The passages and questions are on opposite pages, similar to the actual test.

How to Use This Section

We recommend that you practice several passages per week in preparing for exam.

You may find many words and concepts in this section to be challenging. Don't be surprised if you need to look up many of the words that you encounter in this section! We encourage you to make a list of words that give you trouble, whether they appear in passages, questions, or answer choices. Write down the definition of each word as well as a sentence using the word. You might also want to consider writing down positive or negative associations, any root words that can help you remember the word, or any words that are commonly encountered with that word. Reach out to a trusted educator for help learning new or confusing words or concepts.

Tutorverse Tips!

Remember that on the Middle Level ISEE, there is no penalty for guessing. If you don't know the answer to a question, take your best guess.

Practice Active Reading

We recommend that you read the passage first before attempting to answer the questions. As you read, underline or circle key information like main ideas. Draw arrows between related ideas, or examples that support main ideas. Consider outlining the passage to get a sense for the structure of the passage as well as how the different parts of the passage are related to each other.

Because the questions on each passage will be similar to those that you have practiced, you can keep an eye out for important themes and ideas as you read. This will help save time when you answer the questions.

Identifying Main Ideas & Genres

Think about what the main idea might be as you read the passage. Remember, some passages may appear to fall into multiple genres. For example, a very descriptive passage may also be narrated by the author or a character in the passage. In those instances, think about which two genres might best fit to help you eliminate incorrect answer choices. Here are some clues:

- Narrative Passages – often used to tell a story, such as a memory or a fantasy; may include dialogue, characters, or the word "I"
- Persuasive Passages – often used to persuade or convince the reader of an opinion or idea; may include opinions supported by reasons or facts; may ask the reader to do or agree with something
- Descriptive Passages – often used to describe something, such as a person, place, thing, or event; may be very descriptive, using many adjectives to appeal to the senses
- Expository Passages – often used to explain something, such as a process, or to present facts; may be very logical and sequential; may describe how to do something or explain a concept or idea

Identifying Question Types

- Reading Comprehension questions *are not* listed in order of difficulty. They are ordered based on the order of ideas in the passage. For example, questions related to Line 1 of a passage will be listed before questions related to Line 60.
- Main idea questions tend to be listed first. They often ask about the passage's "primary purpose" or about "what the passage is primarily concerned with."
- Supporting idea questions typically ask you to find something explicitly stated in the passage. Inference items typically ask you to think about ideas and interpret the passage in order to make a conclusion about something you've read. These questions tend not to ask for explicit support.
- Vocabulary questions usually ask what a specific word or phrase "most nearly means."

This section is similar to the actual Middle Level ISEE in that each passage has six questions. The passages and questions are on opposite pages, similar to the actual test.

Directions: Answer the questions following each passage on the basis of what is stated or implied in that passage.

Passage #1

Each year, around the end of November, the residents of Sycamore Lane participate in a tradition. This ritual is as old as anyone on the street can remember. The residents of Sycamore Lane pursue this custom with such enthusiasm and energy that their custom draws crowds from far and wide to pack into their narrow, tree-lined street.

The first preparations take place on the weekend after Thanksgiving Day. Lawns are raked clean of the season's leaves, which are hastily dumped alongside the curb. Metal frames are staked to the ground or attached to rooftops. Stringed lights of every shape, size, color, and length are uncoiled from their eleven-month long cocoons. Soon, a festive mood envelopes the lane.

Each family works to decorate their home: they string up lights on trees, wrap them around the metal frames, and hang them from eaves. Tell-tale signs of the holidays – reindeer, candy canes, and more – are inflated and placed merrily on once leaf-covered lawns. Over the weekend, every house on Sycamore Lane – every tree and every empty space – is covered in lights or other holiday decorations. It's not until everyone on Sycamore Lane has hung the last of their lights that the ceremony can truly begin.

Every year, Mrs. Jones, Sycamore Lane's oldest resident, gives a short speech welcoming family, friends, and hundreds of strangers to the annual lighting festival. At the end of her speech, all lights on the street are extinguished, leaving the crowd standing in a nervous silence and blanketed in an inky darkness.

Then, as if by magic, the silence is broken. The first bars of "Jingle Bells" come from the left; the next bars come from the right, and then from behind – and finally, from all around, as lights begin to flash.

In step with the music, star-shaped white lights twinkle in the trees up and down the street. Christmas trees on every lawn begin to glow like bushy rainbows; candy canes light up red and white; entire homes shimmer like white-hot coals in a fire and dance to the rhythm of the music.

All around the merrymakers is an organized light show set to the jingling, jangling melody of the season. The strangers stand shoulder to shoulder, smiling at one another, feeling within the warm fuzziness of the season's spirit.

Passage #1 Question Set

1. One of the main points of the passage is to

   (A) compare different customs.
   (B) explain a popular tradition.
   (C) list various holiday decorations.
   (D) describe the weather after Thanksgiving Day.

2. The passage provides information to support which of the following statements?

   (A) Decorating Sycamore Lane is exhausting.
   (B) The spectacle on Sycamore Lane is famous.
   (C) The music played during the ceremony is chosen at random.
   (D) Very few people are aware of the Sycamore Lane tradition.

3. The phrase "eleven-month long cocoons" (lines 15-16), compares the stringed lights with butterfly cocoons in order to

   (A) describe the shape of the bulbs.
   (B) depict how the strings are formed to look like butterflies.
   (C) emphasize that stringed lights may only be used once every eleven months.
   (D) show how the beauty of stringed lights are unwrapped after a period of waiting.

4. In line 16, the word "envelopes" most nearly means

   (A) contains.
   (B) letters.
   (C) opens.
   (D) surrounds.

5. According to the passage, the "nervous silence" and "inky darkness" (lines 34-35) are immediately preceded by

   (A) the crowding of strangers onto Sycamore Lane.
   (B) the crowding of residents onto Sycamore Lane.
   (C) the playing of music all around Sycamore Lane.
   (D) a speech from a respected resident of Sycamore Lane.

6. The passage implies that all of the residents of Sycamore Lane coordinate on the decoration of their street because

   (A) it is their most important holiday tradition.
   (B) if they didn't the street would be silent and dark.
   (C) they advertise together to draw a crowd to their street.
   (D) all of the decorations and music on the street are synchronized.

Passage #2

People have used coal as a source of energy for thousands of years. When burned, coal can be used to heat water, cook food, and even generate electricity. But where does coal come from, and how is it formed?

The hard, black rock that we recognize as coal was not always so hard and so black. In fact, it was not always a rock! The story of coal stretches back hundreds of millions of years. It is the story of life and death, of heat and pressure, and of time and chance.

The story of coal begins with plants that existed some 300-400 million years ago. For millions upon millions of years, plants lived and died in an endless cycle. Ferns, trees, and other plant life that died sometimes accumulated in great quantities and were eventually buried by tremendous amounts of soil and rock. Though the process of burying large amounts of dead plant matter usually took many years, sometimes flooding and other geological phenomena helped to cover the plant matter in a shorter period of time.

Once deep underground, the plant matter was subjected to enormous pressure and high temperatures. In addition, acidic water and mud helped to prevent or slow the decay of the plant matter. Together, these forces had the effect of converting the once-living plant matter into peat, a fibrous, brown, soil-like material.

With the right conditions, peat can be transformed into a mineral known as lignite. Lignite is peat that has basically been transformed into a rock, and is brownish-black in color. Sometimes, one can recognize plant structures, such as leaves and stems, in the lignite. Over time, by adding even more heat and pressure, lignite can be transformed into sub-bituminous and bituminous coal. Bituminous coal is the most abundant and commonly recognized form of coal. The rock itself is black and striped with alternating glossy and dull material. When asked to describe the appearance of "coal," people generally describe bituminous coal.

Though coal is relatively plentiful, the coal formation process is long and precarious. Some estimates suggest that each unit of coal starts with as much as five times as much plant matter. Even if this much plant matter were to accumulate (which is no easy feat – think about all of the leaves it would take!), it would take many more years and very specific conditions to transform that plant matter into peat, lignite, and eventually bituminous coal.

Passage #2 Question Set

1. The author would most likely agree with which statement about coal?

    (A) People create coal by killing plants.
    (B) Without coal, people would be unable to heat water or cook food.
    (C) The burning of coal should be replaced with the burning of natural gas.
    (D) Though coal may appear to be a simple rock, it is actually the product of a complex process.

2. The main purpose of the third paragraph (lines 12-23) is to

    (A) describe how coal can be used by people.
    (B) describe the end of the coal formation process.
    (C) describe the middle of the coal formation process.
    (D) describe the beginning of the coal formation process.

3. According to the passage, all of the following factors are necessary to turn lignite into bituminous coal EXCEPT

    (A) acid.
    (B) heat.
    (C) pressure.
    (D) time.

4. In line 47, "precarious" most nearly means

    (A) easily disrupted.
    (B) largely confusing.
    (C) potentially deadly.
    (D) permanently unbalanced.

5. It can be inferred from the passage that the coal formation process

    (A) requires very little plant matter to begin.
    (B) only takes place every 300-400 million years.
    (C) is ongoing, so long as the right conditions exist.
    (D) is a much faster process than previously estimated.

6. The author's attitude towards the coal formation process is best described as

    (A) admiring.
    (B) critical.
    (C) gloomy.
    (D) quizzical.

Passage #3

Most mornings, I need to drag myself out of bed. Waking up is usually a very slow and unpleasant process for me. Most days, it feels like I spend as much time slowly blinking absently at myself in the mirror as I do brushing my teeth and taking a shower.

On days like this, I think back to when I was in middle school. Back then, I had no trouble getting up on Sunday mornings. Waking up wasn't so dreary because I had something special to look forward to. Sundays were the one day a week that the newspaper comic strips were printed in glorious, vibrant color.

Long before my parents even put coffee on, I'd throw back my covers and jump out of bed. Bolting out of my bedroom, I wouldn't bother washing my face or brushing my teeth. Skipping the bathroom entirely, I couldn't get down the stairs quickly enough. Wedging my arms between the wall and the railing, I had developed a great way of skipping steps by half stepping and half swinging down the stairs. In just a few step-swings I'd be downstairs, fumbling to unlock and open the front door.

Stepping outside into the new day, I'd run full-speed across the lawn down to the mailbox. I can still feel my pajamas starting to stick to my ankles as the dew, cold and wet, would soak through the thin fabric. Using the post of the mailbox as a brake, I'd swing myself in front of the mailbox and tear open the little blue plastic door that kept my Sunday treasures dry.

Pulling out the day's paper, I'd run back up to the house. Feet and pajamas still wet, I'd find a spot by the window and sprawl out on the carpet. After finding the comics, I'd toss the rest of the newspaper aside and flip immediately to *Calvin & Hobbes*.

Instead of the usual paneled cartoons, what I'd find instead was a magnificent, half-page spread of Calvin attacking a monster with a ray-gun. The comics always drew me in deeply, and I'd spend fifteen minutes or more reading and soaking in each and every detail. For the rest of the day, I'd imagine myself as Calvin, with a faithful sidekick at my side, getting into all sorts of wacky and crazy adventures.

Passage #3 Question Set

1. Which of the following sentences best expresses the main idea of the passage?

   (A) Color comics are superior to black and white comics.
   (B) The comics are the most important part of the newspaper.
   (C) Getting out of bed is easier with something to look forward to.
   (D) The only reason to wake up in the morning is to read *Calvin & Hobbes*.

2. In line 10, "dreary" most nearly means

   (A) cheerless.
   (B) important.
   (C) thrilling.
   (D) uplifting.

3. The passage suggests that the author

   (A) is currently an adult.
   (B) hates every day but Sunday.
   (C) is no longer in middle school.
   (D) cannot wake up now without having coffee.

4. The author mentions how he "couldn't get down the stairs quickly enough" (lines 18-19) in order to

   (A) show how late he is for school.
   (B) illustrate how hungry he is in the mornings.
   (C) describe what he needs to do to avoid being scolded.
   (D) explain to the reader how excited he is to read his comics.

5. The phrase "Sunday treasures" (line 32), refers to

   (A) the mailbox.
   (B) the morning coffee.
   (C) the newspaper comics.
   (D) the author's imagination.

6. According to the passage, the author would often be cold and wet when reading the comics because

   (A) of the early morning dew.
   (B) he often spilled coffee in his excitement.
   (C) he did not dry off after his morning shower.
   (D) his face would be wet from brushing his teeth.

Passage #4

One of the most visited and recognizable structures in the world, the Eiffel Tower in Paris, France, stretches over 1,000 feet into the sky. Like a narrow, curving pyramid, the tower has four legs planted firmly in the ground, each separated from its adjacent neighbor by a gracefully curved archway. These four bases are aligned with the four points of the compass. Curving up from each leg are the corners of the tower, starting far apart at the four corners of the base and narrowing to a point at the very top of the tower. From the arches up to the top of the tower, the corners are connected by a web of iron latticework. Though the Eiffel Tower's appearance is iconic, there are several little-known details that many admirers fail to appreciate.

The tower has few solid sheets of iron. In some parts of the tower, the latticework is very intricate and easy to miss, a lasting tribute to the workers who manufactured and the designers who created the tower. Another detail which is often overlooked are the names of 72 famous French scientists. The designer of the tower had the names of these mechanics, astronomers, engineers, mathematicians, physicists, doctors, chemists, and more engraved on the few solid sheets of iron on the entire tower. These engravings commemorate and honor the contributions of these great thinkers. One can easily miss such fine details if one does not know where to look.

In fact, it's easy to miss the fact that the color of the tower itself is not painted a uniform shade. The iron tower is painted every several years to prevent it from rusting. Several tons of paint are used to cover the tower each time it is painted. Because of the tower's great height, the paint at the bottom of the tower is darker than at the top. By transitioning from a darker to lighter shade of the same color, the painters of the tower manage to create the illusion that, when viewed from the ground, the tower is uniformly colored. The color of the tower itself has changed over the years, sometimes a Venetian red and at other times a yellow-brown. Eventually, a special color called "Eiffel Tower Brown" was mixed and applied to the tower, as it was determined to be the best complement to the rest of the city.

Passage #4 Question Set

1. Which sentence best expresses the passage's main idea?

   (A) Many people recognize the Eiffel Tower.
   (B) Famous landmarks often have easy-to-miss details.
   (C) The Eiffel Tower's color is its most distinguishing characteristic.
   (D) Visitors to the Eiffel Tower must discover its little known details to have any appreciation of it.

2. In line 20, the word "tribute" most nearly means

   (A) contribution.
   (B) memorial.
   (C) sacrifice.
   (D) tax.

3. According to the passage, each of the French scientists whose names are engraved on the Eiffel Tower

   (A) were friends with the tower's designer.
   (B) voted for the original color of the Tower.
   (C) had a great influence in each of their fields.
   (D) all worked on the design and construction of the Tower.

4. Based on the passage, it is understood that one of the reasons that the tower is painted regularly is because

   (A) painting encourages rusting.
   (B) the color must change every time.
   (C) it helps maintain the integrity of the structure.
   (D) "Eiffel Tower Brown" is the best color to complement the city.

5. According to the author, all of the following are examples of details that visitors can easily miss EXCEPT

   (A) large curved archways.
   (B) intricate latticework.
   (C) the names of French scientists.
   (D) the changing shade of paint color.

6. It can be inferred from the passage that the author would agree with which of the following statements?

   (A) Brown is better than red or yellow.
   (B) The Eiffel Tower has many secrets worth learning.
   (C) The Eiffel Tower is the most iconic structure in the world.
   (D) Commemorating scientists is the most important purpose of the Eiffel Tower.

Passage #5

Many schools require that students wear uniforms. At these schools, students are only permitted to wear certain types of clothing. Rules that govern attire vary widely, but can determine the fit, length, style, and even the color of clothing. Though many students dislike uniforms, there are several reasons why wearing uniforms at school is actually beneficial for students.

People who share customs and traditions grow closer together. Celebrating the same holiday, eating the same foods, and playing the same games brings people closer. Likewise, wearing similar clothing helps create a sense of solidarity. In schools, where there are often students of varying backgrounds and experiences, uniforms help to introduce a deeper sense of community by creating an element common to all students.

Rightly or wrongly, students often focus on how they are different from others rather than on things that they have in common with their peers. By requiring uniforms, schools remove a visible and often distracting source of differences. Some studies have shown that students attending schools that require uniforms form fewer cliques. In short, uniforms help people see past clothing. By removing distractions, uniforms help students focus on truly important things like opinions, thoughts, ideas, and personality.

Uniforms are used often as a way to identify members of a group, and can provide intangible benefits. For example, many businesses require their employees to wear uniforms. These companies understand that uniforms create an air of professionalism about their workers. In some cases, such as with military men and women, wearing a uniform creates a sense of pride and belonging. In this way, uniforms provide emotional benefits to the wearer. Such uniforms are not merely individual articles of clothing, but something greater. They are something symbolic, the embodiment of sacrifice and pride. School uniforms can provide similar benefits.

Many people strive to stand out and be different. Individuality and independence is an important skill to develop. However, being able to work and empathize with others is equally important. So too is developing a sense of solidarity with one's peers. Uniforms help to level the playing field. They help students to see past ever-changing fashion trends; they help students not judge their fellow students by what they wear, but rather by what they say, what they do, and who they are.

Passage #5 Question Set

1. The author would most likely agree with which statement about clothing?

   (A) Clothing can divide or unify people.
   (B) Solidarity is more important than individuality.
   (C) In schools, clothing is not as important as other matters.
   (D) Uniforms will eliminate all sources of conflict in schools.

2. In lines 14-15, the phrase "a sense of solidarity" most nearly means

   (A) confusion.
   (B) formality.
   (C) individuality.
   (D) unity.

3. It can be inferred that the "source of differences" mentioned in line 24 can be

   (A) uniforms.
   (B) clothing styles.
   (C) student communities.
   (D) opinions and personality.

4. The main purpose of the final paragraph (lines 45-55) is to

   (A) explain the importance of individuality.
   (B) describe the intangible benefits of uniforms.
   (C) provide examples of different uniform requirements.
   (D) summarize how uniforms can be beneficial to students.

5. The phrase "level the playing field" (line 51), refers to

   (A) changing fashion trends.
   (B) similar customs and traditions.
   (C) how uniforms can help students.
   (D) types of uniforms worn by athletes.

6. Which of the following best describes the organization of the passage?

   (A) Different types of uniforms are described in detail.
   (B) Specific facts and figures are used to refute a theory.
   (C) An opinion is supported by several reasons and examples.
   (D) A commonly held belief is challenged and eventually upheld.

Passage #6

Tuesday began like any other day. My classmates and I sat in our classroom waiting for the first period bell to ring.

"Quiet down, please," said our teacher, Mr. Bernard. "It's time for rollcall."

It took a minute or so, but eventually my classmates and I began to quiet down. Mr. Bernard did not bother waiting until our side-chatter had stopped completely.

"Ashley Adams," he began.

"Here," responded Ashley.

"Carly Bertrand."

"Present," sniffed Carly, who always seemed to have a cold coming on.

Mr. Bernard went down the list and students responded in kind, until I was next. He had barely finished saying "Skyler" when a deafening crash echoed through the room. The initial sound caused everyone to jump out of their seats and cover their ears. This was followed by the scraping sound of metal coming from the playground.

Our jungle gym was wrecked! The slide was smashed, the monkey bars were twisted every which way, and our swings were nowhere to be seen. In fact, all we could really see was a long ditch stretching from one side of the playground to the other.

"Stay in your seats," commanded Mr. Bernard, as he moved toward the windows to get a better look at what had happened.

I looked at Ashley, who sat next to me, and saw in her wide eyes the reflection of my own shocked expression. As if on cue, she and I – along with the rest of our classmates – jumped out of our seats and ran to the windows, ignoring Mr. Bernard's order.

There was a huge hole in the ground at the far side of the playground – a crater! Shock turned quickly to excitement, awe, and wonder. The classroom buzzed with questions.

"Do you think it's an alien spaceship?"

"No way, it's just a comet."

"I bet it's aliens!"

"It can't be a comet."

We soon found out that a small meteorite had landed in our playground! For the rest of the day, even the teachers were pretty distracted – to say nothing of the students. I don't think anybody learned much that day. In fact, I'm not sure I even got credit for attending class that day – Mr. Bernard never did finish rollcall.

So much for a normal day!

Passage #6 Question Set

1. Which sentence best expresses the passage's main idea?

   (A) Tuesday was a normal day.
   (B) A piece of playground equipment is destroyed.
   (C) A seemingly normal day can sometimes become extraordinary.
   (D) A huge hole in the ground causes a student to not get credit for attending class.

2. It can be inferred that the author's name is

   (A) Ashley.
   (B) Bernard.
   (C) Carly.
   (D) Skyler.

3. In line 18, the word "deafening" most nearly means

   (A) very bright.
   (B) curiously odd.
   (C) extremely loud.
   (D) strangely delicious.

4. The passage suggests in lines 32-37 that the schoolchildren ran to the window

   (A) in order to line up for rollcall.
   (B) in order to be first for recess outside.
   (C) because they did not respect Mr. Bernard.
   (D) because they were curious to see what had made the sound.

5. According to the passage, the jungle gym and monkey bars were destroyed because of

   (A) recess.
   (B) a comet.
   (C) an alien.
   (D) a meteorite.

6. The author's tone when describing the events of meteor crash can best be described as

   (A) annoyed.
   (B) excited.
   (C) outraged.
   (D) somber.

Passage #7

Scientists call a partly enclosed coastal body of brackish water an estuary. An estuary forms when fresh water from rivers or streams flows into the sea. The resulting mix of salt and fresh water forms what is known as brackish water. Estuaries are special environments, as they are influenced by marine and river environments.

Though all estuaries are affected by the tides and contain brackish water, there are many different types of estuaries. One of the principal factors to consider when differentiating types of estuaries is water circulation, which describes how fresh and salt water interact. Under this system of classification, there are four types of estuaries.

In a salt wedge, the output of fresh water from the river is much greater than the inflow of salt water as a result of the tides. In this case, due to the chemical differences between salt and fresh water, fresh water flows atop the salt water. The closer to the mouth of the river, the more fresh water there is; the farther out to sea, the less fresh water there is. Thus, because fresh water floats atop salt water and because there is more salt water farther out to sea, a wedge forms. The closer to the mouth of the river, the less and less salt water present in the estuary.

As the influence of the tides increases, the estuary is said to become partially mixed. In these circumstances, it is no longer necessary that fresh water flow atop salt water. In a partially mixed estuary, as the name suggests, there is some mixing of salt and fresh water into ever-changing layers and bands.

When tidal force exceeds fresh water output, there is a greater mixing of fresh and salt water. The mixing effect is greater than in a partially mixed estuary. This type of estuary is known as vertically homogenous because the fresh and salt water are more equally mixed.

Salt wedge, partially mixed, and vertically homogenous estuaries are all permanent estuaries. This means that the presence of saltwater and freshwater is relatively constant. The fourth type of estuary is one in which the amount of fresh water varies significantly. In some cases, these intermittent estuaries are wholly marine, consisting of saltwater only. Only when fresh water output increases, such as with melting snow or heavy rainfall, does the fresh water mix with the salt water and create a temporary or seasonal estuary.

Passage #7 Question Set

1. One of the main points of the passage is to

   (A) illustrate the best types of estuaries.
   (B) compare salt water estuaries to fresh water estuaries.
   (C) convince the reader of estuaries' environmental importance.
   (D) describe the differences between different types of estuaries.

2. According to the passage, different types of estuaries can be classified by

   (A) salt wedges.
   (B) water circulation.
   (C) diversity of marine life.
   (D) the number of salt water layers.

3. The passage provides information to support which of the following statements?

   (A) Poorly mixed fresh and salt water results in a salt wedge.
   (B) Thoroughly mixed fresh and salt water results in a salt wedge.
   (C) Fresh and salt water that never mixes results in an intermittent estuary.
   (D) Permanently mixed fresh and salt water results in a partially mixed estuary.

4. Based on the passage, one of the factors that influences the mixing of fresh and salt water is

   (A) tidal force.
   (B) boat traffic.
   (C) changing temperatures.
   (D) sediment and nutrient deposits.

5. Which of the following best describes the organization of the passage?

   (A) Examples support an opinion.
   (B) Examples support a general concept.
   (C) A concept is questioned and rejected.
   (D) A series of specific events are described.

6. In line 47, "intermittent" most nearly means

   (A) apparent.
   (B) constant.
   (C) irregular.
   (D) valuable.

Passage #8

It was late July, and with students enjoying summer recess and families on vacation, the small beach town was crowded with both locals and tourists. Everyone had the same idea: head to the beach to flee the oppressive heat and humidity.

Though my friends and I were desperate to find relief in the cool water, we found ourselves trapped in my car. We had gotten a late start to the day, and because of this, we were having a difficult time finding somewhere to park our car.

Every parking space was taken; there wasn't a single stretch of unoccupied asphalt bordering a curb anywhere. We knew that there was no way we were going to get a decent parking space. Though it was just barely after 8:00 a.m., we had to circle the residential blocks like vultures, hoping that someone would get in their car and leave.

As we drove aimlessly in circles, hoping against hope that we might find a vacant parking space, I began to regret not having had the air conditioning in my car fixed. It had been broken for a while but had never really bothered me, as I always kept the windows down. But because we were barely moving, there was hardly a breeze. As a result, the swamp-like humidity in the air was beginning to take its toll on us. We were all sweating buckets.

We could have given up earlier in our search. In fact, we probably should have. Instead, after half an hour of luckless roaming, we were determined not to give up, for doing so would have been to admit that we had wasted our time. At the same time, it didn't look as if we were going to find a parking space. People had, after all, just arrived at the beach not long ago.

Frustrated and growing impatient, we put it to a vote. The majority was in favor of heading home to the pool and air conditioning.

As I steered the car toward the road back home, a shout from the backseat almost sent me crashing into a parked car. Behind us, a car was pulling out onto the road. There was going to be an empty parking space!

The mood in the car improved significantly as I braked and pulled over to the side of the road. Soon, the four of us were walking to the beach, ready to escape to a cooler day.

Passage #8 Question Set

1. One of the main points of the passage is to

   (A) relate a personal experience.
   (B) convince the reader of an opinion.
   (C) advertise the qualities of a particular beach.
   (D) explain to the reader different facts and terms.

2. The author's tone when describing how they circled the residential blocks "like vultures" (lines 16-19) can best be described as

   (A) dreamy.
   (B) hopeless.
   (C) joyful.
   (D) taunting.

3. In line 21, the word "vacant" most nearly means

   (A) empty.
   (B) fulfilled.
   (C) happy.
   (D) intense.

4. The phrase "sweating buckets" (line 29), refers to

   (A) the effect of the heat and humidity on the author and her friends.
   (B) the mood in the car when an empty parking space was spotted.
   (C) the actual amount of sweat that was coming from the author and her friends.
   (D) the relief the author and her friends would feel when jumping into the ocean.

5. The main purpose of the sixth paragraph (lines 38-40) is to describe the

   (A) reason why it is difficult to find a parking space.
   (B) author's state of mind after they found a parking space.
   (C) author's state of mind before they found a parking space.
   (D) actions taken by the author and her friends to find a parking space.

6. According to the author, which event contributed to the finding of an empty parking space?

   (A) A shout from someone outside.
   (B) Accidentally crashing into a parked car.
   (C) The oppressive heat discouraged beachgoers.
   (D) Another car pulled out of its parking space and drove away.

Passage #9

Before me towered a Japanese *torii* gate. Though it stood farther up the mountain's summit, maybe fifty yards away, I could tell that the gate was very big. It loomed, imposing and alone, halfway between where I stood and what seemed to be the top of the mountain. That there were no trees or shrubs this high up the mountain only made the gate seem larger. Rising up from a gravelly carpet of grey flint, shiny silica, and tough granite, the reddish-brown gate outlined the summit and the sky behind it like a picture frame.

Though I was alone with the gate, the rocks, and the sky, I perceived a strange feeling – a presence that I was not, in fact, alone. The huge gate, with its cross-beam resting atop two upright pillars, resembled a crude "n". It seemed to be calling to me, asking me to cross beneath it. Though I had already been climbing for days, I continued to climb up the steep hill toward the gate, heeding its call.

With each step, the *torii* gate grew larger, more powerful, and more mysterious. As I neared, I could tell that on the upright pillars were intricate carvings. I could not read the Japanese inscriptions, but something told me that they were important. All around the pillars were long, perfectly straight columns of script that were perfectly uniform in size and spacing. The closer I drew to the gate, the more I could see. Once I was just in front of the gate, I could see that the markings appeared to have once been painted, as the grooves were not uniformly colored. Centuries of wind and rain must have weathered the pillars, stripping the letters of most of their paint.

To me, the inscriptions echoed what I already felt to be true: that this place was important – sacred, even. Once I crossed the threshold – once I passed beneath the silent and watchful gaze of the *torii* gate – I would be standing in a special place. I could not help myself but to walk through the gate. Though I could have easily walked around it, I felt within me that doing so would have been wrong – even disrespectful.

I inhaled and exhaled slowly. The clear, crisp mountain air cleared my mind and put me at ease.

I looked left, right, then up at the gate, and stepped through the threshold.

Passage #9 Question Set

1. One of the main points of the passage is to

   (A) explain the purpose of *torii* gates.
   (B) describe the world's largest *torii* gate.
   (C) provide advice on mountain climbing.
   (D) describe a powerful experience in detail.

2. According to the first paragraph, all of the following factors made the *torii* gate seem even more striking EXCEPT the

   (A) lack of plant life.
   (B) huge cross-beam.
   (C) summit of the mountain.
   (D) shiny silica and tough granite.

3. The "crude 'n'" (line 17), refers to

   (A) the shape of the gate.
   (B) the appearance of the carvings.
   (C) a strangely shaped rock on the ground.
   (D) the outline of trees in the background.

4. In line 35, "weathered" most nearly means

   (A) worn away.
   (B) carved out.
   (C) painted on.
   (D) fastened securely.

5. According to the author, one of the reasons that he felt his surroundings were sacred was because of

   (A) the watchful gaze of the *torii* gate.
   (B) the freshness of the air on the mountaintop.
   (C) the existence and appearance of the inscriptions.
   (D) the chirping of birds and rustling of small animals in the rocks.

6. The author's tone when describing the appearance of the *torii* gate can best be described as

   (A) awestruck and respectful.
   (B) disbelieving and sarcastic.
   (C) disinterested and confused.
   (D) sentimental and forgiving.

Passage #10

I love the idea of having a vegetable garden in the backyard, don't you? At a time when most Americans are spending more and more money on groceries and produce, having a vegetable garden is a great way to save money on one's monthly food bill. Many people also worry about the health impact of fertilizers and pesticides used to grow food. Growing vegetables at home is the only way to know for certain that your food is completely free of these chemicals.

Not only are vegetable gardens a great way to save money and eat more healthily, but they also encourage people to spend more time outside. People who garden will reap the benefits of physical activity. On top of the physical and financial benefits of having a vegetable garden, many gardeners report a feeling of satisfaction and accomplishment associated with caring for a garden.

Vegetable gardens, in fact, have had a big impact on the course of human history. In times past, people gardened as a matter of necessity. As science progressed, farms adopted more automated and effective agricultural techniques. As a result, people were able to minimize the effects of droughts and pest problems. Combined with improved storage methods and more efficient transportation, food became cheaper and more readily available. As a result, fewer and fewer people needed to grow their own vegetable gardens at home.

One exception to this general trend has been during times of global crises, such as World War I and World War II. As these conflicts surged around the globe, involved countries encouraged their citizens to cultivate "victory gardens," or private and communal vegetable gardens. In 1917, Charles Pack founded the US National War Gardens Commission. By the end of World War I, the Commission helped to promote and organize over five million gardens in the United States. These gardens were planted on both public and private land and helped to ease the burden on the public food supply. The people involved were very resourceful, planting wherever they could: in backyards and parks, as well as on rooftops, in railroad yards, and even in vacant lots. During World War II, First Lady Eleanor Roosevelt planted a victory garden on the White House grounds. More recently, First Lady Michelle Obama mirrored her predecessor by planting a kitchen garden on White House grounds.

Like many other people, I often have an urge to work outside with my hands. Looking back at victory gardens, I can't help but feel envious of these gardeners' resourcefulness and creativity. Today, it often seems as if vegetable gardens are a thing of the past. If more people knew about the benefits of gardening, maybe there would be more vegetable gardens in the world.

Passage #10 Question Set

1. Which sentence best expresses the passage's main idea?

   (A) Sometimes, good ideas can come from the past.
   (B) Saving time is more important than saving money.
   (C) Healthy food should only be grown in personal gardens.
   (D) Technology and science mean there is no need for vegetable gardens.

2. The passage suggests, in the third paragraph (lines 20-31), that there are fewer vegetable gardens today than there were in the past because

   (A) the use of fertilizers is widely accepted.
   (B) there is abundant food and no need to work a garden.
   (C) transportation has caused the cost of food to increase.
   (D) droughts and pest problems are more damaging than they used to be.

3. The term "victory garden" (line 36), refers to

   (A) a nickname used by today's gardeners.
   (B) the healthiness of vegetable gardens.
   (C) how vegetable gardens help athletes become winners.
   (D) the contribution vegetable gardens had toward a war effort.

4. It can be inferred from the passage that Charles Pack would agree with which of the following statements?

   (A) Vegetable gardens are only useful for personal enjoyment.
   (B) Eleanor Roosevelt should not have planted a garden on White House grounds.
   (C) The combined effect of many small vegetable gardens can have a big impact.
   (D) When it comes to food, eating healthily is more important than saving money.

5. In line 56, the word "envious" most nearly means

   (A) capable
   (B) jealous.
   (C) resentful.
   (D) scared.

6. The last paragraph (lines 54-61) suggests that the author

   (A) works outdoors.
   (B) works with her hands frequently.
   (C) wants to start her own vegetable garden.
   (D) is frequently engaged in creative activities.

Passage #11

Painting can be a quick and easy way to add character and depth to a room. To do a good job, painting requires prior planning and proper equipment.

First, think about what part of the room you're painting so you can start moving any furniture or decorations. If you're painting the ceiling, the best thing to do would be to empty the room of furniture entirely. This will give you more room to work and will protect your furniture from getting splattered with paint. If removing the furniture isn't possible, you should group any furniture in one part of the room and cover it with a tarp or cloth. You should only work on the areas of the ceiling where the furniture beneath it has been cleared away. Once these areas are completed, move the furniture to a painted part of the room, and work on the next portion of the ceiling. Though the same principle applies when you're painting the walls, it's actually less complicated than painting the ceiling. This is because you can just group the furniture together in the center of the room, and cover all of it with a tarp or cloth.

Once you've decided how you're going to manage your furniture and safeguard it from painting-related accidents, think about the tools and supplies you'll need. At a minimum, you'll need paint and a brush. If you're painting a large area, you'll also probably need a rolling brush to help cover a larger surface area with each stroke, as well as a tray in which to pour the paint. If you're painting something out of reach, such as the top of a wall or a ceiling, you may want to consider an extension rod for your rolling brush. Otherwise, you'll need to get a footstool or ladder. The extension rod for your brush could save you a lot of time and energy, though it can be more difficult to maneuver and control. In addition to the paint, brush, and these other related tools, you should also consider buying painter's tape. Many people like to use this tape to line edges and corners, as it makes painting easier. One of the great features of this tape is that it doesn't leave residue or pull up paint when removed. Painter's tape is particularly useful wherever two surfaces meet. For instance, it works well when placed at the edge between two walls, along the edge between the wall and the ceiling, or within the nooks and crannies near doorframes and windows.

Now that you're properly prepared, it's time to get to work! Prepare the surfaces by fixing any blemishes and wiping them clean of dust and debris. Once cleaned and blemish-free, mix your paint and pour it into the tray. Coat the brush in enough paint so that it doesn't drip or run down the walls. Finally, paint in broad, multi-directional strokes. Once you're finished, let the paint dry, and apply a second coat if needed.

Passage #11 Question Set

1. The author would most likely agree with which statement about painting a room?

   (A) Painting requires little effort.
   (B) Painting a room is best done on a whim.
   (C) There are many easy ways to improve a room.
   (D) There are many things to consider before and while painting.

2. In line 2, the word "depth" most nearly means

   (A) atmosphere.
   (B) deepness.
   (C) distance.
   (D) length.

3. The passage implies that by not planning ahead,

   (A) painting can be messy and tiring.
   (B) one can save a great deal of time.
   (C) painting can be energizing and efficient.
   (D) one can be confident in the quality of the results.

4. The phrase "nooks and crannies" (line 50), refers to

   (A) areas that benefit from use of painter's tape.
   (B) the best place to store furniture while painting.
   (C) areas that are easy to reach with a rolling brush.
   (D) areas that are easy to reach with an extension rod.

5. The author's tone in lines 53-60 ("Prepare…needed") can best be described as

   (A) aggressive.
   (B) bored.
   (C) objective.
   (D) shocked.

6. According to the passage, a high quality and efficient paint job is made possible by all the following EXCEPT

   (A) careful planning.
   (B) appropriate equipment.
   (C) a group of experienced painters.
   (D) cleaning the surface to be painted.

Passage #12

Since ancient times, people around the world have prized diamonds for their beauty and desired them for their rarity. Diamonds are one of the most coveted and valuable minerals on Earth. These stones come in many different sizes, colors, and qualities. Though all diamonds are precious, certain diamonds exhibit unique qualities, which make them exceptionally valuable. For example, some diamonds are unusually large, while others are unusually colored. Such diamonds are more than just gemstones. They are legends.

Widely regarded as one of the largest gem-quality diamonds ever found, the *Cullinan* diamond was found in a South African mine. The original diamond weighed over 3,106 carats, but was split into over 100 separate stones. The two largest resulting stones, *Cullinan I & II*, were set into the Crown Jewels of the United Kingdom. The *Cullinan I*, the larger of the two, was set into the scepter. The *Cullinan II* was set into the crown. Though *Cullinan I* weighed only 17% of the original, its still-prodigious size earned it the nickname *Great Star of Africa.*

Diamonds are not only prized for their size. They are also valued for their clarity and color – or lack thereof. Discovered in Zaire, the *Millennium Star* is far from the largest diamond in the world. However, the *Millennium Star* is actually the second-largest colorless, flawless diamond in the world. The diamond possesses no internal or external imperfections, nor does it contain any discolorations.

Many diamonds have become famous because of their physical attributes. *Amarillo Starlight, Eye of Brahma, Heart of Eternity*, and *Mountain of Light* are just a few more examples of the many diamonds that have come to embody perfection in either size, color, or quality. Some diamonds, however, transcend mere fame and become truly legendary, despite their physical attributes.

Tavernier Blue, a 115-carat diamond, surfaced some time during the 17th century. A French merchant-traveler by the name of Jean-Baptiste Tavernier sold the diamond to King Louis XIV of France. Louis XIV had the stone recut, after which it became known as *French Blue. French Blue* became part of the French Crown Jewels, and eventually became the property of King Louis XVI and his queen, Marie Antoinette. During the French Revolution, which resulted in the execution of the king and queen, *French Blue* was stolen and never recovered.

Decades after the theft of *French Blue*, a similar but smaller diamond emerged in the United Kingdom. While history is unclear as to how, this diamond became the property of Thomas Hope. It was thereafter known as the *Hope Diamond.* The diamond would go on to change hands many times, becoming the property of jewelers, heiresses, dukes, lords, and possibly even a sultan.

Though the *Hope Diamond* is beautiful by many physical standards, it is the diamond's long, rich, and sometimes mysterious history that truly sets it apart from other famous diamonds. The diamond is surrounded by intrigue, which over time has turned speculation into fact and fact into legend. Many believe the diamond to be cursed, citing as proof the unfavorable fates of many of the diamond's owners. The diamond became so well-known that newspapers around the world published stories about how the diamond had brought misfortune to its owners. Though *Cullinan I* and the *Millennium Star* are estimated to be more valuable than the *Hope Diamond*, it's possible that many more people have heard of the latter than the former. And while color, size, and quality matter when judging diamonds, the *Hope Diamond* suggests that they aren't everything.

Passage #12 Question Set

1. The passage is primarily concerned with

    (A) sharing examples of valuable diamonds.
    (B) documenting the criteria for evaluating diamonds.
    (C) describing the experience of looking at a perfect diamond.
    (D) explaining how diamonds can be valuable for different reasons.

2. According to the passage, the *Millennium Star* is famous as a result of its

    (A) enormous size.
    (B) clarity and color.
    (C) legendary ownership.
    (D) publicity in newspapers.

3. In line 40, "transcend" most nearly means

    (A) become.
    (B) change.
    (C) exceed.
    (D) ruin.

4. According to the passage, while some diamonds are famous for their physical beauty alone, other diamonds become famous

    (A) for their use in industry.
    (B) because of their creative nicknames.
    (C) as a result of their color and size.
    (D) because of their history and ownership.

5. The passage provides information to support all of the following statements EXCEPT

    (A) Many believe the *Hope Diamond* to be cursed because of what happened to Louis XIV.
    (B) When diamonds are cut or recut, the leftover pieces are often lost and destroyed.
    (C) Diamonds are often collected by royalty and included as a part of royal jewelry collections.
    (D) Objective standards that measure diamonds are not the only factors that make diamonds valuable or famous.

6. The passage implies that

    (A) people's perceptions ultimately determine a diamond's worth and fame.
    (B) the number of carats is irrelevant to the evaluation of a diamond's worth.
    (C) the smaller the diamond, the more likely it is to have perfect color and clarity.
    (D) *French Blue* and *Millennium Star* should be more famous than the *Hope Diamond.*

Passage #13

In many ways, the ball of hydrogen and helium at the center of our solar system is mind-boggling. The sun, as this ball of gas is known to us, is almost too big to imagine. Its diameter is more than 100 times greater than Earth's. The sun has a mass more than 300,000 times greater than Earth's. It is the single most massive object in our solar system and accounts for more than 99% of all matter in our solar system. The sun is not only incomprehensibly large, but it is also inconceivably old. Scientists estimate that the sun was formed more than 4.5 billion years ago.

Yet this does not mean that the sun was always – or will always be – the same as it is now.

Scientists hypothesize that the sun formed as a result of a process called "gravitational collapse." This theory states that the gravity where the sun is now became so strong that it continued to attract more and more matter to it. As the matter within the center of the collapse became more and more dense, individual atoms began to fuse together in a process known as nuclear fusion. Nuclear fusion produces tremendous amounts of energy, and has kept the sun shining ever since.

For the past 4.5 billion years, the sun has used up around 600 million tons of hydrogen every second to fuel its nuclear reactions. For the next 5.4 billion years, this process will continue relatively unchanged. However, around its 10 billionth birthday, the sun will start to run out of hydrogen. At this point, the sun will begin to get much bigger, much brighter, and much hotter.

As it is now, the sun is known as a yellow dwarf star. Once the sun runs out of hydrogen, however, it will begin to turn into what is known as a red giant star. Then, every 500 million years or so after that, the sun will double in size until it reaches a size more than 200 times larger than it is today. By then, the sun will be thousands of times brighter than it is today. During this process, Mercury, Venus, and most likely even Earth will be engulfed by the swelling star. The outer planets of our solar system – Jupiter, Saturn Uranus, and Neptune – will experience changes as well. For example, ice that had remained frozen for billions of years will likely begin to melt for the first time.

Just as the sun will eventually run out of hydrogen, it will also eventually run out of helium. Once this happens, the sun becomes unstable. It will constantly be losing matter in powerful solar ejections. Eventually, after many more millions of years, the sun will begin to cool and shrink. Ultimately, the sun will become a white dwarf star with approximately half the mass it has now.

Passage #13 Question Set

1. One of the main purposes of the passage is to explain

    (A) the lifecycle of the sun.
    (B) how nuclear fusion works.
    (C) what will happen to the outer planets.
    (D) how the sun influences the solar system.

2. Which word best describes the author's tone in the first paragraph (lines 1-12)?

    (A) regretful
    (B) confused
    (C) uncertain
    (D) awestruck

3. According to the passage, gravitational collapse

    (A) gave birth to the sun.
    (B) keeps the sun shining.
    (C) increases the mass of the sun.
    (D) increases the temperature of the sun.

4. In line 44, the word "engulfed" most nearly means

    (A) totally ignored.
    (B) utterly isolated.
    (C) partially destroyed.
    (D) completely overwhelmed.

5. The passage implies that ice on the outer planets will eventually melt (lines 46-48) because

    (A) of the sun's gravitational collapse.
    (B) of the hydrogen that escaped from the sun.
    (C) the sun will be much hotter than it has ever been.
    (D) the sun will have half the mass that it does now.

6. Which statement best describes the organization of the passage?

    (A) A fact is compared with an opinion.
    (B) Different theories are compared and contrasted.
    (C) A personal point of view is shared and supported.
    (D) A hypothesis is described chronologically.

Passage #14

Mary found sleep too difficult to capture. For hours, she had been listening to the storm raging outside her window. But it was not only the storm that kept her awake.

Earlier that evening, the five of them had gathered around the fireplace. Byron had found a book of ghost stories, and he read them aloud in his deep, dramatic voice. Combined with the crashing of thunder, it didn't take long for the stories to have the effect Byron wanted. He grinned as he saw the others glance uneasily into the darkness beyond the fireplace. At last, he closed the book and looked around at the others. "I propose a contest," he said. "Let us see which of us can write the best ghost story."

That was very like him – to propose a contest that he would obviously win. The most famous writer in the world, suggesting a writing contest? What chance would the others have?

In her heart, Mary wished she could think of a story good enough to enter the contest. She knew it was foolish to think that a girl still in her teens could compete with Byron for literary achievement.

All her life she had lived in the shadow of her famous parents, both of whom were writers. Her mother had urged women to claim rights equal to those enjoyed by men. Mary had been given her mother's name, and felt in some way that this obliged her to carry on her mother's crusade. Perhaps she could do that by writing a story that was as good as any written by a man.

Lying awake in bed, Mary's mind continued to race. When she was in Germany, she saw a ruined castle. What was its name? Castle Frankenstein. She began to imagine what kind of man might have lived there.

He would be like her boyfriend, Percy, she decided. Curious about new things. Mary had listened as Byron and Percy had discussed the life force. People, animals, birds, fish, plants – all had the power of life. But then, they died, and once that happened, they could not live again. What was it that caused some things to live?

Byron had said a man in Italy had caused a dead frog's leg to move by touching it with electricity. But that had not made the frog come alive.

A bright flash of light and a deep rumble close by startled Mary out of her thoughts. Lightning, she thought. Lightning was a kind of electricity, people said. But how could you use it to bring a frog back to life?

And even if the frog did somehow live again, that would not be a very scary story.

There was a book that Mary had when she was a child. It was filled with pictures. She remembered one in particular. It showed a man, a giant, really, standing over a bed in which a child was sleeping. She had forgotten the story, but she recalled that the picture was frightening.

A lightning bolt split the darkness, and lit up Mary's bedroom. She opened her eyes and saw him there. Saw that strange, giant creature standing over her bed. She pulled the covers over her head. It was only her imagination, she knew. But then she cried out, even though no one could hear: "I have found my story!"

Passage #14 Question Set

1. The main purpose of the passage is to

   (A) discuss the power and cause of life.
   (B) recall the results of a writing contest.
   (C) describe the life and career of a famous author.
   (D) tell about how an author came up with an idea.

2. Mary did not think that she could win the writing contest because

   (A) Byron was a very famous writer.
   (B) her mother told her she was not a good writer.
   (C) she was tired from her travels in Germany.
   (D) Percy told her not to bother competing with Byron.

3. In line 30, "obliged" most nearly means

   (A) desired.
   (B) permitted.
   (C) prevented.
   (D) required.

4. The "deep rumble" referred to in line 49 is most likely

   (A) thunder.
   (B) Percy snoring.
   (C) Mary's empty stomach.
   (D) the fireplace in Mary's room.

5. The passage implies that Mary "pulled the covers over her head (lines 65-66) because

   (A) she was cold.
   (B) she was excited.
   (C) she was startled.
   (D) the lightning was too bright.

6. According to the passage, Mary lay awake in bed because

   (A) she was trying to think of an idea for a story.
   (B) of Byron's scary story earlier in the evening.
   (C) she was confused about the power and causes of life.
   (D) she recalled Castle Frankenstein during her time in Germany.

Passage #15

The Golden Gate Park in San Francisco, California, is a large, green haven that attracts locals and visitors alike. Each year, more than 10 million people pay a visit to the park's 1,000 acres of public land, museums, gardens, statues, and more. Many of these visitors are attracted to one of the oldest and most visited fixtures in the park: the Japanese Tea Garden.

One of the most prominent features of the Tea Garden is the Tea House. The Tea House was actually the home of the Tea Garden's original caretaker, Makoto Hagiwara. The Hagiwaras lived in the wood structure for generations, and held tea ceremonies for visitors. Eventually, the Hagiwaras moved out, and their home was converted into the commercial Tea House that exists today.

From the Tea House, visitors are able to take in the beautiful landscape surrounding them. The garden was designed by Makoto Hagiwara to emulate the gardens of his ancestral home. Makoto imported Japanese plants, animals, and even building materials to add to the Garden's authenticity. He ordered and planted hundreds of blossoming cherry trees, as well as bamboo, azaleas, magnolias, cedars, and maples. He also had a large pond constructed in the center of the Tea Garden, and had koi fish delivered straight from Japan. Even the stones used throughout the garden were specially ordered from Japan.

Also visible from the Tea House are several other iconic structures. One of the most recognizable is the "Treasure Tower" Pagoda. The pagoda has five-tiers and reaches high into the sky. Its red color and distinctive architecture help it to stand out against the backdrop of greenery that surrounds it. The Pagoda today is largely decorative – and, in fact, contains no treasure. Pagodas themselves are deeply rooted in Japanese philosophy. Each of the five tiers represents a different natural element: earth, fire, wind, water, and sky.

Not far from the main entrance is the Moon Bridge, another notable structure in the Tea Garden. Though the Moon Bridge only spans a small, shallow water feature, the footbridge itself has a high, exaggerated arch. The bridge is so-named because its reflection in the water creates a full circle, which resembles the moon. Like the pagoda, the bridge's features are similarly inspired by Japanese philosophy. The steepness of the bridge is designed to slow visitors both physically and mentally. This was to ensure that people enjoying the garden were in the proper frame of mind.

Scattered throughout the Tea Garden are other important – though easily missed – artifacts. For example, at a fork in one of the Tea Garden's many paths is a bronze lantern. Carved in a distinctly Japanese style, the lantern is more than just a beautifully carved work of art. The 9,000-pound fixture was a gift from Japanese students to America, a symbol of friendship after the end of World War II.

Wherever they are in the Tea Garden, visitors are sure to feel immersed in Japanese culture. Every sip of tea – every step along a path – will transport visitors from the hustle and bustle of San Francisco to a peaceful, traditional Japanese garden.

Passage #15 Question Set

1. The main purpose of the passage is to

    (A) convince readers to visit the Japanese Tea House.
    (B) present a chronological history of a particular place.
    (C) present information that supports a specific point of view.
    (D) describe notable qualities of a famous and popular destination.

2. The passage supports which statement about Makoto Hagiwara?

    (A) Makoto Hagiwara's ancestral home was Japan.
    (B) Makoto Hagiwara became rich serving tea to visitors.
    (C) Makoto Hagiwara was skilled at making bronze lanterns.
    (D) Makoto Hagiwara was a trained landscape designer.

3. According to the passage, each tier of the Treasure Tower Pagoda represents

    (A) Buddhist beliefs.
    (B) different elements.
    (C) different types of plants.
    (D) each year the Hagiwaras lived in the garden.

4. In line 47, an "exaggerated arch" is

    (A) unusually steep.
    (B) dangerously steep.
    (C) eccentrically built.
    (D) remarkably unstable.

5. In line 55, "frame of mind" refers to

    (A) a visitor's mood.
    (B) a visitor's physical health.
    (C) a visitor's religious beliefs.
    (D) a gardener's level of interest.

6. According to the passage, the reason Makoto Hagiwara imported Japanese plants, animals, and materials was to

    (A) help blend into his new home.
    (B) make sure the Tea Garden was authentic.
    (C) save money on the cost of the Tea Garden.
    (D) attract more visitors to visit the Tea Garden.

Passage #16

Today is a rare day. In the northeast United States, spring technically lasts for several months. However, there are only a few weeks where the weather is nice enough to be called spring. Spring is wedged between the dry, freezing cold of winter, and the humid, blistering heat of summer. Only in late March do winter's icy, gnarled fingers reluctantly begin to loosen their grip on the weather. April is only slightly better, since it rains more often than not. But May – May is usually the very definition of pleasant.

When I think of a perfect day in May, I can't imagine how it could be better than today. The temperature is just right. It's neither too hot in the sun, nor too cool in the shade. It's neither too dry, nor too humid. Though I'm wearing shorts and a t-shirt, I know I'd be just as comfortable wearing pants and a light sweater.

The sky is a giant sapphire, with not a blemish to be seen. Like a baby in a cradle, I'm rocked half-asleep in my hammock by the gentle breeze. As I lay in the partial shade of an oak tree, I can't help but smile to myself. I'm overcome with happiness – a satisfaction so deep that all my worries melt away.

From a nearby bush comes a sweet melody. Before the bird finishes its song, another joins in. Soon, I'm surrounded by a chorus unlike any other. Try as I may, I can't spot the songbirds. They're too well-hidden behind leaves and branches. Instead, I spot robins with rust-orange breasts hopping around on the lawn, rustling their feathers. Maybe they hop in search of food. Maybe they hop just to hop, and rustle just to rustle.

Here and there, out of the corner of my eye, a flash of bright red – a cardinal. And there, a glimpse of a deep royal blue – a blue jay.

Still, the songbirds sing their songs. I try, with no success, to decipher the hidden message carried in their song. In the end, I give up. Surely they sing just to sing.

As my ears absorb the acoustic treat, my eyes feast on the vibrant colors around me. The scene almost looks too real, like a vivid painting come to life. The magenta fireworks of azalea blossoms compete for my attention with the gentle pink petals of the nearby cherry blossoms. Irises blossom here and there, their rich indigo petals surrounding a golden, powdery stamen.

When will there be another day like today? Maybe tomorrow. Maybe not until next year. Only one thing is certain. Days like this don't come around very often. I don't know the next time I'll have time to enjoy a day like today, so I will savor it all the more.

Passage #16 Question Set

1. The main purpose of the passage is to

   (A) explain a process in great detail.
   (B) convince readers of a certain point of view.
   (C) describe a memorable personal experience.
   (D) compare the weather during different times of year.

2. In line 1, the word "rare" most nearly means

   (A) special.
   (B) unbelievable.
   (C) undercooked.
   (D) unexpected.

3. In line 20, "blemish" can best be interpreted as describing

   (A) humidity.
   (B) stains.
   (C) clouds.
   (D) wind.

4. The melodies that the author heard came from

   (A) robins.
   (B) blue jays.
   (C) cardinals.
   (D) unknown birds.

5. The passage suggests that the author is

   (A) normally very busy.
   (B) employed as a poet.
   (C) a professional gardener.
   (D) a student studying weather.

6. Which best describes the organization of the passage?

   (A) Questions are answered sequentially.
   (B) Events are described in chronological order.
   (C) Plants and animals are presented in order of color.
   (D) Facts are presented to support an argument.

Passage #17

Monoculture is the practice of growing and relying upon a single crop. The practice threatens the security and stability of our food supply. In fact, there are many historical disasters that prove how dangerous monoculture can be. One of the most well-known of these was the Irish Potato Famine of the mid-nineteenth century.

During the seventeenth and eighteenth centuries, Irish Catholics were oppressed by the ruling British powers. The Irish were not allowed to own land, vote, or even to receive an education. The result of this was to trap the Irish in poverty for generations.

By the mid-nineteenth century, the British government found that poverty was rampant in Ireland. One-third of all Irish worked on parcels of land so small that they could not support their families. At the time, two-thirds of Irish were dependent on farming to support their families, even though they had to sell most of their crops to pay rent to their British landlords. Because of this, the only crop that could be grown in sufficient amounts was the Irish Lumper potato. These potatoes were not only used as food for people, but were used also as feed for livestock.

In 1844, Irish newspapers reported on a troubling disease. For two years, this disease had attacked potato crops in America. In 1845, the Gardeners' Chronicle and Horticultural Gazette reported on a strange new potato blight. Though the British government found the reports troubling, they chose to ignore them.

This did nothing to stop the disease from attacking. A few months after its arrival in Europe, the blight spread to Ireland. In 1845, one-third to one-half of all potato crops were destroyed by disease. A year later, in 1846, the disease had destroyed three-quarters of all Lumper potatoes. For the next several years, the amount of potatoes produced shrank to a fraction of what they had once been. As a result, famine and starvation set in, and hundreds of thousands of people died. This drove many to flee the country, seeking refuge in Europe and America.

Americans today have not been forced to accept monoculture, as the Irish were. Instead, Americans embrace monoculture as a matter of convenience. Focusing on growing a single crop means that it can be produced in large quantities. This, in turn, allows the crops to be sold at low prices. In general, Americans appear willing to trade taste, variety, and food security for lower prices.

A prime example of monoculture in America today is the wheat crop. Most of the wheat grown in America and around the world belongs to a single species. This species has many virtues, but also a fatal flaw. It is vulnerable to a disease called stem rust, which is caused by a fungus that very quickly kills otherwise healthy plants. Billions of people around the world rely upon wheat. The destruction of the wheat crop would have results similar to the Irish Potato Famine, only this time, it would happen on a global scale. If the wheat crop were to be decimated by stem rust, we would be faced with global famine and social instability.

For now, the best way to prevent this from happening is to grow a variety of crops. But doing so can be expensive. Are we willing to take a chance on human life in order to save some money? Or will we finally learn from history and do the right thing?

Passage #17 Question Set

1. With which sentence would the author most likely agree?

    (A) People usually learn from history, which generally never repeats itself.
    (B) To avoid mistakes in the future, people should do the sensible thing now.
    (C) The problems of the past have little to do with the problems of the present.
    (D) Having inexpensive crops is more important than having diverse crops.

2. According to the passage, all of the following contributed to the Irish Potato Famine EXCEPT that

    (A) the Irish were not permitted to receive an education.
    (B) the British kept the Irish in poverty for generations.
    (C) the Irish grew a number of different types of potatoes.
    (D) disease wiped out a crop that was heavily relied upon.

3. In line 15, "rampant" most nearly means

    (A) fortified.
    (B) ruined.
    (C) static.
    (D) wild.

4. The passage implies that the Irish Lumper potato of the past and today's wheat crop have all of the following in common EXCEPT which statement?

    (A) Neither crop has a pleasant taste.
    (B) People relied heavily on both crops.
    (C) Both crops are vulnerable to disease.
    (D) The destruction of both crops would be a disaster.

5. The last questions in the passage (lines 70-73), the author's tone can best be described as

    (A) comical.
    (B) indifferent.
    (C) objective.
    (D) passionate.

6. Which best describes the organization of the passage?

    (A) A historical event is discussed in detail.
    (B) A theory is disproven with facts and figures.
    (C) A scientific concept is defined and a process explained.
    (D) A point of view is advanced and supported with examples.

Passage #18

Not every restaurant takes reservations. Some restaurants that don't take reservations have very good reasons not to. One of these reasons is that diners often make reservations but don't show up for their meal. This can be very bad for business. Once diners make a reservation, the restaurant saves a table for those diners. If the diners don't show up, then the table sits empty, instead of accommodating diners who were ready and willing to pay for a meal. Indeed, "no-shows," as the restaurants call such diners, pose a real problem to a restaurant's financial success. No-shows are a reason that many restaurants close.

Still, many diners have come to expect the ability to make a reservation. To help manage the problem of no-shows, many restaurants that do accept reservations have come up with creative ways to make sure diners show up for their reservations.

Some restaurants require a customer to provide his or her credit card information in order to make and hold a reservation. If the diner doesn't show up for the reservation, the restaurant then charges a fee on the credit card. This encourages the diners to show up for their meal. It also helps to offset the cost of keeping a table sitting empty.

Rather than charging reservation holders a fee for a no-show, other restaurants have attempted to put their reservations up for sale or auction. This practice is highly controversial. There are many people who support the practice, and many who dislike the practice. The people who support the practice argue that taking reservations is a service. And, like any other service provided, taking reservations should be something that restaurants should be allowed to charge money for. Supporters also argue that people who pay for their reservations will be more likely to keep them. This, they believe, will prevent the problems posed by no-shows.

The opponents to this practice argue that it flies in the face of hospitality itself. They also suggest that the practice gives an unfair advantage to the wealthy. They argue that other ways, such as requiring a credit card number to hold reservations, are equally effective at managing no-shows.

Perhaps there is a happy middle ground – one that is already employed by some restaurants. Some restaurants that offer fixed-priced meals and dining experiences sell tickets for a specific date and time. These tickets are priced at the cost of the meal, which is known to diners in advance. Effectively, diners buying tickets are pre-paying for their meal. They are therefore highly motivated to show up at the appointed ticket time. In this way customers are not charged more than the cost of their meal, and restaurants will not lose money in the event of a no-show.

Passage #18 Question Set

1. Which sentence best expresses the main idea of the passage?

   (A) Reservations are bad for business and should no longer be offered.
   (B) Restaurants should never be allowed to charge money for reservations.
   (C) There are different ways to provide reservations while also protecting restaurants.
   (D) Though there are many ways to protect restaurants, protecting diners is most important.

2. According to the passage, "no-shows" hurt restaurants because

   (A) restaurants will stop taking reservations.
   (B) diners will see that a restaurant is partly empty, and think that the food is bad.
   (C) there will be bad publicity about how people don't show up for reservations.
   (D) the tables are reserved, and will be empty if diners don't show up for their meals.

3. In line 43, the phrase "flies in the face of" most nearly means

   (A) closely aligns with.
   (B) supports and reinforces.
   (C) represents and embodies.
   (D) undermines and contradicts.

4. The passage suggests that the wealthy will have an "unfair advantage (lines 44-45) because

   (A) only people who can afford to pay will get reservations.
   (B) the poor will never be permitted to dine out at restaurants.
   (C) restaurants will only cook for people who have a lot of money.
   (D) they are more likely to be friends with chefs and restaurant owners.

5. In line 57, "appointed" most nearly means

   (A) approximate.
   (B) nominated.
   (C) required.
   (D) scheduled.

6. Which sentence best describes the organization of the passage?

   (A) One idea is supported and others are discredited.
   (B) An opinion is supported with personal experiences.
   (C) A particular point of view is described and reinforced.
   (D) A problem is presented, and possible solutions discussed.

Passage #19

Agnes had surprised everyone by going to America. By herself. She hadn't even told Eleanora, her best friend, what she had been planning.

Just today, Eleanora had received a letter from Agnes. It was a surprise to see her neat handwriting on the envelope. Eleanora put her hand inside her purse, touching the letter. She had carried it all day long, reading it over and over again.

Agnes had found a job working as a maid in a wealthy family's home. She had her own room in the house and took her meals there, too. So she could save practically everything she earned.

"You wouldn't believe how many buildings there are here," Agnes had written. "And there are so many wagons and carts going from place to place. Everybody moves so fast. But it's so much fun. It seems like nobody goes to bed until ten o'clock or even later! There's something happening all the time."

Agnes liked that, Eleanora knew. Something happening all the time. She was always restless here in Skara, where you had to go to bed early because work started before the sun came up.

What would it be like to live there, Eleanora wondered. She had some money saved from selling needlework. If only…

A light burning in the parlor window shone like a star in the darkness. After opening the front door and putting away her coat, scarf, and boots, she went to turn it out. She was surprised to find Mama there, knitting socks, even though the church bell had already struck eight.

Mama gave her a look, and at first Eleanora feared she might give her a scolding. It was awfully late to be just getting home.

Instead, Mama asked, "Did you and Lars have a good time?"

"Oh. Yes," Eleanora answered, blushing slightly.

After a moment, Mama said, "He didn't say anything you'd want to tell me?"

Eleanora shook her head. "No, Mama. Not yet. But he will. You know Lars."

"By the way," Mama continued, "you didn't let me read the letter that came from Agnes."

Eleanora took off her coat and sat down by the fireplace. "Oh, I threw it away, Mama. She just said some silly things. Nothing you'd be interested in."

Mama put her knitting in a bag and stood up. "I'm going to bed," she said. "You'd better not stay up much later."

"I won't, Mama," promised Eleanora. "I just want to sit by the fire and warm up."

Mama left and Eleanora looked into the remnants of the logs that would soon burn out. She took the letter from her purse and read it one more time. Then, she dropped it into the fire, watching it turn to ash.

If only she wasn't waiting for Lars, Eleanora thought, maybe she could have a life like Agnes.

Passage #19 Question Set

1. The main purpose of the passage is to

   (A) describe the relationship between two friends.
   (B) illustrate someone's thoughts, feelings, and hopes.
   (C) describe the relationship between a mother and her daughter.
   (D) convince the reader that life in America is better than life in Skara.

2. Eleanora feels that going to bed after 10:00 P.M. is

   (A) exotic and unusual.
   (B) ridiculous and impractical.
   (C) unacceptable and pointless.
   (D) customary and not surprising.

3. Eleanora read Agnes' letter many times because

   (A) she had never before left Skara.
   (B) Mama told her to think about moving to America.
   (C) she would like the chance to live a life like Agnes.
   (D) she finds Agnes' actions to be very irresponsible.

4. Based on the passage, it can be inferred that the conversation between Eleanora and her mother took place

   (A) at night.
   (B) in America.
   (C) in the morning.
   (D) in the afternoon.

5. In line 58, "remnants" most nearly means

   (A) inferno.
   (B) pieces.
   (C) smoke.
   (D) sparks.

6. Eleanora burns Agnes' letter because

   (A) she is angry with Agnes.
   (B) the fire was dying and needed more fuel.
   (C) Lars wrote her a more interesting and entertaining letter.
   (D) Lars is more important to her than an exciting life in America.

Passage #20

The small island of Taiwan sits approximately 110 miles off of the coast of China. Despite its size, Taiwan has been making big waves in international relations for decades. To understand these issues, one must first understand Taiwan's history.

Taiwan was originally settled by the ancestors of today's Taiwanese aborigines. By the 17th century, the ethnic Han Chinese had taken control of the island. They integrated the island into the Chinese empire on the continent. Following a war with Japan in the late 19th century, China gave the island of Taiwan to Japan. Eventually, as a part of their terms of surrender following World War II, the Japanese would relinquish their control of the island.

However, the Chinese Civil War complicated the matter. From 1927 to 1937, prior to World War II, two forces within China fought for control of the country. The nationalists, who were loyal to the existing government of China, clashed with the communists, who wanted to overthrow the existing government. The two adversaries temporarily stopped fighting when the Japanese invaded China in World War II. They united and fought together to successfully repel the Japanese. Shortly after the end of World War II in 1946, China's civil war resumed. This time, however, Taiwan was no longer under Japanese control. A new question arose: which China – nationalist, or communist – would control Taiwan?

Fighting in the Chinese Civil War eventually came to a stop in 1949. At that time, the leader of the communist forces, Mao Zedong, proclaimed Beijing to be the capital of the newly founded People's Republic of China (PRC). The nationalist forces, led by Chiang Kai-shek, left mainland China for Taiwan. There, he proclaimed Taipei to be the capital of the Republic of China (ROC).

For decades thereafter, the PRC and ROC have operated independently. The relationship between the PRC and the ROC is complicated. The PRC maintains that it is the only legitimate Chinese country. It argues that the ROC has continued to operate as an illegitimate government ever since the 1949 founding of the PRC. This is because the Chinese Civil War never came to a legal end, since there was no peace treaty or armistice. Therefore, they believe, both the PRC and the ROC belong to the same country, which is controlled by the PRC. The ROC in Taiwan disagrees. The ROC argues that it meets internationally agreed-upon requirements of being an independent country.

Other countries' view of the situation is best described as political. In 1952, the United Nations suggested that the Chinese communists of the PRC were rebels against the ROC. In 1971, however, the United Nations officially recognized the government of PRC as the only representative of China to the United Nations. Since then, the PRC has refused diplomatic relations with any state that officially recognizes the ROC. However, the PRC does not view economic, cultural, or other such exchanges as "official recognition." The United States, for example, is a long-time ally of the ROC. It has supported Taiwan through the sale of military arms and training. The United States acknowledges – rather than "officially recognizes" – the PRC's claim that Taiwan is a part of China.

Despite the fact that both the ROC and the PRC conduct trade with other countries – and with one another – the political conflict between the ROC and the PRC has not yet been resolved. Though many of the people living in the ROC and the PRC share a common ancestry, a final resolution to the question of Taiwan's independence does not seem likely.

Passage #20 Question Set

1. With which statement would the author most likely agree?

   (A) Control over Taiwan is a complicated issue.
   (B) The United Nations should officially support Taiwan.
   (C) The ROC should be an independent country and control Taiwan.
   (D) The Chinese Civil War was an unfortunate series of events.

2. In line 24, "adversaries" most likely means

   (A) colleagues.
   (B) opponents.
   (C) peers.
   (D) relatives.

3. The passage suggests that if a peace treaty or armistice had concluded the Chinese Civil War,

   (A) the PRC would not be able to claim control over the ROC.
   (B) the war would have ended with less violence and bloodshed.
   (C) Japan would not have relinquished control over the island of Taiwan.
   (D) other countries would not have acknowledged either the PRC or ROC.

4. The author cites which of the following as a reason why other countries' view of Taiwan is "political" (lines 57-58)?

   (A) The conflict between the PRC and the ROC was settled legally.
   (B) Japan never officially gave Taiwan to either the PRC or the ROC.
   (C) The United Nations first rejected the PRC, then later accepted it.
   (D) The United States influences other countries' opinions about Taiwan.

5. Which best describes the organization of the passage?

   (A) A specific process is explained in detail.
   (B) An opinion is supported using historical facts.
   (C) A problem is described and solutions proposed.
   (D) A modern problem is explained with historical causes.

6. The author's attitude toward the issue of Taiwan's independence can best be described as

   (A) neutral.
   (B) favorable.
   (C) unfavorable.
   (D) disbelieving.

Passage #21

For students of abstract expressionist art, perhaps no artist is as influential and famous as Jackson Pollock.

Pollock was born in 1912 in Wyoming, and was the youngest of five brothers. He grew up in various places throughout the American West, including Arizona and California. Pollock was not much of a student. In fact, he was expelled from two different high schools.

In 1930, at the age of 18, Pollock followed one of his older brothers to New York City. There, despite his lack of success in traditional academic settings, he studied art under Thomas Benton. At the time, Pollock did not identify strongly with his mentor's artistic interests. However, many of Pollock's biographers agree that some of Benton's artistic styles and philosophies had a great influence on Pollock. Many art historians believe that Pollock's artistic independence is due in part to his time learning from Benton.

It was difficult to be an artist during the late 1930s and early 1940s. The effects of the Great Depression were at their worst. Yet, thanks to the federal government's Works Progress Administration, many artists – Pollock among them – were able to find work in the Federal Art Project.

During this time, Pollock barely managed to keep his head above water. Finally, in 1943 he signed a contract with Peggy Guggenheim. Guggenheim would go on to be one of Pollock's primary paying patrons. Pollock was commissioned to produce a massive work for Guggenheim, measuring 8 feet tall by 20 feet long. This work helped to launch his career. It propelled him toward artistic stardom.

With help from Guggenheim, Pollock bought a home and art studio on Long Island, New York. There, he began experimenting with new techniques, including his now-famous "drip" method of painting. In this technique, Pollock would lay a canvas on the floor of his studio and would use flinging, pouring, splattering, and dripping motions to apply paint to the canvas. This was a technique previously unseen in Western art, and earned Pollock critical acclaim. Pollock, and the iconic paintings he created, were, to the art community, one and the same. *Time* magazine even gave Pollock the nickname "Jack the Dripper."

Then, as suddenly as he began, Pollock stopped using the drip style in his work. By the 1950s, Pollock had moved on to experimenting with new artistic styles and methods. These works did not sell as well as his drip paintings. Many art historians agree that Pollock's iconic style was so popular that it limited the appeal of his later works. Art collectors were simply not interested in Pollock's departure from his famous drip paintings.

Tragically, Pollock died in a car crash in 1956 at only 44 years old. Though Pollock's life was cut short, his paintings and bold artistic integrity live on even today. Many of Pollock's most famous drip paintings can be viewed in prestigious museums, including the Metropolitan Museum of Art in New York City.

Passage #21 Question Set

1. One of the main purposes of the passage is to

    (A) describe the life and work of an artist.
    (B) compare one style of art with another.
    (C) tell the story of a particular work of art.
    (D) encourage more people to become artists.

2. According to the passage, which factor led to Pollock's widespread popularity?

    (A) the Works Progress Administration
    (B) a favorable article in *Time* magazine
    (C) the patronage of Peggy Guggenheim
    (D) his education in Arizona and California

3. In line 47, "critical acclaim" most nearly means

    (A) high praise.
    (B) severe criticism.
    (C) negative critique.
    (D) widespread disapproval.

4. According to the passage,

    (A) Pollock's most iconic painting style was developed on Long Island.
    (B) Pollock created the nickname "Jack the Dripper" for *Time* magazine.
    (C) Pollock donated many of his works to the Metropolitan Museum of Art
    (D) Pollock's later works did not sell well because they were too similar to his drip paintings.

5. It can be inferred from the passage that

    (A) Pollock pursued art because he hated high school.
    (B) Pollock may not have fully realized the effect his mentor had on him.
    (C) Pollock's iconic style was created despite Thomas Benton's influence.
    (D) Pollock never would have gone to New York City if not for his brothers.

6. The author's tone in the passage can best be expressed as

    (A) critical.
    (B) solemn.
    (C) objective.
    (D) humorous.

Passage #22

A blue unlike any other shimmered all around me. It was almost as if I was walking around inside the world's largest sapphire. This was a blue that I had never seen before. It was constantly shifting, alive, as I put one foot in front of the other. This blue was that of pure ice, hundreds of feet thick. Even with my sunglasses on, the dancing of the blue light was bright and blinding.

I stopped for a moment to take stock of my situation. Somewhere in the back of my mind, the pulsing of a coming headache registered dimly. I ignored it, took a breath, and looked up. Beyond the jagged crack, thirty or forty feet above me, was the sky.

Thankfully, I had not fallen into this crevasse. I had simply walked into the crack in the side of a glacier, along with a few other hikers. We were exploring Franz Josef Glacier in New Zealand, one of the most unique glaciers in the world. Its lowest point was only a thousand feet above sea level. The glacier itself was surrounded by a temperate rainforest. The temperature was much warmer than I had expected, especially considering the fact that I was walking on, and surrounded by, a fortress of ice.

The walls of the crevasse were slippery and smooth. All around me, the ice wasn't so much melting as it was sweating, covering itself in a fine sheen. The bottom of the crevasse was so narrow that I half-shuffled and half-slid through the crack. I often needed to suck in my breath to slide between the two walls. It suddenly dawned on me that I hadn't taken a full breath since the beginning of the walk.

I stopped again, this time, to try and catch my breath. I stared into the pure and flawless ice just inches in front of my face, trying to glimpse the very soul of the glacier. There was nothing to obstruct my view – no air bubbles or blemishes for my eyes to linger on. I stared hundreds of years into the past at snowfall that had piled up and become ice under its own weight. I was looking at snow that had fallen when man first walked on the moon – snow that had fallen when the world's earliest explorers first sailed around the world. The past, I realized, was the essence of the glacier.

Walking the glacier was a profound experience. I remember that walk like it was yesterday. The beauty of the experience will be forever burned into my memory.

Passage #22 Question Set

1. The primary purpose of the passage is to

   (A) recount a vivid dream.
   (B) describe how blue a glacier is.
   (C) tell about a memorable experience.
   (D) illustrate how dangerous glaciers can be.

2. The sapphire mentioned in line 3 represents the

   (A) ice.
   (B) sky.
   (C) snow.
   (D) melting water.

3. The passage provides all of the following as evidence to support the fact that the Franz Josef Glacier is unique EXCEPT

   (A) its elevation.
   (B) the temperature around it.
   (C) the landscape surrounding it.
   (D) the number of people who visit it.

4. According to the passage, the author needed to hold his breath because

   (A) he was very nervous.
   (B) his surroundings were very narrow.
   (C) the other hikers were smoking.
   (D) there was too much water everywhere.

5. The passage provides information to answer which question?

   (A) How are glaciers formed?
   (B) How old is the Franz Josef Glacier?
   (C) Why was the author hiking on the glacier?
   (D) What was the temperature during the author's walk?

6. In line 49, "profound" most nearly means

   (A) exaggerated.
   (B) regrettable.
   (C) touching.
   (D) unremarkable.

Passage #23

Many scientists agree that the earth's climate is changing. They believe that this change has a major impact on the environment. These scientists warn that a warming global climate has many catastrophic side effects. Some examples of these effects include rising sea levels and more powerful and destructive storms, like hurricanes and tornadoes. One of the main causes of this climate change is the buildup of greenhouse gases in the atmosphere. These gases include carbon dioxide, methane, nitrous oxide, and ozone. They are called greenhouse gases because they trap heat in the atmosphere, and imitate the effect of a greenhouse on the entire planet.

Because of these dangerous consequences, scientists have been researching different ways to reduce the amount of greenhouse gases. One way is to remove carbon dioxide, which is one of the most powerful greenhouse gases, from the atmosphere. This is a process known as "carbon sequestration." There are many ways to accomplish this. One of the most effective methods is to use the power of nature itself.

All around the world, there are natural processes that give off carbon dioxide and those that absorb carbon dioxide. Some processes give off more carbon dioxide than they absorb. These are known as "carbon sources." Other processes absorb more carbon dioxide than is given off. These are known as "carbon sinks." By using carbon sinks, scientists believe that we can help reduce the amount of carbon dioxide in the atmosphere. One of the most effective carbon sinks on the planet are the world's oceanic ecosystems.

The key to carbon sequestration begins at the base of the food chain. Phytoplankton are organisms that use light, water, and carbon dioxide to grow. These organisms produce oxygen as a side effect of photosynthesis. They live in the world's oceans and are extremely abundant. Some estimates suggest that phytoplankton contribute between 50% and 85% of the world's oxygen. In fact, it is thought that phytoplankton have balanced the earth's carbon dioxide and oxygen levels since the early Precambrian era. This would mean that phytoplankton have been regulating Earth's atmospheric gases for over 4 billion years!

Many scientists believe that we should increase the number of phytoplankton in the world's oceans. They believe that this would mean less carbon dioxide in the atmosphere. Yet phytoplankton cannot live on carbon dioxide alone. They require other nutrients, like iron, to thrive. Some scientists suggest that people should "fertilize" the oceans with iron nutrients, like how people fertilize soil to make plants grow. The idea is that increasing the amount of iron in the oceans will increase the number of phytoplankton. This would then increase the amount of carbon dioxide that is removed from the atmosphere.

Passage #23 Question Set

1. Which sentence best expresses the main point of the passage?

   (A) People should "fertilize" the oceans with iron nutrients.
   (B) People can work with nature to help reduce greenhouse gases.
   (C) Phytoplankton alone will solve the problem of a warming climate.
   (D) Phytoplankton have been regulating Earth's atmosphere for over 4 billion years.

2. The passage implies that reducing the amount of greenhouse gases in the atmosphere would have which effect?

   (A) less frequent and less powerful storms
   (B) a decrease in the number of carbon sinks in the world
   (C) an increase in the number of phytoplankton
   (D) an increase in the amount of iron in the world's oceans

3. A process that increases the amount of carbon dioxide in the atmosphere is called

   (A) a carbon sink.
   (B) a carbon source.
   (C) a greenhouse gas.
   (D) carbon sequestration.

4. In line 42, "abundant" most nearly means

   (A) ample.
   (B) ancient.
   (C) important.
   (D) scarce.

5. The author's tone when discussing the amount of time phytoplankton have been regulating greenhouse gases (lines 44-49) can best be described as

   (A) angry.
   (B) frantic.
   (C) grateful.
   (D) impressed.

6. According to the passage, an increase in the number of phytoplankton in the world's oceans would require additional

   (A) ozone.
   (B) nitrous oxide.
   (C) iron nutrients.
   (D) carbon sequestration.

Passage #24

I knew that we were due for a thunderstorm.

The clouds – once white and fluffy – were angry and dark as coal. The air was tinged a sickly greenish-yellow. A barely-audible buzzing – an electrical humming, almost – played on the edge of my hearing. The little hairs on the back of my neck and on my arms stood on end.

Even without looking at the weather forecast, I knew that we were due for some bad weather. I had witnessed this same scene unfold before me time and time again. And each time, we were in for a big storm.

There were a number of things I needed to do, and I ran through the checklist in my mind: close the windows; close the storm shutter; get flashlights and candles ready; double check my battery supply. As I went around the house on autopilot, checking batteries and closing windows, a deep rumbling rolled over my house. The storm was coming, and thunder was its herald.

A few drops of rain quickly gave way to a deafening deluge, a million nails being hammered into my roof. The wind began a relentless campaign to break into my house, shaking my storm shutters violently and searching for gaps in my windows. The thunder, once a gentle bass in the distance, split the air like a giant's war drums, shaking the contents of my house.

Through the slats of my shutters came a blinding flash, casting a striped shadow against the walls and floors of my living room. The lightning was followed by a violent peal of thunder, sending one of my picture frames crashing to the floor. Somewhere out there, the branches of a tree – a victim of the wind or lightning – fell to the earth, taking with it the electrical lines that powered my home.

But for the lightning and the weak glow from my candle and flashlight, I sat in near darkness and waited for the storm to pass.

Passage #24 Question Set

1. One of the main points of the passage is to

   (A) describe different features of thunderstorms.
   (B) explain the scientific causes of a thunderstorm.
   (C) list the proper steps to take before a big storm.
   (D) illustrate a personal encounter with a strong storm.

2. According to the passage, the author knows that a storm is coming primarily due to

   (A) his neighbors.
   (B) his observations.
   (C) the newspaper report.
   (D) the television forecast.

3. In line 25, the word "campaign" most nearly means

   (A) defense.
   (B) effort.
   (C) idea.
   (D) requirement.

4. The phrase "million nails being hammered" (lines 23-24), refers to

   (A) the sound of rain hitting the room.
   (B) the sound of construction next door.
   (C) the sound of thunder in the distance.
   (D) the sound of shutters flapping in the wind.

5. According to the passage, the power outage was influenced by

   (A) giants in the sky.
   (B) the thunder or rain.
   (C) either the wind or the lightning.
   (D) construction in the neighborhood.

6. The author would support which of the following statements about powerful storms?

   (A) Preparation can prevent the most severe storms.
   (B) All clouds announce the arrival of a thunderstorm.
   (C) There is little to be frightened about strong thunderstorms.
   (D) After preparing, there is little to do but wait for a storm to pass.

Passage #25

Trees are an invaluable part of our ecosystem. They provide us with many benefits, some of which we are only beginning to understand.

Have you ever walked, hiked, or exercised in the blazing summer sun? Well, if you exercised in the shade, you'd feel between 10 and 15 degrees cooler. That's because trees absorb sunlight and use that energy to grow. According to the USDA Forest Service, trees that are properly placed around buildings can reduce air conditioning needs by 30%. This can help reduce the amount of energy used for climate control by between 20-50%.

Another way that trees benefit our environment is by absorbing carbon dioxide from the atmosphere. Trees use carbon dioxide from the atmosphere as an ingredient in their cellular processes. This is helpful to the environment because carbon dioxide is a powerful greenhouse gas. Greenhouse gases, like carbon dioxide, trap heat in our atmosphere, causing temperatures on Earth to increase. Estimates suggest that a single tree can capture between 18 and 50 pounds of carbon dioxide per year! And trees do more than just provide us with a beautiful, inexpensive way to absorb carbon. In the process of converting carbon dioxide into energy, trees release oxygen into the atmosphere. Thus, together with other organisms, trees provide us with the very air that we breathe!

In addition to removing excess carbon from the atmosphere, adding oxygen to the air, and keeping things shady and cool, trees also help fight soil erosion. Deep roots hold soil together and help prevent landslides. Trees basically form giant underground nets that help prevent soil from washing away in the rain. Furthermore, trees help to block even the strongest of winds, which would otherwise whip up dust and strip the land of fertile topsoil. Trees also contribute to replenishing the soil itself. Every autumn in temperate climate zones, colorful fallen leaves decompose into minerals and nutrients that enrich the soil.

Trees are also important to our physical health. Many trees bear fruit that are fit for human consumption. Even those that do not are important to insects and animals that help pollenate our crops. Not only do trees produce things that are good to eat, but they have also contributed to our fight against illnesses and cancers. For example, a drug that is used to treat asthma was developed using a tree in the Amazon rainforest. An anti-cancer drug has been derived from a tree found in the Pacific Northwest.

The value people receive from trees comes not only in the form of foods, medicines, shade, and oxygen. Many people receive spiritual or other personal value from trees. Trees, being majestic in size and diverse in shape and color, are beautiful to behold. People have planted trees as living monuments to life-changing events (like the birth of a child) that grow with the people they commemorate. The personal, spiritual, and aesthetic value of trees is not only intangible, but can also help increase the economic value of a home or property.

The next time you take a break from the heat under the shade of a tree, think about just how amazing trees really are. The more people appreciate trees and what they do for us, the better off we'll be.

Passage #25 Question Set

1. The author would be most likely to agree with which of the following statements?

   (A) An increase in temperatures is the cause of greenhouse gases.
   (B) The most important thing trees do for people is create shade.
   (C) People often take trees for granted and fail to appreciate their value.
   (D) The medicine trees provide are more important than the fruit they bear.

2. According to the passage, trees can help people save energy

   (A) by fighting soil erosion.
   (B) if planted around buildings.
   (C) by capturing carbon dioxide.
   (D) if used to produce medicines.

3. The "nets" mentioned in line 36 refer to

   (A) the roots of trees.
   (B) soil underground.
   (C) strong winds and dust.
   (D) carbon in the atmosphere.

4. In line 46, "bear" most nearly means

   (A) consume.
   (B) experience.
   (C) produce.
   (D) support.

5. The passage provides information to answer all of the following questions EXCEPT

   (A) How can trees help keep people fed?
   (B) How do trees help prevent the loss of soil?
   (C) How have trees helped people fight disease?
   (D) How are trees dispersed through various climates?

6. Which best describes the organization of the passage?

   (A) An opinion is supported by a number of facts.
   (B) A theory is described and then discredited.
   (C) A problem is stated and solutions proposed.
   (D) One point of view is supported while another is disproven.

Passage #26

When Justin arrived in San Francisco for the first time, he only had one thing on his list: to bike across the Golden Gate Bridge.

The only thing he knew about the Golden Gate Bridge was what he had read about in his travel guide. He knew, for instance, that the suspension bridge was well over a mile long and weighed nearly 900,000 tons. He also knew that the steel used in the construction of the bridge was manufactured along the East Coast and shipped through the Panama Canal all the way to San Francisco. He also knew that the Golden Gate Bridge wasn't painted an ordinary shade of orange – it was painted a distinctive vermilion-orange.

After dropping off his small backpack at a friend's apartment, he rented a bike and started pedaling for the bridge.

Justin took a scenic route along the bay, riding along the water's edge. He settled into a leisurely pace and tried to soak in the sights. There were many things to look at: boats, islands, far away trees and buildings, storefronts and pedestrians. But his eye was always drawn to the Golden Gate Bridge, which towered proudly in the background.

Justin's travel guide did little to prepare him for the graceful beauty of the bridge. It didn't matter that the bridge was painted vermilion-orange. What mattered was that the vermilion-orange seemed to set fire to the bay as it stood in stark contrast to the blue waters and grey skies. It didn't matter that the two main towers rose nearly 750 feet into the air. What mattered was that these towers stood like giants guarding the bay.

Eventually, Justin began to make his way across the massive bridge. While his travel guide had at least given him some idea as to the size, shape, and color of the bridge, it did little to prepare him for the beauty of the view. Standing at the very middle of the span, Justin looked eastward toward the bay. Behind him, the setting sun cast furious rays the color of the bridge itself over the Bay Area. Countless buildings, cars, and windows caught the light and bounced it back his way. Justin raised his hand to his eyes against the beauty of the dazzling fire and molten gold.

"This must be why they call it the Golden Gate Bridge," he thought aloud.

Passage #26 Question Set

1. Which sentence best expresses the passage's main idea?

   (A) San Francisco is a beautiful city.
   (B) Bridges are a top tourist destination.
   (C) Suspension bridges are the most beautiful of all bridges.
   (D) Experiencing something first hand and reading about it can be very different.

2. In line 14, the word "distinctive" most nearly means

   (A) bright.
   (B) unique.
   (C) familiar.
   (D) obvious.

3. Which of the following supports the idea that Justin prepared for his visit in advance?

   (A) He trained on his bike at home.
   (B) He read many facts about the Golden Gate Bridge.
   (C) He purchased his airplane tickets many months beforehand.
   (D) His friend had been living in San Francisco for many years already.

4. The main purpose of the fifth paragraph (lines 27-36) is to

   (A) compare Justin's expectations with his real experiences.
   (B) describe the actual appearance of the Golden Gate Bridge.
   (C) explain common misconceptions about the Golden Gate Bridge.
   (D) convince the reader that Justin's travel guide is incorrect.

5. The phrase "set fire to the bay" (line 31), is used to describe

   (A) the colors of the sunset.
   (B) how Justin feels after a long bike ride.
   (C) the precise color painted on the bridge.
   (D) the effect of the bridge's color on its surroundings.

6. Which of the following best describes the organization of the passage?

   (A) An opinion is expressed.
   (B) Several travel tips are shared.
   (C) A personal experience is shared.
   (D) Directions are provided in order.

Passage #27

Like many others who grew up in suburban America, my childhood home had a grass lawn in both the front and back yards. Many of my memories involve those lawns: picnicking with family on the soft grass under an oak tree; playing tag with friends until dusk, arms and legs stained green; knocking up clumps of grass as I learned how to kick a soccer ball or swing a golf club; the unmistakably pungent, herbal smell of freshly cut grass.

Given all of these pleasant memories, and knowing how important grass lawns are in American culture, I was dismayed to learn that maintaining grass lawns can have many negative effects on the environment.

Think about everything it takes to cultivate and maintain a luscious, green lawn: seeds, fertilizers, herbicides, pesticides, water, lawn mowers, waste removal, and time. According to some estimates, approximately 25 million acres of land in the United States are devoted to grass lawns. An incredible 50-70% of all residential water usage is intended to keep our lawns green. Recently, the Environmental Protection Agency (EPA) has estimated that as many as 70 million pounds of pesticides are used each year to keep our lawns insect-free. And, in order to keep grass at a pleasant height, the average American spends 40 hours a year mowing the lawn. According to the EPA, gas mowers represent approximately 5% of air pollution in the United States.

In my mind, the real question is: why does a lawn have to be a certain way, and if it does, is this ideal worth all the time and resources that we spend trying to achieve it? Rather than fighting nature with herbicides, maybe we should tolerate other types of plant life on our lawns, such as clover, dandelion, and other plants typically deemed to be weeds. Rather than draining rivers dry to water our lawns in naturally dry areas, maybe we should think about other ways to landscape our properties in places where grass doesn't thrive naturally. Rather than mindlessly doing what we have always done for our lawns, maybe we should think about less harmful, less expensive ways to care for our lawns – ways that don't harm other parts of our environment or drain our limited resources.

I love the look and feel and smell of grass lawns as much as the next person, and I certainly do not believe that we should ban or outlaw grass lawns. I understand that over time, we as a nation have accepted the idea that a home must have a yard, and that a yard must have a perfectly manicured grass lawn. Though this may be right for some people, it might not be right for everyone. I just think we should spend some time thinking about the consequences of our actions rather than just doing what everyone else is doing.

We might have more time to enjoy nature if we spent less time trying to fight it.

Passage #27 Question Set

1. The author would most likely agree with which statement about gardening and lawn care?

   (A) Spending time gardening makes everyone happy.
   (B) Appearances are more important than anything else.
   (C) Lawns and gardens should be maintained at any cost.
   (D) People should not be afraid to challenge norms and traditions.

2. The author's tone in the first paragraph (lines 1-10) can best be described as

   (A) apathetic.
   (B) empathetic.
   (C) regretful.
   (D) sentimental.

3. In line 13, the word "dismayed" most nearly means

   (A) disappointed.
   (B) encouraged.
   (C) inspired.
   (D) unfazed.

4. The passage suggests that the author would agree with which of the following statements?

   (A) Lawns are an irreplaceable aspect of American culture.
   (B) Irrigation must be used wherever there is not enough water.
   (C) Fertilizers are helpful and should be used wherever desired.
   (D) People should consider using electric or man-powered lawn mowers.

5. According to the passage, all of the following are mentioned as reasons why maintaining a lawn can be wasteful EXCEPT

   (A) that maintenance wastes water.
   (B) that lawns are visually pleasing.
   (C) that lawn mowers contribute to air pollution.
   (D) that time spent caring for lawns could be better spent on other things.

6. Which of the following best describes the organization of the third paragraph?

   (A) An opinion is refuted.
   (B) A number of policies are described in order.
   (C) A series of events are presented chronologically.
   (D) Various facts and statistics are presented to support an opinion.

Passage #28

Easter Island is a small island in the southeastern Pacific Ocean. One of the island's greatest claims to fame are the moai, large, human-shaped sculptures carved from a single piece of stone. On Easter Island, many of the surviving moai were buried to their shoulders. As a result, these large stone sculptures became mistakenly known as the "Easter Island heads." Many mysteries surround the moai. One such mystery is how the sculptures were moved around the island.

Many of the moai scattered around the island were carved from the same rock quarry on the island. This meant that the rock was somehow moved from the quarry to the moai's final destination. The average moai weighed approximately 14 tons. Some sculptures were significantly larger – even in excess of 80 tons. Most of the moai were created between the 13th and 16th centuries. This was long before modern construction equipment could help move the massive rocks. As a result, historians are unsure precisely how the native islanders were able to accomplish such a feat.

Oral histories describe how powerful rulers wielded supernatural or divine powers. These rulers were said to have caused the statues to come to life and walk themselves around the island. Though many considered such stories to be outlandish, critics had difficulty coming up with an alternative explanation.

One early theory was that the islanders transported quarried rock across the island by means of a conveyer belt system. This theory stated that trees were cut down and used as rollers, across which the giant stones could be moved. However, by the time Europeans arrived on Easter Island in the 18th century, the island was completely treeless. This only deepened the mystery of the moai, which persists even today.

More recently, some archaeologists and historians attempted to "walk" moai replicas across the island. They did so by tying ropes around the head and the base of the replica, rocking the replica from side to side. The team was able to shuffle the replica forward, which they considered proof that such a methodology was likely employed by the island's old inhabitants.

However, not everyone was convinced. Some historians and archaeologists questioned the basic premise behind the "walking" experiment. They argued that the replica used in the "walk" was not representative of actual moai weight, and that the replica did not behave as a real moai would have. Thus, they argued, no definite conclusions could be drawn from the "walking" experiment.

We are no closer to discovering the definitive truth behind how the Easter Island natives moved the moai than we were decades ago. For all we know, perhaps the moai really did get up and walk themselves.

Passage #28 Question Set

1. Which sentence best expresses the passage's main idea?

    (A) Moai are beautiful sculptures found on Easter Island.
    (B) Islands in the Pacific are a popular tourist destination.
    (C) Despite different theories, some historical mysteries remain unsolved.
    (D) Island natives may have used an unusual "walking" technique to transport sculptures.

2. The author's tone when describing the weight of the moai (lines 16-18) can best be described as

    (A) academic.
    (B) biased.
    (C) confused.
    (D) proud.

3. In line 30, the word "outlandish" most nearly means

    (A) absolutely true.
    (B) not unreasonable.
    (C) unbelievably strange.
    (D) perfectly reasonable.

4. Historians and archaeologists who question the "walking" experiment would likely support which of the following statements?

    (A) Real moai could not be easily shuffled around the island.
    (B) Moai were controlled by magic and commanded to walk around the island.
    (C) European visitors destroyed the only records containing the moai's secrets.
    (D) It is more likely that trees were used to help carry the moai across the island.

5. According to the fourth paragraph, the "conveyer belt system" theory described in lines 32-40 is questionable because

    (A) oral histories contradict the concept.
    (B) the moai were too heavy to be rolled across tree trunks.
    (C) there have not been trees on Easter Island for hundreds of years.
    (D) the islanders actually used tools brought by early European visitors.

6. According to the passage, historians and archaeologists know that moai were transported around the island because

    (A) oral traditions passed through generations detail the movement.
    (B) inscriptions on the moai record their exact path across the island.
    (C) European visitors witnessed the construction and transportation of the moai.
    (D) they originated from the same rock quarry, and moai are scattered around the island.

Passage #29

I looked forward to biology class every day. In fact, you could even say that I loved biology class. The different topics fascinated me, and I would sit in class furiously taking notes about everything from cell division to the Krebs Cycle.

At the beginning of the school year, my teacher, Mr. Smith, grouped everyone in the class into pairs. Each pair consisted of two lab partners, who would work on projects together throughout the year and be graded on those projects together.

I liked and generally got along with my lab partner, Charlie. For the most part, we worked well together, sharing responsibilities equally. We'd meet up after school to work on our projects, compare notes, or study for the next test. Still, we'd sometimes argue about whose turn it was to check the petri dish or who was supposed to note our observations about Spot, the class plant. We weren't exactly friends, but we didn't dislike each other, either. We were happy to work together, but that was about it.

Things went along as they always did until the day that Mr. Smith announced our next project. We were going to dissect a frog and examine the inside of its body! My heart skipped a beat – I had been looking forward to this project since I first read about it on our class syllabus!

Charlie, however, did not share my enthusiasm.

As we stared down at the pale frog lying on the shiny metal dissection tray, Charlie leaned over, gripped my arm, and whispered, "I don't think I can do this. I think I'm going to be sick."

Charlie's face was shrouded in panic and fear. I could tell by the pleading, searching look in Charlie's eyes that this was a pure and powerful anxiety.

"Don't worry about it," I smiled. "I'll handle this one. You can help with the next project that we have."

Charlie nodded and seemed relieved, if not a little bit surprised at my generosity.

For my part, I put on my gloves and started to go to work.

At first, Charlie was fine. We examined the exterior of the frog, and identified a few interesting features as we listened to Mr. Smith's instructions. I picked up my scalpel and made the first incision.

Almost immediately, Charlie's face turned a shade curiously akin to the frog that we were dissecting.

As I lengthened the incision, exposing the most intimate parts of the frog, Charlie bolted out of the classroom, knocking over lab stools and papers on the way out.

Passage #29 Question Set

1. Which of the following sentences best expresses the main purpose of the passage?

   (A) A friendship is recalled.
   (B) Scientific theories are debated.
   (C) A memory about school is described.
   (D) Detailed scientific processes are explained.

2. In line 37, the word "pleading" most nearly means

   (A) approving.
   (B) desperate.
   (C) hopeful.
   (D) passive.

3. Because of Charlie's reaction mentioned in lines 43-44, it can be inferred that

   (A) Charlie thought the author was not nice.
   (B) Charlie did not expect the author to act kindly.
   (C) Charlie actually enjoyed the frog dissection project.
   (D) the teacher instructed the author to be friendly toward Charlie.

4. According to the passage, Charlie ran from the room as a direct result of

   (A) the author's thoughtful words.
   (B) seeing the author cut into the frog.
   (C) knocking over lab stools and papers.
   (D) seeing the frog simply laying on the tray.

5. The phrase "Charlie's face turned a shade curiously akin to the frog" (line 52-53), refers to

   (A) the author's actions.
   (B) an involuntary reaction.
   (C) Charlie's everyday appearance.
   (D) an accident involving Charlie and the frog.

6. Which of the following best describes the organization of the passage?

   (A) A point of view is defended with facts.
   (B) A number of differing opinions are compared.
   (C) Specific definitions are illustrated with examples.
   (D) Events are told in the order that they happened.

Passage #30

People have cultivated and consumed the seeds of different types of plants for thousands of years. The seeds of wheat, rye, and oat plants are just some examples of the grains that people eat. One way of eating grains is by grinding it into a powder. Today, we know this powder as flour, which can be used in cooking in many different ways. However, before flour can be ground (or milled, as it is known in the food business), grain must first be harvested, threshed, and then winnowed.

Taking place at the end of the growing season, the harvest was a time for farmers to gather mature crops. In the case of grain plants, the harvest process consisted of reaping, or the cutting down of grain producing plants. Traditionally, the harvest was extremely labor intensive because entire fields of crop needed to be harvested by hand. For generations, farmers used tools such as the scythe or sickle to cut down grain bearing crops. Such tools were essentially long, curved blades that were carried by hand and swung in an arc to cut down plants. Though people became extremely skilled at wielding their tools, the harvest of grains was still very time consuming.

After the grain crop was harvested, farmers would prepare to separate the grain kernels from the rest of the plant. This process was known as threshing, and was accomplished in a number of different ways. One method of hand threshing involved spreading the harvested grain plants on a floor and beating it with a flail, which was essentially a long staff with a short, heavy rod that swung from one end. By swinging the staff, the short rod would smash into the grain crop and separate the grain from the rest of the plant. Threshing grain by hand was very time consuming, taking about an hour to produce a bushel of wheat. Because of the labor intensity of threshing, people often used creative means to make the process more efficient. One such method was to use oxen or mules to walk repeatedly over the grain crop that had been laid out on the floor.

While threshing removes the grain from the larger plant, leaving straw behind as a byproduct, the grain kernels themselves would still be protected by a thin skin, called chaff. In order to remove the chaff from the grain and separate any pests from the crop, farmers engaged in a process called winnowing. Most simply, winnowing consisted of tossing the threshed grain into the air such that the wind would carry away the thin chaff. The grains would then fall back to the ground or into a basket for collection and storage. As with harvesting and threshing, winnowing was also an arduous process, and many tools were developed to help improve the process. Such tools as the winnowing fan and winnowing fork helped to simplify the process.

Passage #30 Question Set

1. Which of the following sentences best expresses the main purpose of the passage?

   (A) Different types of crops are compared.
   (B) One process is compared with another.
   (C) The different steps of a process are explained.
   (D) The appearance of various tools are described in detail.

2. The passage suggests that, once harvested, grain must be

   (A) threshed.
   (B) winnowed.
   (C) laid out to dry in the sun.
   (D) used immediately in the production of flour.

3. According to the passage, people used the scythe and sickle because doing so

   (A) helped them harvest crops quickly.
   (B) improved their ability to mill flour.
   (C) allowed them to quickly remove the chaff from the grain.
   (D) made separating grain kernels from the plant more efficient.

4. According to the passage, the use of tools and animal labor was influenced by

   (A) boredom and idle creativity.
   (B) royal decrees and farming laws.
   (C) the dangerous nature of grain production.
   (D) the time-consuming nature of grain production.

5. The author's tone in the passage can best be described as

   (A) amused.
   (B) bored.
   (C) fascinated.
   (D) impartial.

6. In line 58, the word "arduous" most nearly means

   (A) artistic and beautiful.
   (B) casual and enjoyable.
   (C) difficult and tiring.
   (D) simple and repetitive.

Quantitative Reasoning & Mathematics Achievement

Overview

The Middle Level ISEE contains two separate math sections.

In the Quantitative Reasoning section, you may be asked to estimate, compare and contrast amounts, interpret charts and graphs representing data, and calculate probability. In this section, there are two types of questions and two parts on the exam: Word Problems and Quantitative Comparisons. This section tests your ability to understand broader, more abstract math questions and does not require elaborate calculations.

In the Mathematics Achievement section, you may be asked to apply mathematical rules, procedures, concepts, and formulas to solve questions. This section tests concrete math skills and may require calculations as well as knowledge of some mathematical terms and vocabulary.

Both of these sections are linked by common skills outlined further below.

- *Numbers and Operations* – You may be evaluated on your understanding of various numerical operators and concepts. You may also be asked to understand the conceptual nature of numbers including integers, fractions, decimals, and percents.
- *Algebra* – You may be asked to understand algebraic functions, including the use of symbols in functions. You may also be asked to analyze expressions and equivalent expressions. You may also be asked to interpret graphs and tables as they relate to algebraic functions.
- *Geometry* – You may be asked to understand geometric figures, including the identification of those figures as well as how they interact with a coordinate grid and 3-dimensional space.
- *Measurement* – You may be asked to use mathematical formulas to measure different dimensions and qualities of both 2-dimensional and 3-dimensional shapes, including area, perimeter, and volume.
- *Data Analysis and Probability* – You may be asked to look at a data set, graph, or chart and from it draw conclusions or make inferences. You may also be asked to understand statistical concepts and probabilities.

On the Actual Test

In the Quantitative Reasoning section of the Middle Level ISEE, you will encounter 37 questions, which you will have 35 minutes to complete. There will be between 18-21 Word Problems and 14-17 Quantitative Comparisons.

In the Mathematics Achievement section, you will encounter 47 questions, which you will have 40 minutes to complete.

Most answer choices will be ordered from greatest to least or least to greatest.

As with other sections of this exam, a portion of these questions will be unscored, though you will not know which questions are unscored. Five questions from each section are unscored.

In This Practice Book

Because both Quantitative Reasoning and Mathematics Achievement test the same common skills, they are combined in this workbook by topic.

Any topic that may be covered in the Quantitative Comparison portion of the test will include several Quantitative Comparison practice problems in this workbook, which can be found at the end of each topic.

The full list of topics can be found in the table of contents at the beginning of this workbook.

How to Use This Section

As determined by your study plan, including the results of your diagnostic test, we encourage you to focus on the topics that are most challenging to you. Because there may be material on this test that you have not yet learned in school, we encourage you to seek additional help from trusted educators. Bring the materials to your tutor or teacher if you need additional enrichment in any given topic.

The questions in each section are progressive. This means that they start out easier, but then become more and more difficult as they build on more nuanced concepts related to that topic. Don't get discouraged if you find some questions difficult. Instead, consider asking a trusted educator to help you better understand the material.

Mixed Practice

We've added Mixed Practice question sets designed to review each topic area throughout the book. Whether with a tutor, parent, or by yourself, working through these question sets is a great way to quiz yourself and ensure you remember key concepts come test day!

Tutorverse Tips!

You won't be able to use a calculator to perform complex calculations. So, if as you answer a question things start to get more and more complicated, take a step back and think about what the question is asking you to do. If necessary, use the answer choices themselves to help you arrive at the correct answer by plugging them into formulas or expressions.

As far as scratch paper goes, the official test booklets do have blank pages at the end for scrap paper and students are allowed to use them. However, they are not allowed to tear them out of their booklets; they will need to flip back and forth to use them. Students taking the test digitally are allowed a single sheet of scrap paper, meaning space is limited either way!

You do not have to memorize unit conversion tables (for instance, the number of feet in a mile), as any such information will be provided. However, metric unit conversions will not be provided (i.e. the number of milliliters in a liter).

Remember that on the Middle Level ISEE, there is no penalty for guessing. If you don't know the answer to a question, take your best guess.

Numbers & Operations

Integers

1. What is the value of the numerical expression $-952 + 1{,}650$?

   (A) $-1{,}302$
   (B) -698
   (C) 698
   (D) 1,302

2. $6 \div 3 + 4 \times (5 - 2) =$

   (A) 12
   (B) 14
   (C) 18
   (D) 20

3. Which of the following choices, when divided by 3, leaves a remainder of 2?

   (A) 45
   (B) 55
   (C) 65
   (D) 75

4. Which number, when squared, will NOT leave a units digit of 9?

   (A) 33
   (B) 37
   (C) 39
   (D) 43

5. Elmo started with four ducks. Each duck then laid between 4 and 8 eggs. After all the ducklings hatched, what is the difference between the largest and smallest number of ducks Elmo could have now?

   (A) 16
   (B) 20
   (C) 28
   (D) 32

6. $154 \times 359 =$

   (A) 54,274
   (B) 55,286
   (C) 56,298
   (D) 57,302

7. Over the course of three days, a wild leopard will sleep an average of 12 hours per day. If the leopard slept 10 hours on the first day, how many combined hours will the leopard sleep on the second and third day?

   (A) 2
   (B) 13
   (C) 24
   (D) 26

8. 6 cats can catch a total of 12 mice in 1 day. How many days would it take 12 cats to catch 96 mice?

   (A) 2
   (B) 3
   (C) 4
   (D) 6

9. What is the largest prime number less than 100 with a units digit of 9?

   (A) 69
   (B) 79
   (C) 89
   (D) 99

10. What is the sum of all the positive integers up to 15, inclusive?

    (A) 104
    (B) 105
    (C) 119
    (D) 120

Quantitative Comparison Practice

Answer Choices:

(A) The amount in column A is greater.
(B) The amount in column B is greater.
(C) The two amounts are equal.
(D) The relationship cannot be determined from the information provided.

	Column A	Column B
11.	The product of two distinct, positive, odd integers	2

	Column A	Column B
12.	$2^0 + 2^1 + 2^2 + 2^3 + 2^4$	2^5

Fractions

1. The circle shown is divided into equal parts.

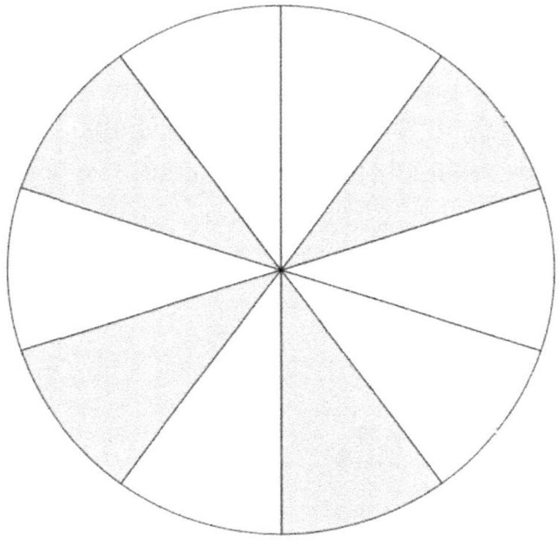

What part of the circle is shaded?

(A) $\frac{2}{5}$

(B) $\frac{1}{2}$

(C) $\frac{3}{5}$

(D) $\frac{4}{5}$

2. What is the value of the expression $\frac{5}{6} \times \frac{1}{4}$?

(A) $\frac{1}{6}$

(B) $\frac{5}{24}$

(C) $\frac{13}{12}$

(D) $\frac{4}{3}$

3. What is the value of the expression $\frac{7}{9} \div \frac{5}{6}$?

(A) $\frac{2}{3}$

(B) $\frac{35}{54}$

(C) $\frac{12}{15}$

(D) $\frac{14}{15}$

4. What is the value of the expression $\frac{1}{2} + \frac{2}{3}$?

(A) $\frac{3}{5}$

(B) $\frac{6}{7}$

(C) $\frac{7}{6}$

(D) $\frac{5}{3}$

5. What is the value of the expression $\frac{4}{5} - \frac{2}{3}$?

(A) $\frac{2}{15}$

(B) $\frac{1}{5}$

(C) $\frac{1}{3}$

(D) $\frac{1}{2}$

6. What is $1 + \frac{1}{2} + \frac{1}{4} + \frac{1}{8} + \frac{1}{16} + \frac{1}{16}$?

(A) $\frac{3}{23}$

(B) 1

(C) $\frac{33}{16}$

(D) 2

7. What is the value of the expression $3\frac{2}{3} \times 2\frac{1}{2}$?

(A) $5\frac{3}{5}$

(B) $6\frac{1}{3}$

(C) $9\frac{1}{3}$

(D) $9\frac{1}{6}$

8. $x = \frac{1}{3} + \frac{1}{9} + \frac{1}{27} + \frac{1}{81}$. Which of the following inequalities is true?

(A) $0.40 < x < 0.50$
(B) $0.33 < x < 0.40$
(C) $0.25 < x < 0.33$
(D) $0.03 < x < 0.25$

9. Carly bought 20 pencils. She used $\frac{1}{4}$ of them. How many does she have left?

(A) 1
(B) 5
(C) 10
(D) 15

10. Dara bought a bag containing 10 pieces of chocolate. She ate $\frac{1}{3}$ of the bag. How many whole pieces of chocolate remain?

(A) 3
(B) 6
(C) 7
(D) 9

11. Wayne's duffel bag contains only hockey pucks and baseballs. There are 7 fewer hockey pucks than baseballs. If there are 12 baseballs, what fraction of the duffel bag's contents are hockey pucks?

(A) $\frac{5}{17}$

(B) $\frac{5}{12}$

(C) $\frac{7}{17}$

(D) $\frac{12}{17}$

12. Alex ate $\frac{1}{3}$ of a pie. Bob ate $\frac{2}{5}$ of what was left by Alex. The pie had 15 slices. How many slices are left after Bob and Alex both ate their slices?

(A) 2
(B) 4
(C) 6
(D) 8

13. Flora made a bowl of punch. $\frac{1}{3}$ of the punch was coconut water, and $\frac{2}{5}$ was cranberry juice. What fraction of the punch was ingredients other than coconut water or cranberry juice?

(A) $\frac{4}{15}$

(B) $\frac{5}{8}$

(C) $\frac{11}{15}$

(D) 4

14. A recipe for granola makes one cup of granola. The recipe calls for $\frac{1}{3}$. cup of oil and $\frac{1}{6}$ cup of honey. If Gavin made 6 cups of granola, what is the total number of cups of oil and honey he used?

(A) 1
(B) 2
(C) 3
(D) 4

15. Which of the following fractions terminates when expressed as a decimal?

(A) $\frac{1}{6}$

(B) $\frac{1}{7}$

(C) $\frac{1}{8}$

(D) $\frac{1}{9}$

16. A pet store only sells cats and dogs. There are 4 more cats than dogs $\frac{4}{9}$ of the animals are dogs. How many cats are there?

(A) 8
(B) 18
(C) 20
(D) 36

17. Emily was assigned a novel to read for her English class. She finished half the book on Monday and 90 pages on Tuesday. If she still has $\frac{1}{8}$ of the book left to read, how many pages are left to read?

(A) 30 pages
(B) 90 pages
(C) 144 pages
(D) 240 pages

Quantitative Comparison Practice
Answer Choices:
(A) The amount in column A is greater.
(B) The amount in column B is greater.
(C) The two amounts are equal.
(D) The relationship cannot be determined from the information provided.

	Column A	Column B
18.	$2\frac{7}{12}$	$\frac{18}{7}$

	Column A	Column B
19.	$1-\frac{1}{2}-\frac{1}{3}$	x, if $x^2=\frac{1}{36}$

	Column A	Column B
20.	The number of distinct digits in the decimal form of $\frac{2}{11}$	The number of distinct digits in the decimal form of $\frac{7}{9}$
21.	The number of distinct digits in the decimal form of $\frac{1}{7}$	7

Decimals

1. If $W = 0.2020$, $X = 0.22$, $Y = 0.1987$, and $Z = 0.18888$, which value is greatest?

(A) W
(B) X
(C) Y
(D) Z

2. $12.6 - 2.77 + 0.004 =$

(A) 9.834
(B) 9.840
(C) 9.934
(D) 10.834

3. $1.23 \div 1.2 =$

(A) 0.1025
(B) 1.0250
(C) 10.250
(D) 102.50

4. What is the quotient when 0.16 is divided by 0.008?

(A) 0.2
(B) 2
(C) 20
(D) 200

5. $\frac{5}{8} =$

(A) 0.58
(B) $0.6\overline{22}$
(C) 0.625
(D) 1.6

6. $1.25 \times 4\frac{1}{5} =$

(A) 4.25
(B) 4.75
(C) 5.20
(D) 5.25

7. $0.02 \times \frac{1.01}{0.01} =$

(A) 0.505
(B) 0.99
(C) 1.01
(D) 2.02

8. If $\frac{n}{n+1} = 0.95$, what is n?

(A) 9
(B) 18
(C) 19
(D) 20

9. A kangaroo jumped 6 feet forward. A wallaby jumped 5 feet forward. How many times longer was the kangaroo's jump than the wallaby's?

(A) 0.8
(B) 1.2
(C) 1.6
(D) 6.5

10. A wildlife reserve for big cats has 16 cheetahs and 6 jaguars. How many times fewer jaguars are there than cheetahs?

(A) 3.750
(B) 3.375
(C) 0.625
(D) 0.375

11. When traveling from the United States to a foreign country, where the currency is called the arn, 25 arns is equal to 22 dollars. To the nearest cent, how much is 11 arns worth?

(A) $0.50
(B) $9.68
(C) $12.50
(D) $50.00

Quantitative Comparison Practice

Answer Choices:

(A) The amount in column A is greater.
(B) The amount in column B is greater.
(C) The two amounts are equal.
(D) The relationship cannot be determined from the information provided.

	Column A	Column B
12.	0.32	$\frac{8}{25}$

	Column A	Column B
13.	The product of $0.\overline{33}$ and 2.25	1

Andrew had two different U.S. coins (quarter, dime, nickel, penny) in his pocket.

	Column A	Column B
14.	The difference between the maximum and minimum value of the coins in his pocket	$0.48

	Column A	Column B
15.	$0.5 \times 0.7 \times 250$	$0.32 \times 0.4 \times 250$

15 frogs escaped from a hungry tuna. This accounts for 0.75 times the original number of frogs.

	Column A	Column B
16.	The original number of frogs	11.25

	Column A	Column B
17.	$800 \div 0.5 \times 0.25 \times 0.75$	$1.2 \times 20 \div 1.5 \times 10$

	Column A	Column B
18.	$80n$, if $0.25 < n < 0.75$	$20m$, if $2.5 < m < 3.5$

n and m are both integers.

	Column A	Column B
19.	n, if $\frac{1}{n}$ terminates as a decimal, and $5 < n < 10$	m, if $m \div 30 = 0.2$

Percents

1. Which of the following expressions is NOT equal to $\frac{22}{16}$?

   (A) $\frac{44}{32}\%$
   (B) $1\frac{3}{8}$
   (C) 137.5%
   (D) $\frac{11}{8}$

2. In one week, a certain cat caught mice on Tuesday, Thursday, and Sunday. To the nearest whole percent, what percentage of days of the week did the cat **not** catch a mouse?

   (A) 75%
   (B) 57%
   (C) 42%
   (D) 33%

3. Jesse answered 80% of the questions correctly on a math test. He answered 10 questions incorrectly. How many questions were on the math test?

   (A) 20
   (B) 40
   (C) 50
   (D) 90

4. A certain group consists of exactly 50 women and 50 men. In this group, 25 people are left-handed. 15 of the left-handed people are men. What percent of the women are right-handed?

   (A) 20%
   (B) 40%
   (C) 50%
   (D) 80%

5. A number is decreased by 30%, and then the new number is decreased by another 30%. What is the percent decrease from the original number?

   (A) 49%
   (B) 51%
   (C) 60%
   (D) 90%

6. A number is increased by 10%, and then the new number is decreased by 10%. What is the percent change from the original number?

   (A) 0%
   (B) 1%
   (C) 10%
   (D) 20%

7. At the beginning of the year, there are 80 songbirds living in an aviary. For three months straight, the population grows by 50% each month. How many birds are in the aviary at the end of the three-month period?

   (A) 200
   (B) 240
   (C) 270
   (D) 360

8. A rectangle has a width of 20 ft. and a length of 20 ft. If the length is increased by 25% and the width is decreased by 15%, what is the change in the area of the rectangle?

   (A) 25
   (B) 40
   (C) 84
   (D) 425

9. A rectangle has a width of 30 ft. and a length of 20 ft. If the length is decreased by 20% and the width is decreased by 30%, what is the percentage decrease in the area of the rectangle?

(A) 25%
(B) 44%
(C) 50%
(D) 60%

10. Jerry and Jordan picked up a total of 500 pieces of garbage while cleaning up the park. Jerry picked up 100 more pieces of garbage than Jordan did. What percent of the 500 pieces of garbage did Jerry pick up?

(A) 20%
(B) 40%
(C) 60%
(D) 80%

11. The Luthors first played 15 games and lost 80% of them. Then, they won their next 5 games. After they played a total of 20 games, what percentage of games did the Luthors win in total, if they never had a tied game?

(A) 20%
(B) 35%
(C) 40%
(D) 85%

12. David took 40% of the chocolates that were in a gift box. Eric took 25% of what was left by David. If there were 27 chocolates left after David and Eric each took chocolates, how many chocolates were originally in the gift box?

(A) 18
(B) 24
(C) 36
(D) 60

13. On Tom's baseball team, all the 9 players got to bat 4 times. If they had a total of 12 hits, to the nearest whole percent, what percentage of the at-bats resulted in hits?

(A) 33%
(B) 44%
(C) 50%
(D) 55%

14. Francis used 20% of the pages in her notebook in the first week she had it. In the second week she had it, she used 25% of the remaining pages. If there were 30 pages left after the two weeks, how many pages were originally in the journal?

(A) 40
(B) 45
(C) 50
(D) 75

15. A triangle has a base of 10 ft. and a height of 25 ft. If the base is decreased by 10% and the height is increased by 20%, what is the change in the area of the triangle?

(A) 10
(B) 15
(C) 30
(D) 45

16. Sharon made 75% of the free-throws that she took during a basketball season. If she missed a total 20 free-throws all season, how many free-throws did she make?

(A) 55
(B) 60
(C) 75
(D) 80

Quantitative Comparison Practice

Answer Choices:

(A) The amount in column A is greater.
(B) The amount in column B is greater.
(C) The two amounts are equal.
(D) The relationship cannot be determined from the information provided.

	Column A	Column B
17.	$\frac{1}{5}$	$22.\overline{22}\%$

In a barrel of 40 apples, 8 were rotten.

	Column A	Column B
18.	20%	The percentage of rotten apples in the barrel

One nickel, two dimes, and three quarters lie on a table.

	Column A	Column B
19.	The percentage of the total value on the table made from quarters	75%

In a certain animal shelter, there are 20 cats. 8 are Burmese cats, 6 are Persians, and 6 are Turkish Angoras.

	Column A	Column B
20.	The percentage of all cats in the shelter that are Burmese cats	The percentage of non-Burmese cats that are Persian cats

	Column A	Column B
21.	Out of the first 20 positive integers, the percent that are evenly divisible by 3	33%

M is between 50 and 75. N is between 125 and 150.

	Column A	Column B
22.	M% of 400	N% of 120

Out of 50 children, 40% of them speak French, 30% speak Spanish, and 20 of the children speak neither.

	Column A	Column B
23.	10%	The percentage of children who speak both French and Spanish

The small pond contains only 6 yellow fish and 9 red fish. The big pond contains twice as many yellow fish and at most 23 blue fish.

	Column A	Column B
24.	The total percentage of yellow fish, out of all fish in both ponds	35%

Factors, Multiples, Primes

1. If $2^x = 64$, then $x =$

   (A) 6
   (B) 8
   (C) 16
   (D) 32

2. What is the greatest common factor of 3 and 17?

   (A) 1
   (B) 3
   (C) 17
   (D) 51

3. The least common multiple of 6, 7, and 11 is which of the following?

   (A) 77
   (B) 154
   (C) 231
   (D) 462

4. What is the least common multiple of 135 and 75?

   (A) 75
   (B) 135
   (C) 210
   (D) 675

5. What is the greatest common factor of 84 and 144?

   (A) 12
   (B) 24
   (C) 42
   (D) 72

6. What is the greatest common factor of 216 and 144?

   (A) 12
   (B) 24
   (C) 36
   (D) 72

7. Which of the following is **not** a factor of 90?

   (A) 3
   (B) 4
   (C) 5
   (D) 6

8. Which of the following numbers is prime?

   (A) 1,303
   (B) 1,313
   (C) 1,353
   (D) 1,383

9. Which of the following represents 25^3 in terms of 5?

   (A) 5^2
   (B) 5^4
   (C) 5^6
   (D) 5^8

10. How many positive integer factors does 36 have?

   (A) 4
   (B) 6
   (C) 8
   (D) 9

11. Which of the following choices has an odd number of positive integer factors?

   (A) 7
   (B) 9
   (C) 11
   (D) 13

12. If $3^y = 81$, then $y =$

   (A) 4
   (B) 6
   (C) 9
   (D) 27

13. What is the greatest common factor of 10, 25, and 205?

(A) 1
(B) 2
(C) 5
(D) 10

14. What is the least common multiple of 140 and 35?

(A) 35
(B) 140
(C) 210
(D) 4,900

15. Which is **not** a factor of 100?

(A) 2
(B) 3
(C) 4
(D) 5

16. How many positive unique integer factors does 24 have?

(A) 4
(B) 6
(C) 8
(D) 12

Quantitative Comparison Practice
Answer Choices:
(A) The amount in column A is greater.
(B) The amount in column B is greater.
(C) The two amounts are equal.
(D) The relationship cannot be determined from the information provided.

	Column A	Column B
17.	The least common multiple of 8 and 27	The least common multiple of 24 and 54

	Column A	Column B
18.	The greatest common factor of 36 and 27	The greatest common factor of 30 and 24

	Column A	Column B
19.	The largest prime number between 10 and 20	The value of xy if $2^x \times 3^y = 2{,}592$

	Column A	Column B
20.	A prime number between 1 and 10	The value of xy if $2^x \times 5^y = 100$

Estimation

1. Mrs. Jones asks her class to estimate the answer for the expression: 411 ÷ (11 × 19). Which of the following choices is the closest estimate?

(A) 2
(B) 3
(C) 4
(D) 5

2. Which of the following choices is closest to $(289 \div 31)^2$?

(A) 10
(B) 20
(C) 50
(D) 100

3. The approximate value of the expression $(248 \div 53)^2 - 2^2$ is

(A) 9
(B) 20
(C) 40
(D) 54

4. The value of $\sqrt{25} + \sqrt{40}$ is between which two integers?

(A) 7 and 8
(B) 8 and 9
(C) 10 and 11
(D) 11 and 12

5. Which of the following choices is closest to $\sqrt{197 \div 49}$?

(A) 2
(B) 4
(C) 16
(D) 40

6. Shanice is putting a lawn in her backyard. She wants the length of the lawn to be between 11-15 feet and the width of the lawn to be between 8-10 feet. If sod costs $2 per square foot, approximately how much will she spend on the lawn?

(A) $120
(B) $190
(C) $240
(D) $300

7. The area of Richard's kitchen is 156 square feet. His kitchen floor is made up of equally-sized square tiles. If his kitchen has 22 tiles, approximately how big is each tile, in square feet?

(A) 5
(B) 6
(C) 8
(D) 15

8. Andy wants a bigger garden. The length of his garden is 12 feet and the width of his garden is 5 feet. He expands the length by 6.7 feet and the width by $5x$ feet. If the new area is 200 square feet, which of the following choices is the closest to the value of x?

(A) 1
(B) 2
(C) 3
(D) 5

9. Lindsay collects rainwater in a rectangular container. It has a square base with an area of 8 square inches. The rain has filled the container up to somewhere between the 7–11-inch marks. Approximately how much rainwater, in cubic inches, has filled up the container?

(A) 50
(B) 75
(C) 110
(D) 125

10. Judith works at a deli where she sells meats and cheeses. A customer comes in and picks out some salami. He also picks out 5 different cheeses that cost between $0.50 and $2.00 an ounce. The customer's total comes out to $15.00. If the customer bought 4 ounces of cheese, approximately how much did he pay for salami?

(A) $7
(B) $8
(C) $10
(D) $13

11. Fred is given the values of a triangle. For this triangle, the base is $21x$ inches, the height is 4.5 inches, and the area is 290 square inches. Which of the following choices is closest to the value of x?

(A) 3
(B) 4
(C) 5
(D) 6

12. Earth has a diameter of approximately 7,917.5 miles. Which of the following is closest to the approximate circumference around the equator?

(A) 8,000
(B) 16,000
(C) 24,000
(D) 26,000

13. Carla sells donuts by bike every day, rain or shine. On rainy days, she can only sell between 10-14 dozen donuts. On sunny days, she sells between 25-35 dozen donuts. This next week, the forecast predicts 3 rainy days and 4 sunny days. If she sells a dozen donuts for $10, approximately how much money can she expect to make this week?

(A) $1,100
(B) $1,500
(C) $2,000
(D) $2,500

14. Toni is in a triathlon, which consists of running, cycling, and swimming. She can complete the swimming course in 45-60 minutes. She can finish the running portion in between 90-110 minutes. If she completes the entire race in 230 minutes, approximately how long does it take her to complete the biking portion?

(A) 60 minutes
(B) 75 minutes
(C) 90 minutes
(D) 95 minutes

15. Bob's popular restaurant is having a sandwich special for 11 days. Profit is revenue minus cost. Bob is spending between $475-$575 to make all the sandwiches. Bob lets 50 customers come in per day, who spend on average between $9.50-$12.50 per sandwich. Approximately how much profit is Bob going to make from the special?

(A) $2,500
(B) $4,500
(C) $5,500
(D) $6,500

16. Randy is writing a book and can draft 750-1,000 words per day, working 5 days per week. He plans to spend 50-70 weeks writing before submitting his first draft to his editor. His editor charges $10-$15 per page, depending on how much editing is needed. If the book can fit about 500 words per page, about how much did the editing cost?

(A) $4,000
(B) $6,000
(C) $8,000
(D) $10,000

17. The area of Fred's bathroom is 147 square feet. His bathroom floor is made up of equally-sized square tiles. If his bathroom has 77 tiles, approximately how big is each tile in square feet?

(A) 2
(B) 5
(C) 70
(D) 75

18. Meghan is using a bucket with a circular bottom to wash her car. The area of the bottom of the bucket is 9 square inches. If she uses a hose to fill the container between 11 – 15 inches. Approximately how much water, in cubic inches, has Meghan filled up the bucket?

(A) 90
(B) 95
(C) 120
(D) 150

19. Andrew delivers pizza every day, rain or shine. On rainy days he usually delivers 35 – 45 pies. On sunny days he usually delivers 10 – 12 pies. The forecast for next week predicts 2 rainy days and 5 sunny days. If Andrew normally gets a tip of around $5 for each pie, approximately how much money can he expect to make in tips?

(A) $255
(B) $500
(C) $650
(D) $2,000

Numbers & Operations Mixed Practice

1. What is the largest prime number less than 150 with a units digit of 7?

(A) 7
(B) 137
(C) 147
(D) 149

2. What is the sum of all the positive integers up to 19, inclusive?

(A) 187
(B) 188
(C) 189
(D) 190

3. What is the value of the expression $\frac{3}{8} \times 2\frac{1}{3}$?

(A) $\frac{5}{12}$
(B) $\frac{7}{8}$
(C) $\frac{10}{11}$
(D) $6\frac{1}{24}$

4. Jordan bought 50 pencils. She used $\frac{2}{5}$ of them. How many does she have left?

(A) 5
(B) 10
(C) 20
(D) 30

5. $3.15 \div 2.8 =$

(A) 0.024
(B) 1.125
(C) 2.125
(D) 11.25

6. An aquarium has 18 whales and 4 penguins. How many times fewer penguins are there than whales?

(A) 72.14
(B) 45.00
(C) 4.50
(D) 4.456

7. Mary answered 40% of the questions correctly on a math test. She answered 30 questions incorrectly. How many questions were on the math test?

(A) 10
(B) 30
(C) 40
(D) 50

8. Larry drank 30% of a carton of milk in the first week he had it. In the second week he had it, he drank 20% of the remaining milk. If there were 112 mL left after the two weeks, how much milk was originally in the carton?

(A) 56 mL
(B) 112 mL
(C) 200 mL
(D) 225 mL

9. What is the least common multiple of 40 and 28?

(A) 4
(B) 56
(C) 80
(D) 280

10. Which of the following is **not** a factor of 45,636?

(A) 3
(B) 4
(C) 5
(D) 6

11. The approximate value of the expression $(362 \div 18)^2 - 6^2$ is?

(A) 180
(B) 244
(C) 364
(D) 400

12. Max's bookstore held a magazine special for 8 days. Max spent between \$325 – \$445 to get the magazines. Max let 50 customers come in per day, who spent on average between \$7.50 – \$10.50 per magazine. Approximately how much profit did Max make from the special?

(A) \$1,250
(B) \$2,125
(C) \$3,215
(D) \$3,600

13. Which of the following represents 16^5 in terms of 4?

(A) 4^4
(B) 4^6
(C) 4^8
(D) 4^{10}

14. What is the value of the expression $\frac{4}{6} \div \frac{2}{3}$?

(A) 1

(B) $\frac{3}{2}$

(C) $\frac{4}{9}$

(D) $\frac{2}{3}$

15. What is the value of the numerical expression $-237 - (-783)$?

(A) 546
(B) –546
(C) – 1,020
(D) 1,020

16. Compare the following and choose the correct answer:

Column A	Column B
$4\frac{6}{15}$	$\frac{67}{14}$

(A) The amount in column A is greater.
(B) The amount in column B is greater.
(C) The two amounts are equal.
(D) The relationship cannot be determined from the information provided.

17. Compare the following and choose the correct answer:

Column A	Column B
Out of the first 24 positive integers, the percent that are evenly divisible by 4	24%

(A) The amount in column A is greater.
(B) The amount in column B is greater.
(C) The two amounts are equal.
(D) The relationship cannot be determined from the information provided.

18. Compare the following and choose the correct answer:

Column A	Column B
The greatest common factor of 48 and 60.	The least common multiple of 4 and 6.

(A) The amount in column A is greater.
(B) The amount in column B is greater.
(C) The two amounts are equal.
(D) The relationship cannot be determined from the information provided.

Algebraic Concepts

Solving Algebraic Equations

1. In the equation $3x - 10 = 11$, what is the value of x?

(A) $\frac{1}{3}$
(B) 3
(C) 7
(D) 21

2. What is the value of y in the equation $25 = \frac{5}{y} - 5^2$

(A) 0.1
(B) 0
(C) 1
(D) 10

3. If $q + r = 9$, then which expression is equal to r?

(A) 4.5
(B) $9 - q$
(C) $9 + q$
(D) 9

4. If $8y = 75$, what is the value of 150 in terms of y?

(A) $4y$
(B) $8y$
(C) $12y$
(D) $16y$

5. In the equation $y = \frac{5}{x}$, what is the value of xy?

(A) $\frac{1}{5}$
(B) $\frac{4}{5}$
(C) 4
(D) 5

6. What is the value of m in the equation $10 = \frac{m}{3} + 3m$?

(A) 3.0
(B) 7.5
(C) 10.0
(D) 30.0

7. In the equation $x^2 - 4 = 5$, what is the value of x if $x < 0$?

(A) -3
(B) -4
(C) -5
(D) -9

8. For what value of x is $x - \frac{1}{4}x = 12$?

(A) 3
(B) 4
(C) 16
(D) 48

9. If $12a + 12 = ba + b$, what is the value of b?

(A) 2
(B) 6
(C) 12
(D) 24

10. If $\frac{x}{2} + \frac{x}{5} = 16$, which of the following choices **must** be equivalent to $\frac{x}{4} + \frac{x}{10}$?

(A) 8
(B) 12
(C) 24
(D) 32

11. What is the value of x in the equation $\frac{6 + 3y}{2x - 4} = \frac{3}{4}$?

(A) $12y + 36$
(B) $6y + 6$
(C) $2y + 6$
(D) $y + 6$

12. The expression $\frac{x}{y}\left(\frac{y}{x}+\frac{x}{z}\right)$ is equal to which of the following expressions?

(A) $1+\frac{2x}{yz}$
(B) $1+\frac{x^2}{yz}$
(C) $\frac{x}{y}+\frac{x^2}{yz}$
(D) $2xy+\frac{x^2}{yz}$

13. If $3x + 4y = y$, which of the following choices **must** be equivalent to $9x + 9y$?

(A) 0
(B) 3
(C) $12y$
(D) $12x$

14. If $7x - 8y = x - 2y + 1$, which of the following choices **must** be equivalent to $12x - 12y$?

(A) 0
(B) 1
(C) 2
(D) 6

15. If $13x + 9 = 7$, what is the value of $13x - 3$?

(A) -5
(B) -3
(C) 0
(D) 7

16. If $q(a + b) = 60$ and $aq = 10$, what is the value of bq?

(A) 6
(B) 10
(C) 50
(D) 70

17. Which of the following answer choices is NOT equivalent to the equation $6=\frac{1}{x}+5$?

(A) $1=\frac{1}{x}$
(B) $0=\frac{1}{x}-1$
(C) $6x = 5x + 1$
(D) $6+x=\frac{1}{x}+5x$

18. The expression $y^2 + 2y - 6$ is equal to which of the following answer choices?

(A) $4y - 6$
(B) $2(2y - 3)$
(C) $y + y + y + y - 6$
(D) $y \times y + y + y - 6$

19. Which of the following choices is equivalent to the expression $(3 \times (1 + 2)) \div (4 - 1)$?

(A) $\frac{3(1+2)}{4-1}$
(B) $\frac{3\times1+2}{4-1}$
(C) $\frac{3(1+2)}{4}-1$
(D) $3\left(\frac{1+2}{4}-1\right)$

Quantitative Comparison Practice

Answer Choices:

(A) The amount in column A is greater.
(B) The amount in column B is greater.
(C) The two amounts are equal.
(D) The relationship cannot be determined from the information provided.

$\sqrt{x+1} = 9$

	Column A	Column B
20.	x	81

$x^2 = y$

	Column A	Column B
21.	y, if $x = -3$	y, if $x = 2$

$y - 3 = x + 2$

	Column A	Column B
22.	x	y

In the expression $\frac{1}{n}$, $n > 0$.

	Column A	Column B
23.	The value of the expression if $n < 1$	The value of the expression if $n > 1$

$\frac{1}{6} = \frac{x+1}{3}$

	Column A	Column B
24.	x	0

$\frac{x}{7} = \frac{x-2}{14}$

	Column A	Column B
25.	2	x

In the equation below, $x > 0$

$y - 5 = x^2 + 1$

	Column A	Column B
26.	The value of y when $x = 2$	The value of x when $y = 106$

$y^2 = z$

	Column A	Column B
27.	z, if $y = -1$	y, if $z = 1$

Ratios, Proportions, & Scale Factor

1. If $\frac{3}{4} = \frac{6}{x}$, what is the value of x?

(A) 3
(B) 4
(C) 6
(D) 8

2. If $\frac{24}{32} = \frac{36}{x}$, what is the value of x?

(A) 12
(B) 16
(C) 48
(D) 64

3. 1 twez = 5 yorz
1 twez = 0.2 jimp

Stephen has 100 yorz and 20 jimp. If he exchanges the yorz and jimp for twez according to the rates above, how many twez will he receive?

(A) 20
(B) 100
(C) 120
(D) 504

4. In a hotdog eating contest, Ichigo always drinks $\frac{1}{3}$ glass of water for every 6 hotdogs he eats. If he drinks 3 glasses of water, how many hotdogs must he have eaten?

(A) 6
(B) 18
(C) 27
(D) 54

5. Circle R has a diameter of 10 cm. What is the circumference of a circle similar to circle R with a scale factor of $\frac{2}{5}$?

(A) 2π
(B) 4π
(C) 5π
(D) 8π

6. At Frank's Fun Zone, June earns 3 tickets for every 8 points scored on arcade games. If June earned 39 tickets, how many points did she score?

(A) 15
(B) 24
(C) 48
(D) 104

7. A recipe for salad dressing uses 3 ounces of oil for every 2 ounces of vinegar. If a restaurant needs to make exactly 20 ounces of salad dressing, how many ounces of oil will it need?

(A) 4
(B) 5
(C) 8
(D) 12

8. According to a cake recipe, 25 pounds of butter are needed to make 300 cakes. At this rate, how many pounds of butter are needed to make 6 cakes?

(A) $\frac{1}{2}$ pound
(B) 1 pound
(C) 2 pounds
(D) 4 pounds

9. A model of a real sailboat is built where 1 inch represents 3 yards. If the model is 5 feet long, how long is the real ship? *(Note: 1 foot = 12 inches)*

(A) 15 yards
(B) 60 yards
(C) 180 yards
(D) 540 yards

10. The scale on a blueprint of a building states that 30 feet is represented by 0.25 inches. If a wall is 40 feet long, how many inches long will it be on the blueprint?

(A) $\frac{1}{5}$

(B) $\frac{1}{3}$

(C) $\frac{1}{4}$

(D) $\frac{1}{2}$

11. At a zoo, the ratio of polar bears to giraffes is 9:5. What is the total number of polar bears and giraffes if there are 36 polar bears?

(A) 20
(B) 56
(C) 72
(D) 76

12. Triangle XYZ is similar to triangle ABC. The length of $\overline{XY}$ is 6 cm, and the length of $\overline{AB}$ is 3 cm. If the length of $\overline{YZ}$ is 4 cm, what is the length of $\overline{BC}$?

(A) 2 cm
(B) 4 cm
(C) 5 cm
(D) 6 cm

13. Rectangle $ABCD$ is similar to rectangle $WXYZ$.

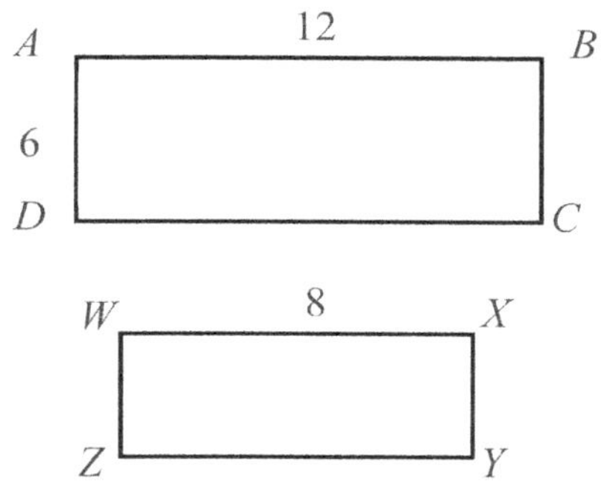

What is the length of side XY?

(A) 4
(B) 5
(C) 6
(D) 8

14.

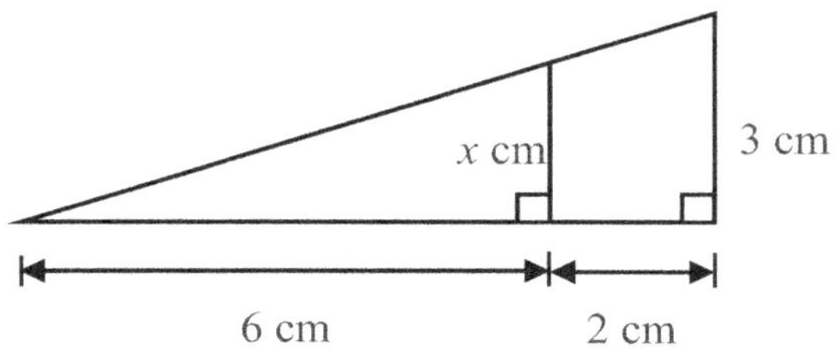

In the figure above, what is the value of x?

(A) $\frac{9}{4}$

(B) $\frac{4}{3}$

(C) $\frac{4}{9}$

(D) $\frac{3}{4}$

Quantitative Comparison Practice

Answer Choices:

(A) The amount in column A is greater.
(B) The amount in column B is greater.
(C) The two amounts are equal.
(D) The relationship cannot be determined from the information provided.

$$\frac{5}{6} = \frac{6}{x}$$

	Column A	Column B
15.	x	7

At 1 P.M., a 60-foot building casts a 50-foot shadow.

	Column A	Column B
16.	The length of the shadow cast by a 5-foot tall person at the same time and place	5

As part of his New Year's resolution, Geoff is determined to run a mile for every 200 calories he eats. Geoff enjoys eating pizza, each slice of which contains 300 calories. Geoff also enjoys eating hamburgers, each of which contains 200 calories.

	Column A	Column B
17.	The number of miles Geoff must run if he eats 2 slices of pizza	The number of miles Geoff must run if he eats 1 slice of pizza and 1 hamburger

	Column A	Column B
18.	x, if $\frac{4}{9} = \frac{12}{x}$	y, if $\frac{y}{3} = \frac{12}{y}$

Triangle X (not shown) has sides that measure 3 in, 4 in, and 5 in.

	Column A	Column B
19.	The shortest side of a triangle similar to triangle X with a scale factor of $\frac{7}{3}$	The longest side of a triangle similar to triangle X with a scale factor of $\frac{7}{5}$

1 kehl = 5 tae
3 verv = 10 tae

	Column A	Column B
20.	3 kehl	3 verv

Triangle *ABC* is similar to Triangle *DEF*.

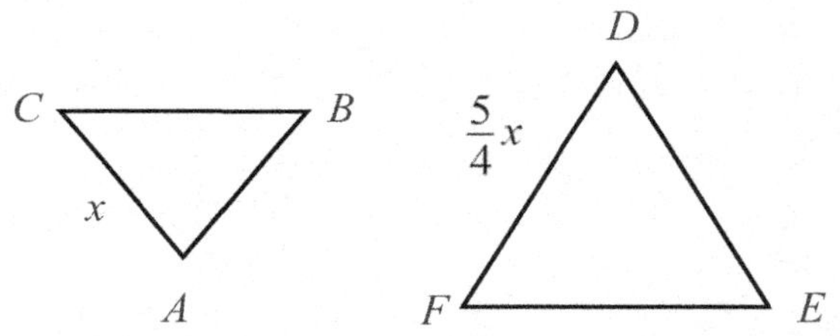

Note: Figures not drawn to scale.

	Column A	Column B
21.	The length of side *EF*	The length of side *CB*

In preparing for Halloween, Penelope likes to give trick-or-treaters a package of sliced apples for every seven pieces of candy that she gives. This Halloween, Penelope will hand out 13 packages of sliced apples.

	Column A	Column B
22.	The total number of sliced apple packages and pieces of candy given out this Halloween	104

A map has a scale of 3 cm = 700 km.

	Column A	Column B
23.	The actual distance between two towns that are 5 cm apart on the map	1,200 km

The school board decided that during each school day, students must have 15 minutes of exercise for every hour of classroom learning. The entire school day is 6 hours long, and consists entirely of exercise, classroom learning, and an hour for lunch.

	Column A	Column B
24.	The total amount of time students spent exercising	The total amount of time students spent NOT in classroom learning

The ratio of apples to bananas to oranges in a bowl is 3:4:5.

	Column A	Column B
25.	The number of bananas, if there are 60 oranges	The number of apples, if there are 60 bananas

Functions & Patterns

1. Siloam has x dollars. Jefferson has twice as many dollars as Siloam. In terms of x, how many dollars does Jefferson have?

(A) 2
(B) $2x$
(C) $x + 2$
(D) $x \div 2$

2. Mr. Dobson has been teaching math for four years less than twice as long as Mrs. Simons. If Mrs. Simons has been teaching math for x years, which of the following expressions represents the number of years that Mr. Dobson has been teaching math?

(A) $2x - 4$
(B) $2x + 4$
(C) $2(x - 4)$
(D) $2x - 2 \times 4$

3. Brent mowed m lawns. Jessica mowed 4 more lawns than Brent. Which of the following expression represents the total number of lawns Brent and Jessica mowed?

(A) $2m$
(B) $m + 4$
(C) $2m + 4$
(D) $6m - 4$

4. If a represents an odd integer, which of the following expressions represents the next odd integer greater than a?

(A) $a + 1$
(B) $a + 2$
(C) $a + 3$
(D) $2a - 1$

5. Patrick has 7 quarters, 3 dimes, and 1 penny. Which expression represents the amount of money, in dollars, that Patrick has?

(A) $7 \times 0.25 \times 3 \times 0.10 \times 0.01$
(B) $7 \times 0.25 + 3 \times 0.10 + 0.01$
(C) $7 \times 25 \times 3 \times 10 \times 1$
(D) $7 \times 25 + 3 \times 10 + 1$

6. A salad company charges $5 for a basic salad, plus an extra $0.35 for each topping. Which expression represents the cost, in dollars, of a salad with x toppings?

(A) 5.35
(B) $5.35x$
(C) $5x + 0.35$
(D) $5 + 0.35x$

7. When a certain number is tripled, and the result is decreased by 5, the resulting number is 43. What is the original number?

(A) 16
(B) 33
(C) 48
(D) 40

8. If 7 less than four times a number is 41, what is 3 times the number?

(A) 12
(B) 29
(C) 36
(D) 41

9. Micaela is two more than twice Loris's age. If Micaela is 22 years old, how old is Loris?

(A) 9
(B) 10
(C) 12
(D) 20

10. Ansuz read four more than three times as many books as Herene did. If Ansuz read 28 books, how many books did Herene read?

(A) 3
(B) 4
(C) 8
(D) 13

11. In one week, Martin jogged 8 times the number of kilometers Norman did. Together, they jogged a total of 63 kilometers. How many kilometers did Martin jog in that week?

(A) 7
(B) 9
(C) 28
(D) 56

12. Jacob and Kelly have a total of 50 books. If Jacob has 4 more books than Kelly, how many books does Jacob have?

(A) 23
(B) 25
(C) 27
(D) 29

13. In any given amount of time, a machine can sew together 10 times as many articles of clothing as a human can. In one day, a machine and a human can sew together a combined 440 articles of clothing. How many articles of clothing did the machine sew together?

(A) 40
(B) 44
(C) 396
(D) 400

14. If Paul has x nickels, and he has 5 more dimes than nickels, which expression represents the amount of money, in dollars, that Paul has?

(A) $x + 5x$
(B) $0.15x + 0.5$
(C) $0.05x + 0.5x$
(D) $0.05x + 0.6x$

15. For every quarter in his pocket, John also has 5 pennies in his pocket. If the total value of the coins in John's pocket is $5.40, how many quarters does John have in his pocket?

(A) 18
(B) 21
(C) 22
(D) 23

16. For every 7 dimes in his pocket, Jordana has 1 quarter. If the total value of the coins in Jordana's pocket is $4.75, how many dimes does Jordana have in her pocket?

(A) 5
(B) 14
(C) 35
(D) 45

17. Kevin has 2 fewer nickels than quarters. The total value of Kevin's coins is $1.10. How many nickels does Kevin have?

(A) 1
(B) 2
(C) 4
(D) 6

18. In triangle *PQR*, angle *R* is a right angle, and angle *P* is 9 more than two times angle *Q*. How many degrees is angle *P*?

(A) 27
(B) 56
(C) 63
(D) 81

19. If the degree measures of the angles in a quadrilateral are in the ratio 1:2:3:4, what is the degree measure of the smallest angle?

(A) 10
(B) 27
(C) 36
(D) 40

20. If the degree measures of the angles in a triangle are 1:3:5, what is the degree measure of the largest angle?

(A) 20
(B) 60
(C) 90
(D) 100

21. Aza runs 8 miles per hour, and Maya runs 6 miles per hour. If Maya has a 10-mile head start, after how many hours of running along the same path will Aza catch up to Maya?

(A) 0.2
(B) 1.4
(C) 4.0
(D) 5.0

22. When a certain number is doubled, and the result is increased by 8, the resulting number is 30. What is the original number?

(A) 8
(B) 11
(C) 19
(D) 22

23. Janice is four more than three times Ethan's age. If Janice is 55 years old, how old is Ethan?

(A) 11
(B) 12
(C) 17
(D) 18

24. In one week, Betty ran 4 times the number of laps Jane did. Together, they ran a total of 75 laps. How many laps did Betty run in that week?

(A) 15
(B) 20
(C) 45
(D) 60

25. Mike and Raphael have a total of 60 flashcards. If Mike has 18 more flashcards than Raphael, how many flashcards does Mike have?

(A) 18
(B) 21
(C) 39
(D) 42

Slope

1. What is the slope of the line represented by $y = 3x - 4$?

   (A) -4
   (B) -1
   (C) 3
   (D) 4

2. What is the slope of the line represented by $y = \frac{1}{4}x - 6$?

   (A) -6
   (B) $\frac{1}{4}$
   (C) -4
   (D) 6

3. What is the slope of a line that is parallel to the line represented by $y = -\frac{3}{4}x - 2$?

   (A) $-\frac{4}{3}$
   (B) $-\frac{3}{4}$
   (C) $-\frac{1}{2}$
   (D) -2

4. What is the slope of a line that is perpendicular to the line represented by $y = 3x + 1.5$?

   (A) 3
   (B) 1.5
   (C) $-\frac{1}{3}$
   (D) -3

5. Which equation represents a line that is parallel to the line represented by $y = -\frac{1}{3}x + 3$?

   (A) $y = \frac{1}{3}x - 3$
   (B) $y = -\frac{1}{3}x + 6$
   (C) $y = 3x + 6$
   (D) $y = -3x + 3$

6. What is the equation of a line perpendicular to the line represented by $y = 4x + 3$?

   (A) $y = -\frac{1}{4}x + 3$
   (B) $y = \frac{1}{4}x - 3$
   (C) $y = -4x + 3$
   (D) $y = 4x - 3$

7. Michael is driving cross-country at an average of 70 miles per hour. Which equation expresses Michael's distance, y, after some hour(s), x?

   (A) $y = 70 + x$
   (B) $70x = y - 70$
   (C) $y = 70x$
   (D) $x = 70y$

8. The rental cost of a computer, c, depends on the number of hours, h, that the computer is rented, which can be represented by the equation $c = 60 + 10.25h$. In this equation, 10.25 represents

   (A) the total cost of renting the computer.
   (B) the minimum cost of renting the computer.
   (C) the additional cost of renting the computer per hour.
   (D) the initial cost of renting the computer

9. The following graphs plot the descent of four different elevators. Which elevator is the slowest?

(A)

Elevator A

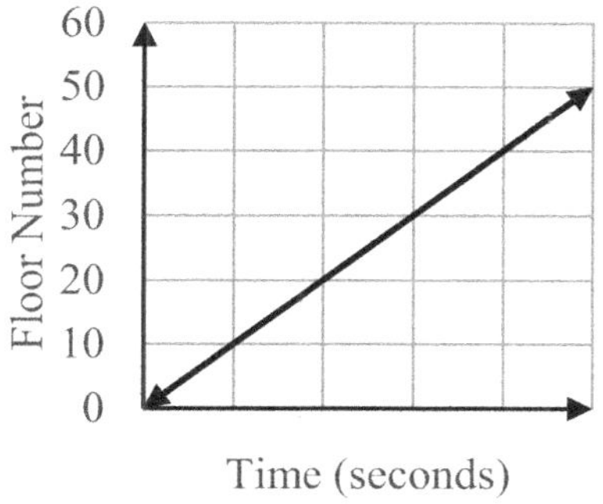

(B)

Elevator B

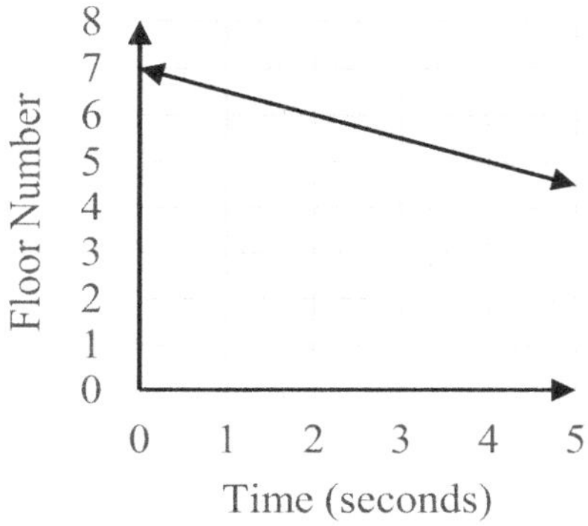

(C)

Elevator C

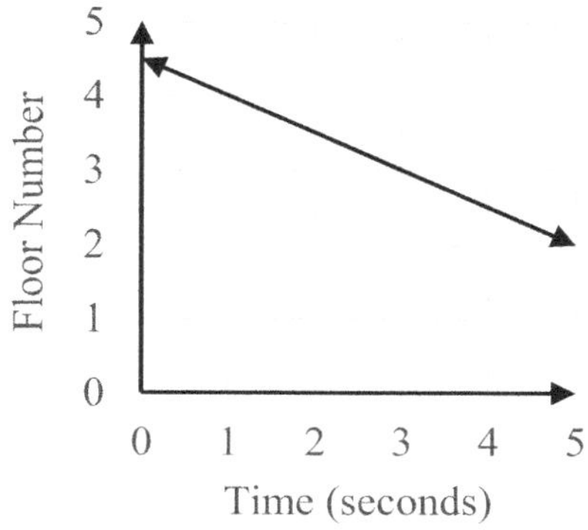

(D)

Elevator D

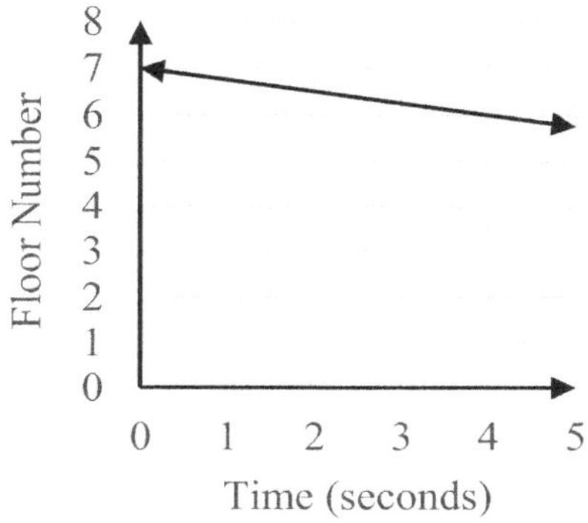

10. The table below represents the number of bacteria in a petri dish after a certain period of time.

Time	Population
0	2
1	4
2	6
3	8

Which of the following choices represents the growth of the bacteria population, y, over time, x?

(A) $y = x^2$
(B) $y = 4x$
(C) $y = 2x + 2$
(D) $y = 4x + 2$

11. The cost of a phone call, c, depends on the number of minutes, m, spent on the call, which can be represented by the equation $c = 0.30 + 0.10m$. In this equation, 0.10 represents

(A) the total cost of a phone call.
(B) the minimum cost of the phone call.
(C) the additional cost of the call per minute.
(D) the number of minutes spent on the call.

12. Carly is paid \$0.25 for each newspaper she delivers, plus a flat rate of \$20 per day. Which of the following graphs represents the amount of money Carly earns for delivering n newspapers?

(A)

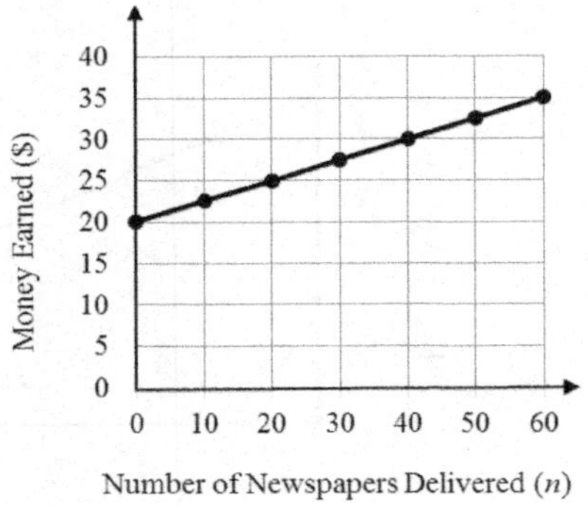

(B)

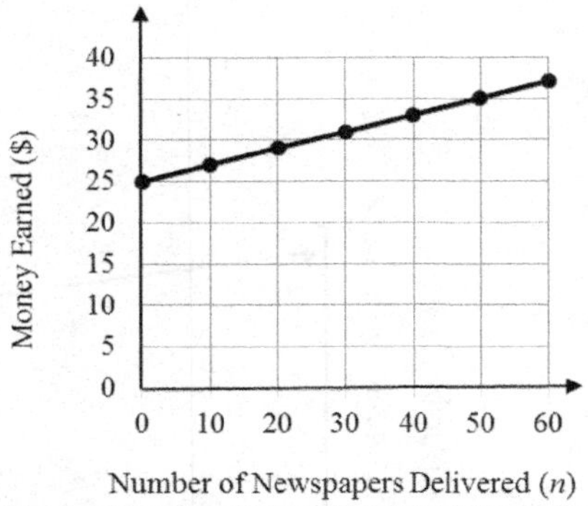

(C)

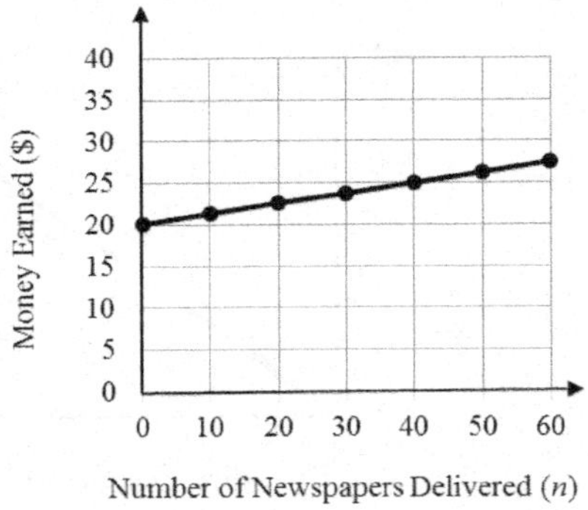

(D)

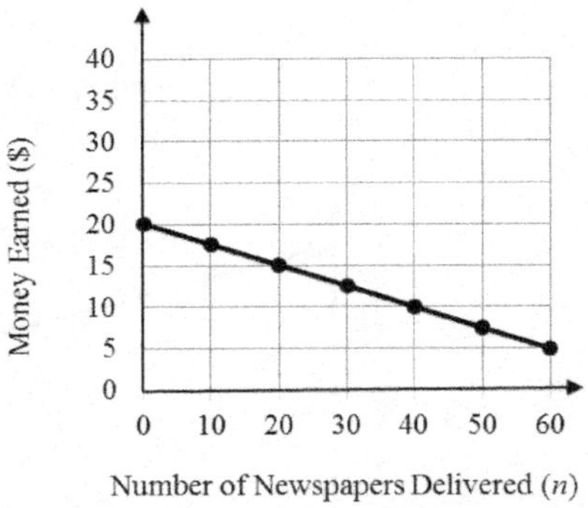

13. The graph below charts the rate at which a certain container's contents leaks over time.

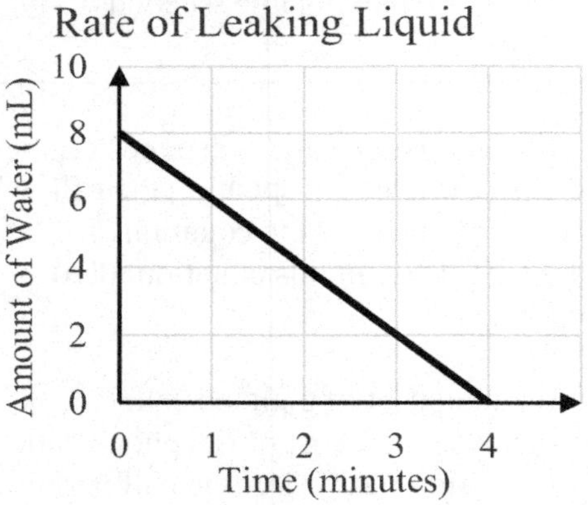

Which of the following equations expresses the amount of water in the container at any given point in time?

(A) $y = 2x + 4$
(B) $y = 2x + 8$
(C) $y = -2x + 4$
(D) $y = -2x + 8$

Quantitative Comparison Practice
Answer Choices:
(A) The amount in column A is greater.
(B) The amount in column B is greater.
(C) The two amounts are equal.
(D) The relationship cannot be determined from the information provided.

Over a certain amount of time, x, the distance traveled on a certain highway is represented by y. The equation that represents the distance Tori travels along the highway is $y = 55x + 10$. The equation that represents the distance Ash travels along the highway is $y = 55x + 50$.

	Column A	Column B
14.	The speed of Ash's car	The speed of Tori's car

	Column A	Column B
15.	The slope of the line $y = \frac{1}{2}x + 12$	The slope of the line $3x + 6y = 9$

The tables below show the height, in inches, of two different plants.

Week	Plant X	Plant Y
0	42	25
2	45	28
6	51	34
10	57	40

	Column A	Column B
16.	The rate of growth of Plant X from Week 0 to Week 2	The rate of growth of Plant Y from Week 6 to Week 10

Algebraic Concepts Mixed Practice

1. If $4x + 6y = 12$, which of the following choices **must** be equivalent to $16x + 24y$?

   (A) 16
   (B) 24
   (C) 48
   (D) 72

2. If $m - n = 12$, then which expression is equal to n?

   (A) 6
   (B) m – 12
   (C) 12 – m
   (D) 12

3. At a museum, the ratio of paintings to sculptures is 7:8. What is the total number of paintings and sculptures if there are 49 paintings?

   (A) 100
   (B) 105
   (C) 120
   (D) 150

4. On John's Game Show, Nancy earns 8 points for every 2 questions she got correct. If Nancy earned 40 points, how many questions did she answer correctly?

   (A) 10
   (B) 16
   (C) 20
   (D) 40

5. If x represents an even integer, which of the following expressions represents the next even integer greater than x?

(A) $x + 1$
(B) $x + 2$
(C) $x + 3$
(D) $2x - 1$

6. Isla ran six more than two times as many laps as Ada did. If Isla ran 20 laps, how many laps did Ada run?

(A) 6
(B) 7
(C) 14
(D) 26

7. The graph below charts the rate at which a balloon deflates over days.

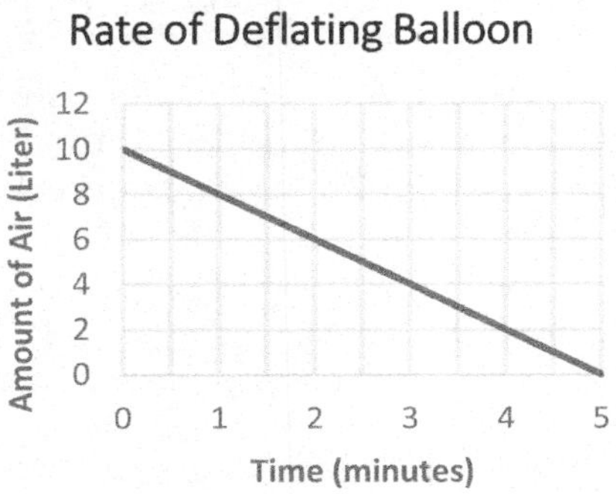

Which of the following equations expresses the amount of air in the balloon at any given point in time?

(A) $y = x + 2$
(B) $y = 2x + 10$
(C) $y = -2x + 2$
(D) $y = -2x + 10$

8. What is the slope of a line perpendicular to the line represented by $y = 2x + 9$?

(A) $y = -\frac{1}{2}x + 4$
(B) $y = \frac{1}{2}x + 9$
(C) $y = -2x + 4$
(D) $y = 2x + 9$

9. An amusement park charges $15 for an adult ticket, plus an extra $7.55 for each children's ticket. Which expression represents the cost of admission, in dollars, for an adult with x child(ren)?

(A) 7.55
(B) $15x$
(C) $15x + 7.55$
(D) $15 + 7.55x$

10. The expression $y^2 - 9$ is equal to which of the following answer choices?

(A) $y - 3$
(B) $y + 3$
(C) $(y + 3)(y - 3)$
(D) $y(y - 3)$

11. Circle Q has a diameter of 12 cm. What is the circumference of a circle similar to circle Q with a scale factor of $\frac{1}{4}$?

(A) 2π cm
(B) 3π cm
(C) 4π cm
(D) 8π cm

12. The table below represents the number of eggs in a farm after a certain period of time.

Time	Population
0	5
2	10
4	15
6	20

Which of the following choices represents the growth of the egg population, y, over time, x?

(A) $y = 5$
(B) $y = \frac{5}{2}x + 5$
(C) $y = x + 5$
(D) $y = 5x + 2$

13. Lauren and Amy have a total 26 folders. If Lauren has 5 more than 2 times as many folders as Amy, how many folders does Amy have?

(A) 5
(B) 7
(C) 9
(D) 11

14. Compare the following and choose the correct answer:

$$y = \frac{2}{5}x + 20$$

Column A	Column B
The slope of the line perpendicular to the above function.	The slope of the line parallel to the above function.

(A) The amount in column A is greater.
(B) The amount in column B is greater.
(C) The two amounts are equal.
(D) The relationship cannot be determined from the information provided.

15. Compare the following and choose the correct answer:

A model has a scale of 2 in = 150 ft.

Column A	Column B
The actual height of a building 20 in on the model.	500 yd.

(A) The amount in column A is greater.
(B) The amount in column B is greater.
(C) The two amounts are equal.
(D) The relationship cannot be determined from the information provided.

16. Compare the following and choose the correct answer:

$$x^2 = y$$

Column A	Column B
x	y

(A) The amount in column A is greater.
(B) The amount in column B is greater.
(C) The two amounts are equal.
(D) The relationship cannot be determined from the information provided.

Measurements

Formulas

1. $A = \frac{1}{2}LW$. If A is 35 and W is 14, what is L?

(A) 2
(B) 3
(C) 4
(D) 5

2. In the figure below, the square has an area of 16 units^2.

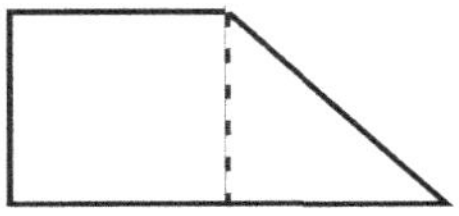

The triangle has a perimeter of 12 units. What is the perimeter of the trapezoid outlined by the solid line?

(A) 12 units
(B) 16 units
(C) 20 units
(D) 24 units

3. The area of the trapezoid shown below is 150 sq. ft.

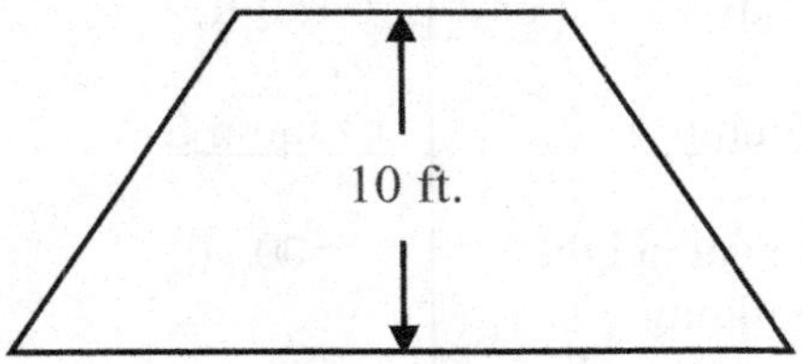

Note: $A = h\frac{(b_1 + b_2)}{2}$.
What is the length of the base labeled x?

(A) 5.0 ft.
(B) 7.5 ft.
(C) 10.0 ft.
(D) 20.0 ft.

4. A trapezoid is shown below, and has an area of 120 in^2.

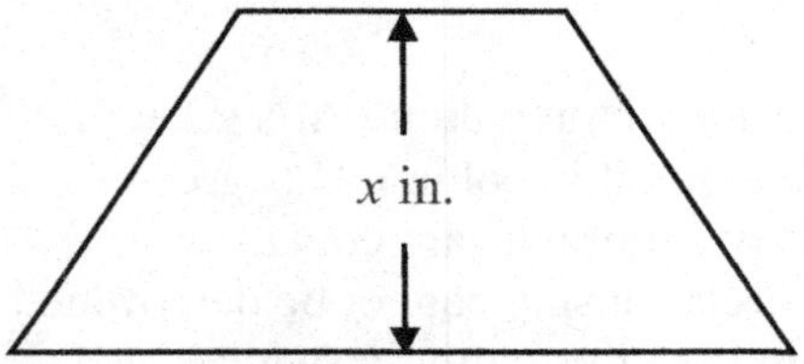

Note: $A = h\frac{(b_1 + b_2)}{2}$.
What is the height of this trapezoid?

(A) 1 in^2
(B) 2 in^2
(C) 8 in^2
(D) 15 in^2

5. What is the sum of the lengths of a trapezoid's bases if its area is 26 and its height is 4? *Note: area of a trapezoid* = $h\frac{(b_1 + b_2)}{2}$.

(A) 13
(B) 20
(C) 24
(D) 26

6. A gallon of paint can cover 25 square feet. If a circular swimming pool has a radius of 5 feet, what is the minimum number of gallons of paint that is needed to paint the entire floor of the pool?

(A) 3
(B) 4
(C) 5
(D) 6

7. If the area of a circle is 150 in^2, which of the following is closest to its circumference?

(A) 14 in.
(B) 21 in.
(C) 42 in.
(D) 56 in.

8. The base of the rectangular prism shown below has an area of 24 in^2.

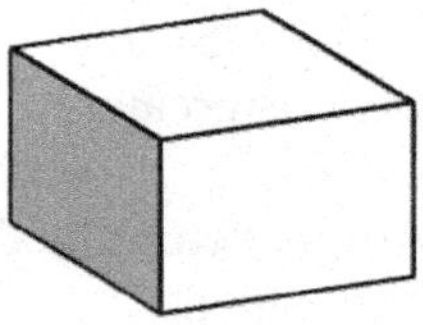

If the volume of the prism is 48 in^3, what is the height of the prism?

(A) 2 in.
(B) 4 in.
(C) 16 in.
(D) 24 in.

9. The volume of a sphere is equal to $\frac{4}{3}\pi r^3$. If a sphere has a diameter of 6 m, what is its volume?

(A) 36π m^3
(B) 108π m^3
(C) 288π m^3
(D) 512π m^3

10. The volume of a cube is 27 cm^3. What is the surface area of the cube?

(A) 3 cm^2
(B) 9 cm^2
(C) 27 cm^2
(D) 54 cm^2

11. What is the height of the trapezoidal prism shown below, if it has a volume of 60 units^3? *Note: the volume of a trapezoidal prism is* $(l)(h)\left(\frac{b_1+b_2}{2}\right)$.

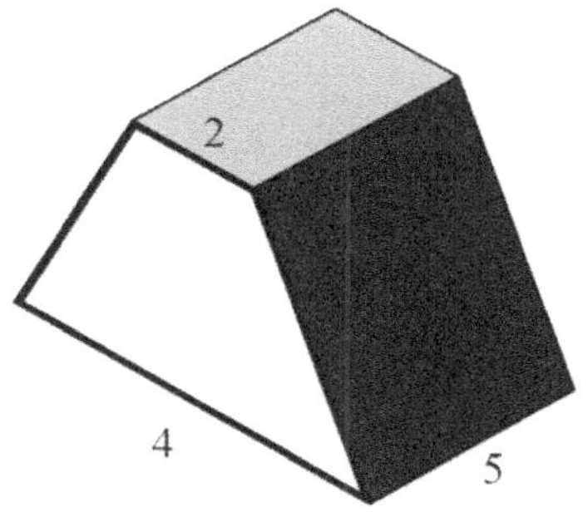

(A) 1 unit
(B) 2 units
(C) 3 units
(D) 4 units

12. What is the volume of a square pyramid if its height is 9 inches and its base has a 4-inch side? *Note: the volume of a square pyramid is* $\frac{lwh}{3}$.

(A) 48 in^3
(B) 72 in^3
(C) 144 in^3
(D) 272 in^3

13. If the slant height (h) of a square pyramid is 4 mm, and the side of its base (s) is 2 mm, what is the surface area of the pyramid, in square millimeters? *Note: surface area of a square pyramid* $= s^2 + \frac{4sh}{2}$.

(A) 8
(B) 12
(C) 16
(D) 20

14. The base of a triangular pyramid is shown below.

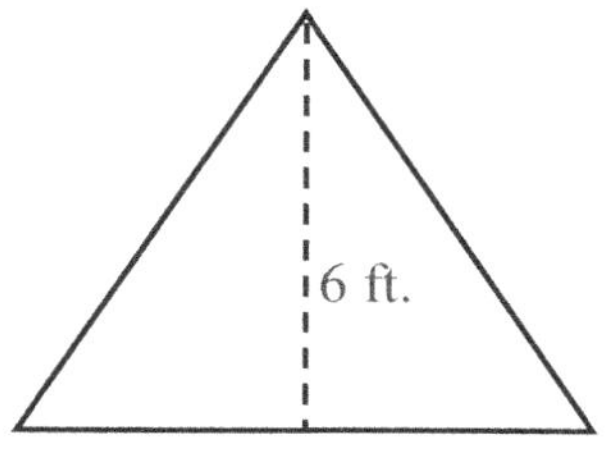

If this pyramid is 10 feet tall, what is the volume of the pyramid?

(A) 40 ft^3
(B) 60 ft^3
(C) 80 ft^3
(D) 120 ft^3

15. A right circular cylinder is shown below. *Note: the volume of a cylinder is* $(\pi)(r)^2(h)$.

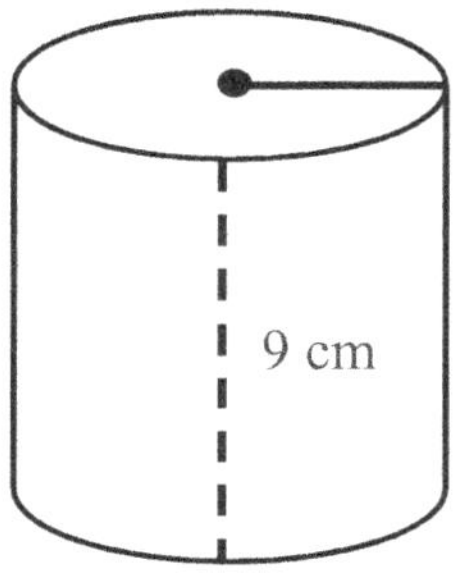

If the volume of this cylinder is 108 cm^3, which is closest to the radius of the base?

(A) 2 cm
(B) 5 cm
(C) 10 cm
(D) 12 cm

Units

1. A cherry lollipop weighs 85 milligrams. What is the lollipop's weight in grams?

(A) 0.085 g
(B) 0.85 g
(C) 8.5 g
(D) 85.0 g

2. A ham that has a mass of 3,500,000 milligrams. What is the ham's mass in kilograms?

(A) 0.35 kg
(B) 3.5 kg
(C) 35.0 kg
(D) 350.0 kg

3. A can of sparkling water weighs 355 milliliters. What is the can's weight in liters?

(A) 0.0355 L
(B) 0.355 L
(C) 3.55 L
(D) 35.5 L

4. At 4:00p, the altitude of a kite is 100ft. If the kite begins descending at a constant rate of 2 yards every hour, at what time does the kite have an altitude of 70ft? *Note: 1 yard = 3 feet.*

(A) 6:00p
(B) 7:00p
(C) 8:00p
(D) 9:00p

5. To decorate for the holidays, Bart wants to cover a wall in his home with wrapping paper, which is sold by the square yard. What is the minimum amount of wrapping paper, in square yards, he will need in order to cover the wall if the wall measures 6 ft. wide by 12 ft. tall? *Note: 1 yd. = 3 ft.*

(A) 8 sq. yds.
(B) 16 sq. yds.
(C) 24 sq. yds.
(D) 72 sq. yds.

6. Andrea is making a blanket measuring 5ft by 4 ft. She is purchasing fabric for this project that is sold by the square inch. How many square inches of fabric does she need to purchase for this blanket? *Note: 1 ft = 12 inches.*

(A) 20 sq. in.
(B) 240 sq. in.
(C) 2,400 sq. in.
(D) 2,880 sq. in

7. In the morning, a buoy in a certain tidal bay shows that the water beneath it is 16 feet deep. The depth of the water beneath the buoy decreased by 6 inches each hour for the next 6 hours. What was the depth of the water beneath the buoy 6 hours later? *Note: 1 foot = 12 inches.*

(A) 13
(B) 16
(C) 19
(D) 36

8. Jake runs the 100-meter dash. In a season, he runs this race 17 times. By the end of the season, how many kilometers has he run?

(A) 0.17 km
(B) 1.7 km
(C) 17.0 km
(D) 1,70.0 km

9. If Marisa is 5 feet 8 inches tall, what is her height in meters? *Note: 1 inch = 2.5 cm*

(A) 1.7 m
(B) 5.8 m
(C) 17.0 m
(D) 168.0 m

10. A snail travels at a rate of 6.1 centimeters per hour. After 100 hours, how many meters has the snail travelled?

(A) 0.061 meters
(B) 0.61 meters
(C) 6.1 meters
(D) 61 meters

11. Darcy is building a model of a library. The library takes up approximately 640,000 square feet. Darcy is making the floor of the model with 1-inch tiles, each representing 6,400 square feet. Which choice is closest to the number of square feet that Darcy's model will take up? *Note: 1 foot = 12 inches*

(A) 0.7 sq. ft.
(B) 1.0 sq. ft.
(C) 8.3 sq. ft.
(D) 64.0 sq. ft.

12. Julia wants to ship a vase to her grandson. If the vase has a volume of 2.5×10^7 cubic millimeters, which of the following expressions could be the dimensions of a box big enough to fit the vase?

(A) 0.3 cm × 0.3 cm. × 0.3 cm.
(B) 3 cm. × 3 cm. × 3 cm.
(C) 30 cm. × 30 cm. × 30 cm.
(D) 30 mm. × 30 mm. × 30 mm.

Geometry

Geometric Objects

1. A square has an area of 64 square centimeters. What is its perimeter, in centimeters?

(A) 16
(B) 32
(C) 64
(D) 256

2. A square has a perimeter of 64 centimeters. What is its area, in square centimeters?

(A) 16
(B) 32
(C) 64
(D) 256

3. The figure below was built using the individual small cubes.

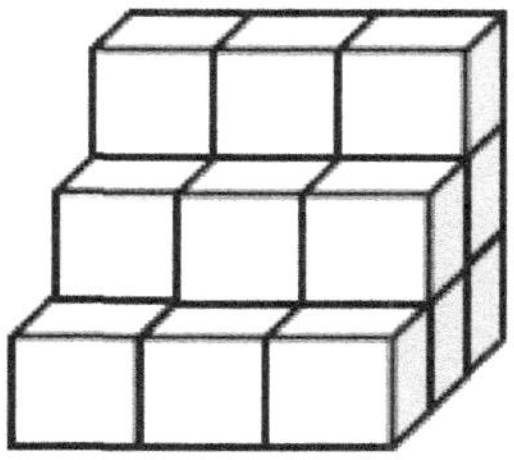

How many individual small cubes were used to build the figure above?

(A) 9
(B) 12
(C) 15
(D) 18

4. Each square in the grid shown has an area of 3 in^2.

What is the area of the shaded region?

(A) 11 in^2
(B) 30 in^2
(C) 33 in^2
(D) 36 in^2

5. The shaded figure has a total area of 44 ft^2.

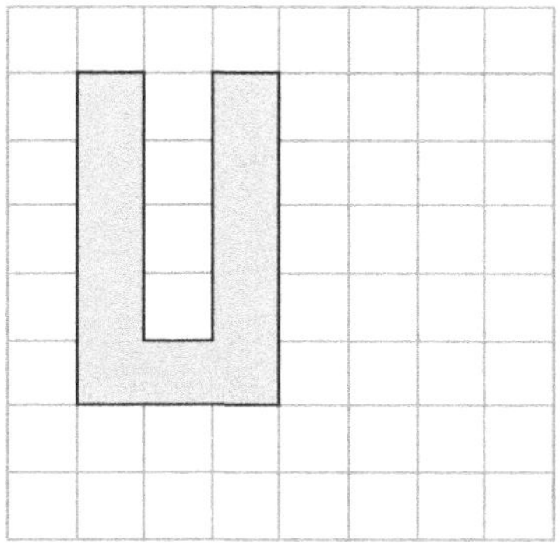

What is the length of a side of a square in the grid?

(A) 2 ft.
(B) 4 ft.
(C) 11 ft.
(D) 22 ft.

6. A large square has had a smaller square cut from its top left corner, as shown.

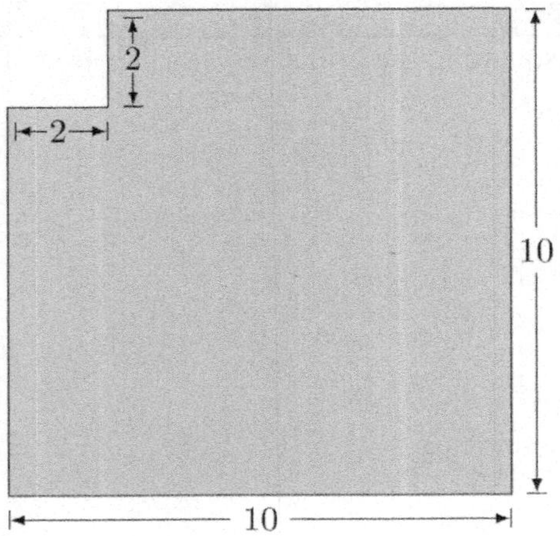

Which expression represents the area of the shaded region?

(A) 8×8
(B) $10 - 4$
(C) $100 - 2$
(D) $10^2 - 2^2$

7.

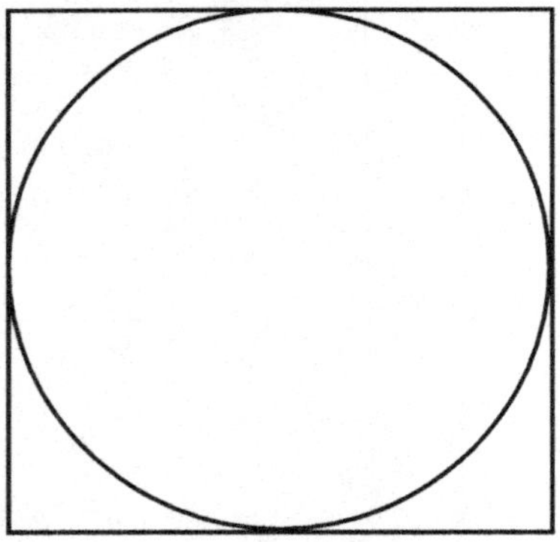

A circle is inscribed in a square, as shown above. If the area of the circle is 36π sq. cm., what is the area of the square?

(A) 36 sq. cm.
(B) 48 sq. cm.
(C) 96 sq. cm.
(D) 144 sq. cm.

8.

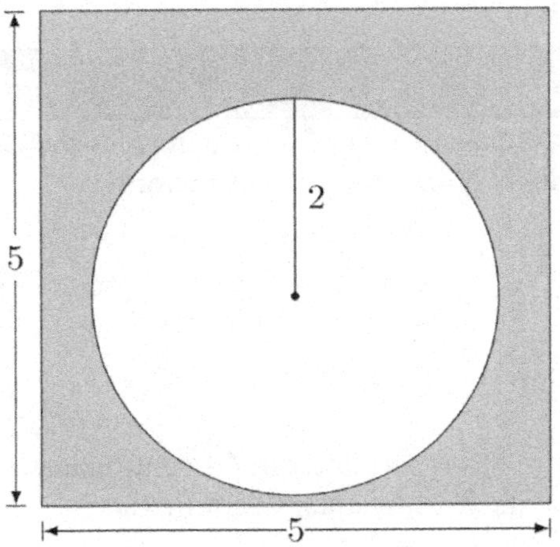

Which expression represents the area of the shaded region if the circle's radius is 2?

(A) 4π units^2
(B) 25 units^2
(C) $25 - 4\pi$ units^2
(D) $25 - 2\pi$ units^2

9. Rectangle ACDF has an area of 200 sq. cm. ABEF and BCDE are squares.

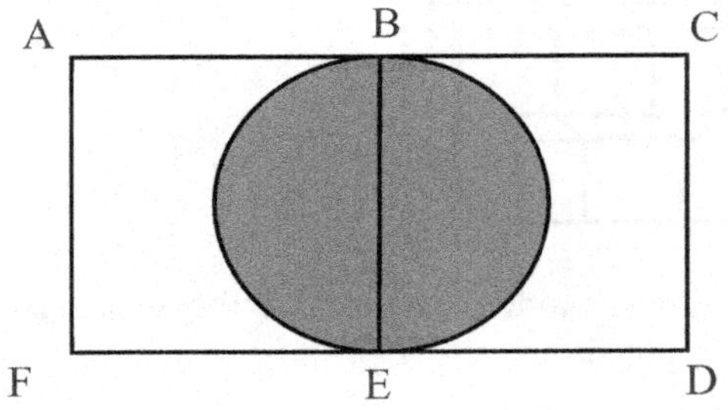

What is the area of the unshaded portion of ACDF if BE represents the diameter of the circle formed by the shaded portion?

(A) 100 sq. cm.
(B) 25π sq. cm.
(C) $8 - \pi$ sq. cm.
(D) $200 - 25\pi$ sq. cm.

10. The figure shows a square with a square portion missing.

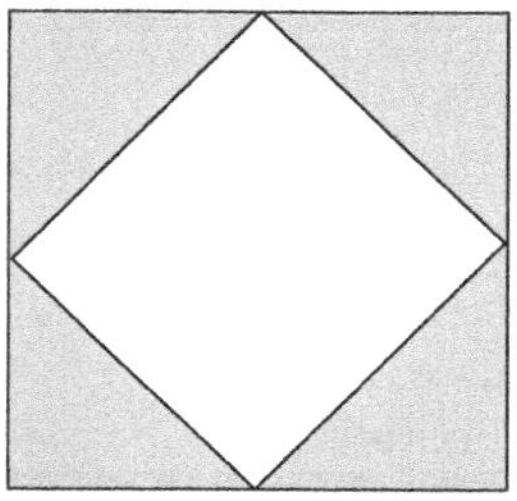

If the large square has a side length of 6 inches, what is the area of the shaded region?

(A) 6 in^2
(B) 9 in^2
(C) 12 in^2
(D) 18 in^2

11. Use the figure shown below to answer the question.

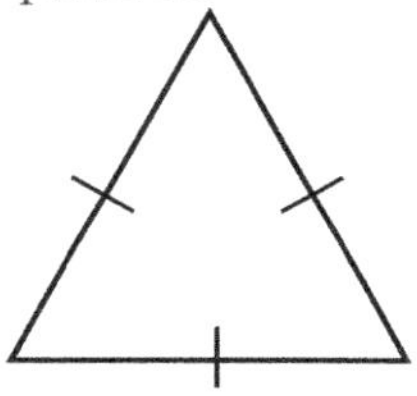

Which type of triangle is shown above?

(A) right
(B) obtuse
(C) scalene
(D) equilateral

12. Use the figure shown below to answer the question.

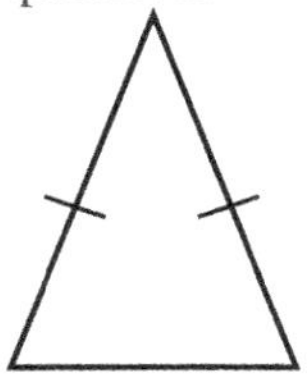

Which type of triangle is shown above?

(A) scalene
(B) isosceles
(C) equilateral
(D) equiangular

13. Use the figure shown below to answer the question.

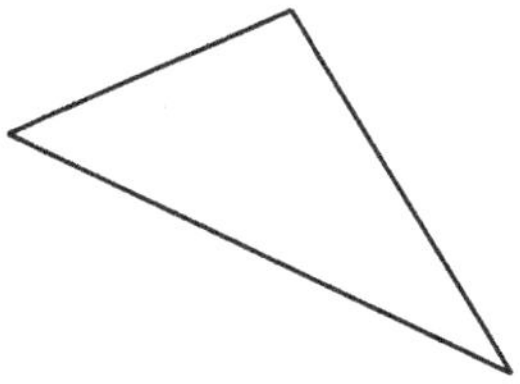

Which type of triangle is shown above?

(A) scalene
(B) isosceles
(C) equilateral
(D) equiangular

14. Which of the following statements is always true?

(A) An obtuse triangle is always an equiangular triangle.
(B) An obtuse triangle can never be a scalene triangle.
(C) An obtuse triangle can never be an isosceles triangle.
(D) An obtuse triangle can never be an equilateral triangle.

15. Which of the following statements is true?

(A) An equilateral triangle is never an acute triangle.
(B) An equilateral triangle could be a right triangle.
(C) An equilateral triangle could be an obtuse triangle.
(D) An equilateral triangle is always an acute triangle.

16. Use the figure shown below to answer the question.

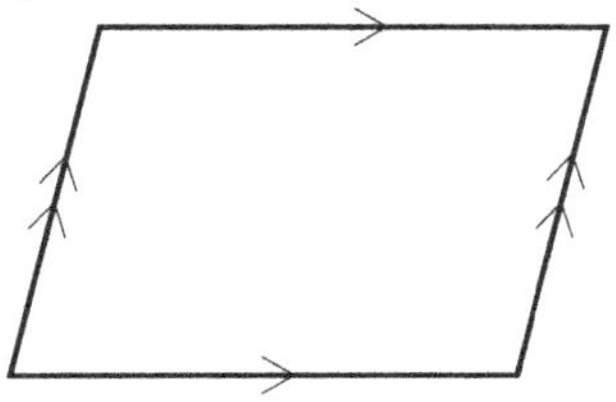

Which type of quadrilateral is shown above?

(A) rhombus
(B) trapezoid
(C) rectangle
(D) parallelogram

17. Use the figure shown below to answer the question.

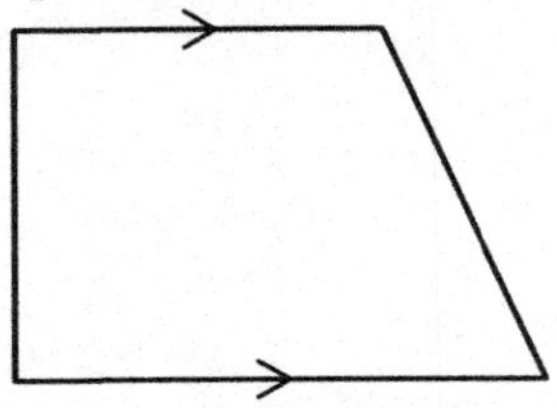

Which type of quadrilateral is shown above?

(A) kite
(B) rhombus
(C) trapezoid
(D) parallelogram

18. All of the following are always true EXCEPT for which statement?

(A) All squares are rectangles, but not all rectangles are squares.
(B) All rhombuses are rectangles, but not all rectangles are rhombuses.
(C) All squares are also rhombuses, but not all rhombuses are squares.
(D) All rhombuses are parallelograms, but not all parallelograms are rhombuses.

Quantitative Comparison Practice

Answer Choices:

(A) The amount in column A is greater.
(B) The amount in column B is greater.
(C) The two amounts are equal.
(D) The relationship cannot be determined from the information provided.

	Column A	Column B
19.	The sum of all angles in a rhombus	The sum of all angles in an irregular trapezoid

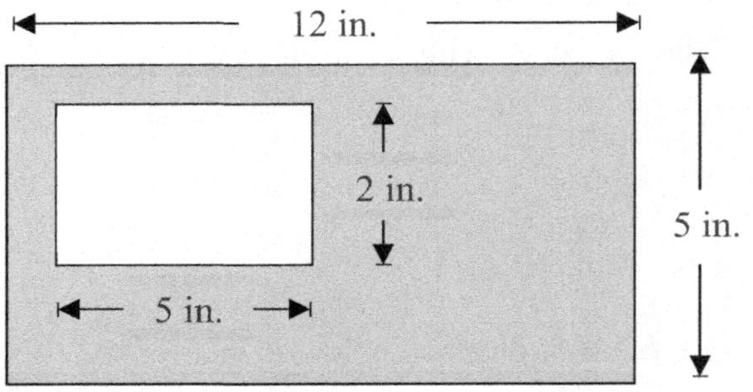

Note: Figures are not drawn to scale.

	Column A	Column B
20.	The area of the shaded region	50 in^2

Coordinates

1. The grid shows two vertices of a right triangle.

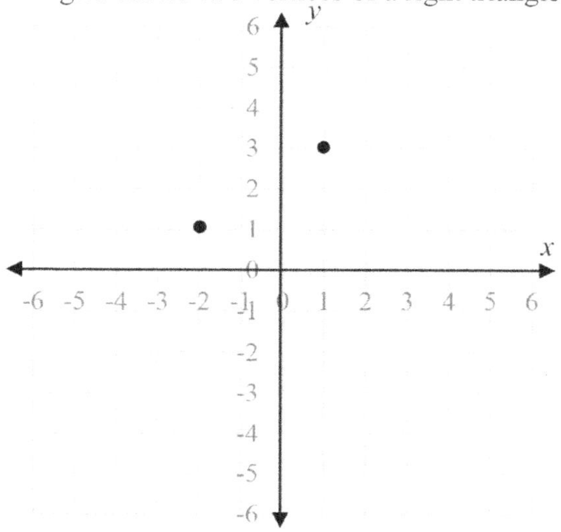

Which could be the coordinates of the third vertex of the right triangle?

(A) (1,1)
(B) (0,1)
(C) (−1,3)
(D) (−1,−3)

2. The grid shows three vertices of an isosceles trapezoid.

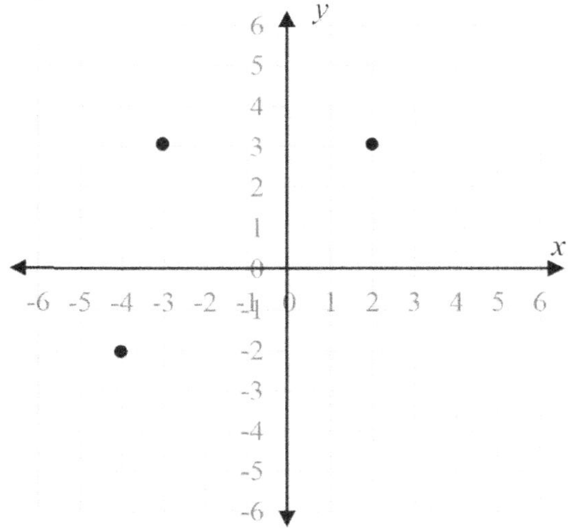

Which could be the coordinates of the fourth vertex of the trapezoid?

(A) (−3,−2)
(B) (−3,2)
(C) (3,−2)
(D) (3,2)

3. The grid shows two vertices of an obtuse triangle.

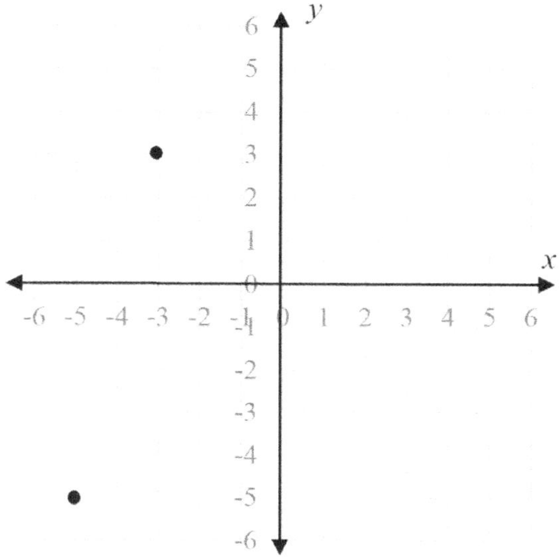

Which could be the coordinates of the third vertex of the obtuse triangle?

(A) (2,0)
(B) (5,−3)
(C) (6,−3)
(D) (−6,−2)

4. Triangle A is shown below.

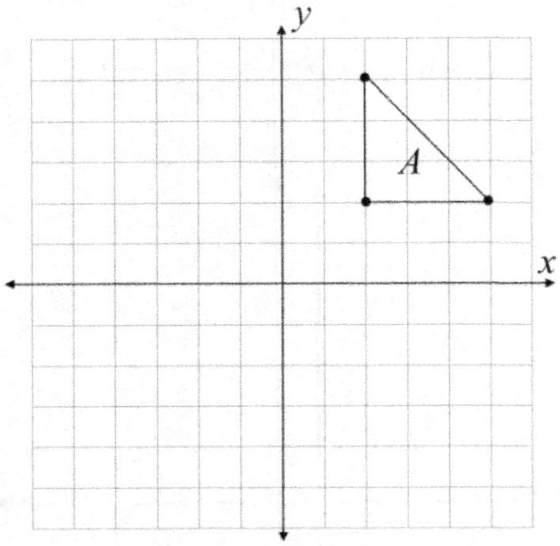

Which diagram shows Triangle A after a translation?

(A)

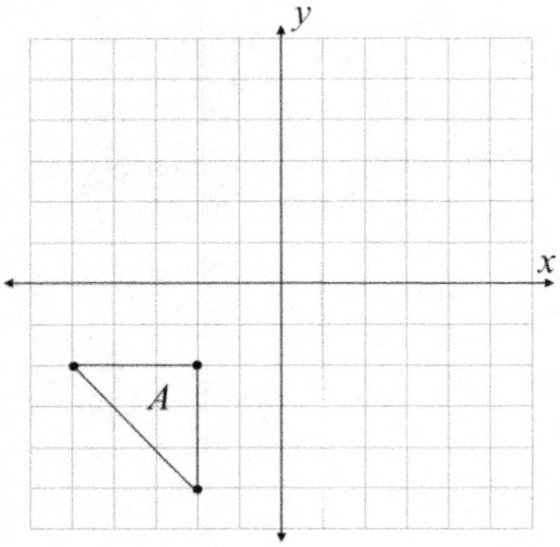

(B)

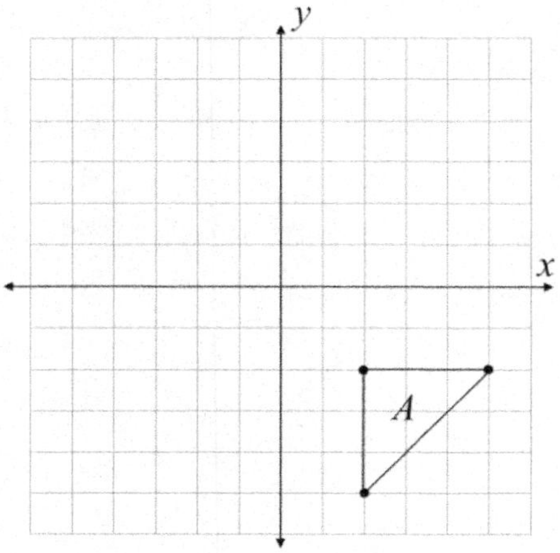

(C)

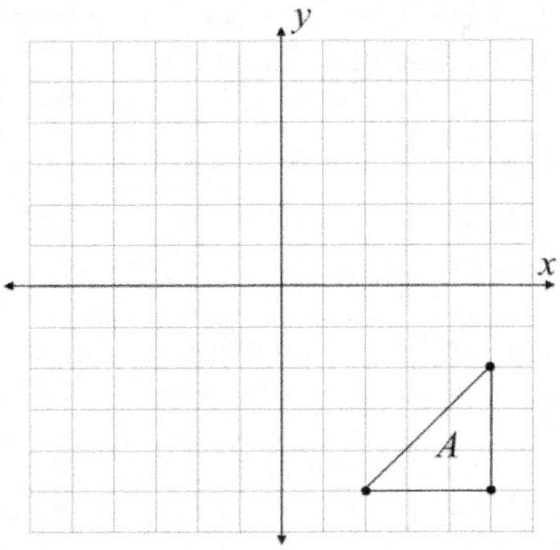

(D)

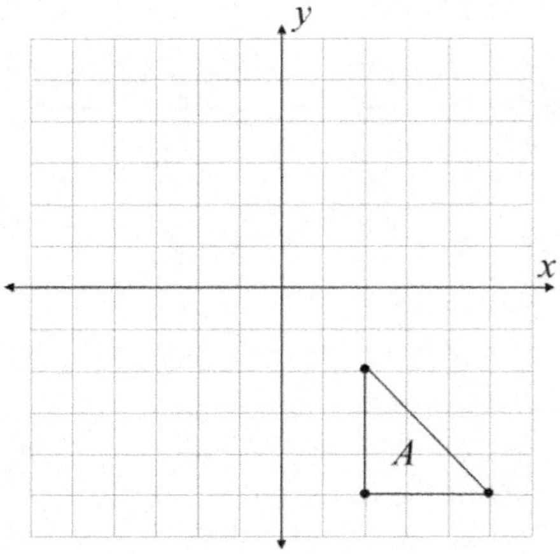

5.

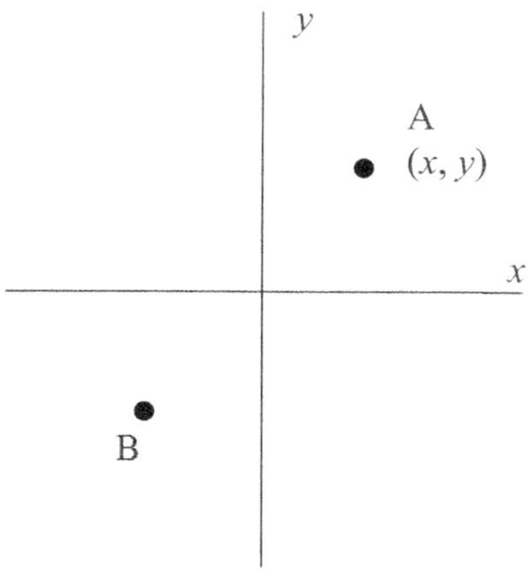

In the above figure, A and B are equidistant from the origin. Which of the following could be the coordinates of point B?

(A) $(-x,-y)$
(B) $(-x,y)$
(C) $(x,-y)$
(D) (y,x)

6. Three vertices of a rectangle are (–5,7), (–2,7) and (–2,–1). Which could be the coordinates of the fourth vertex of the rectangle?

(A) (1,7)
(B) (–2,4)
(C) (–6,1)
(D) (–5,–1)

7. Three vertices of a square are (2,3), (7,3) and (2,–2). Which could be the coordinates of the fourth vertex of the square?

(A) (7,–2)
(B) (4,–2)
(C) (–1,3)
(D) (7,1)

8. On a coordinate-plane, what is the area of a rectangle with points at (3,3), (3,1), (0,1), and (0,3)?

(A) 2 units^2
(B) 3 units^2
(C) 4 units^2
(D) 6 units^2

9. On an *xy*-plane, the center of a certain circle is located at the origin. A line segment is drawn from the origin to point (–3,0), and represents the circle's radius. What is the area of the circle?

(A) -9π
(B) -6π
(C) 6π
(D) 9π

10. On an *xy*-plane, the center of a certain circle is located at (17,53). The circle is then rotated clockwise 180° around the origin. At what point is the center of the new circle?

(A) (–17,53)
(B) (17,–53)
(C) (53,–17)
(D) (–17,–53)

11. Point Q is located on a coordinate plane at (–10,19). If Q is rotated clockwise 90° around the origin, what will be the coordinates of the new point, Q''?

(A) (19,10)
(B) (10,19)
(C) (10,–19)
(D) (19,–10)

12. Point P is located on a coordinate plane at (17,53). If P is rotated counterclockwise 90° around the origin, what will be the coordinates of the new point, P''?

(A) (53,–17)
(B) (–17,–53)
(C) (–53,–17)
(D) (–53,17)

Measurements & Geometry Mixed Practice

1. If the area of a circle is 225π in^2, which of the following is its circumference?

(A) 12π in.
(B) 15π in.
(C) 25π in.
(D) 30π in.

2. A right circular cylinder is shown below. *Note: the volume of a cylinder=* $(\pi)(r)^2(h)$.

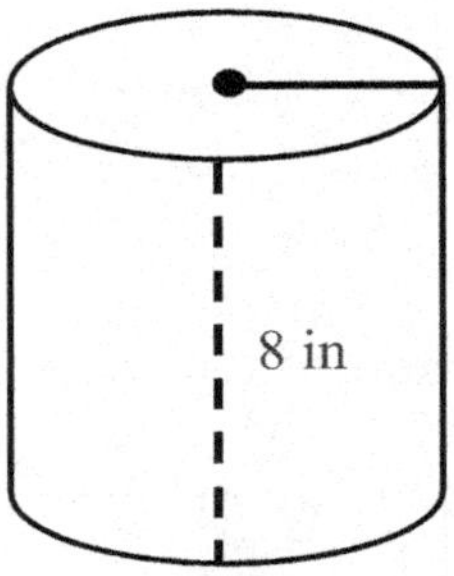

If the volume of this cylinder is 384 in^3, which is closest to the diameter of the base?
(A) 4 in.
(B) 6 in.
(C) 8 in.
(D) 10 in.

3. The figure shows a square with a square portion missing.

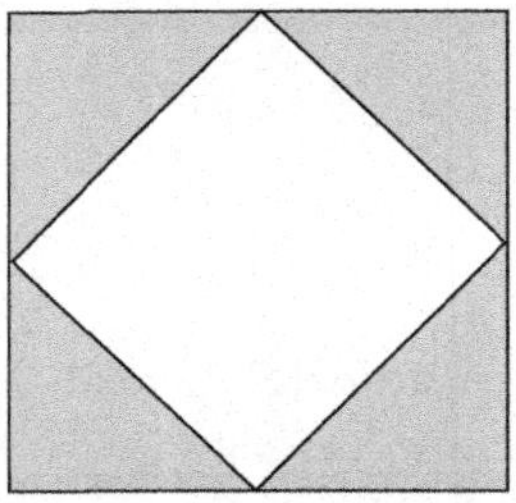

If the large square has a side length of 10 inches, what is the area of the unshaded region?

(A) 10 in^2
(B) 25 in^2
(C) 50 in^2
(D) 100 in^2

4. Which of the following statement is always true?

(A) All rhombus are squares.
(B) All squares are rhombus.
(C) All parallelograms are trapezoids.
(D) All rectangles are squares.

5. Point J is located on a coordinate plane at (5, –12). If J is rotated counterclockwise 90° around the origin, what will be the coordinates of the new point, J'?

(A) (5, 12)
(B) (12, 5)
(C) (5, –12)
(D) (–12, 5)

6. Which point on the coordinate plane is located exactly 5 units from (7, 1)?

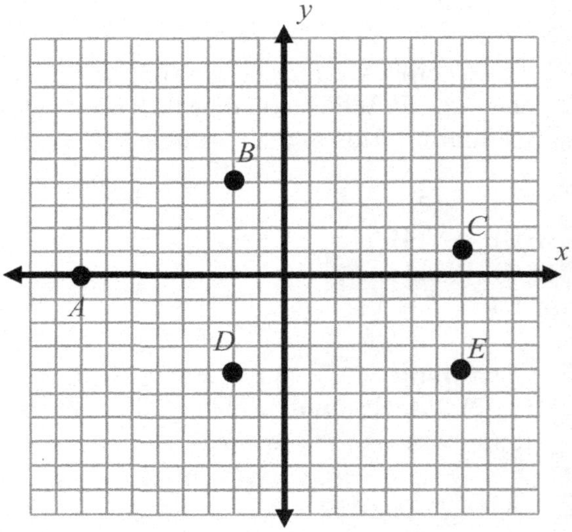

(A) *A*
(B) *B*
(C) *D*
(D) *E*

7. What is the area of a right triangle with the shortest side of 5 units and longest side of 13 units?

(A) 12
(B) 24
(C) 30
(D) 48

8. A cheetah runs at a rate of 35 meters per second. After 4 hours, how many kilometers has the cheetah run?

(A) 8400 meters
(B) 105 kilometers
(C) 140 kilometers
(D) 504 kilometers

9. A bucket of water weighs 16 pints. What is the bucket's weight in gallons?

(A) 1 gallons
(B) 2 gallons
(C) 3 gallons
(D) 4 gallons

10. Line segment *AB* has endpoints on the circle. *AB* has a length of 8 and it does not pass through the center of the circle.

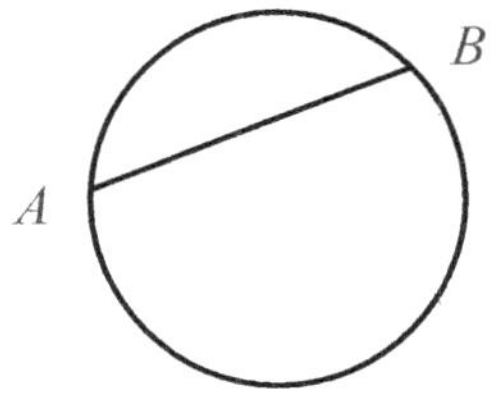

Which of the following could be the circumference of the circle? *(Note: $C = \pi d$)*

(A) 10π
(B) 8π
(C) 6π
(D) 4π

11. On a coordinate-plane, the following points are graphed: (4,6), (4,1), and (2,1). Where is the fourth point of the rectangle?

(A) (2,2)
(B) (2,4)
(C) (2,6)
(D) (4,6)

12. Compare the following and choose the correct answer:

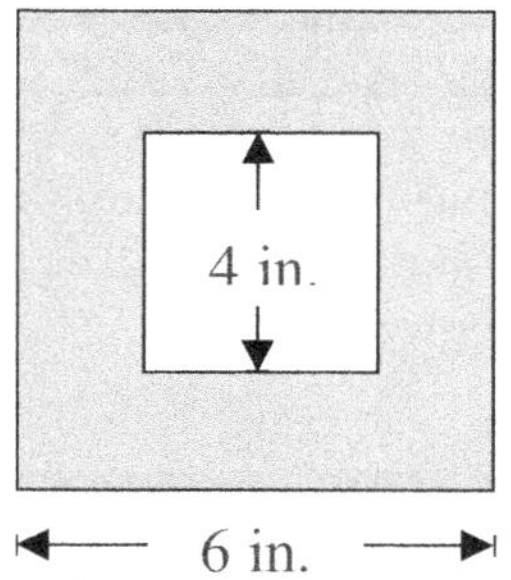

Note: the two shapes are squares.

Column A	Column B
The area of the unshaded region	The area of the shaded region

(A) The amount in column A is greater.
(B) The amount in column B is greater.
(C) The two amounts are equal.
(D) The relationship cannot be determined from the information provided.

13. Compare the following and choose the correct answer:

Column A	Column B
0.01 kiloliter	100 liter

(A) The amount in column A is greater.
(B) The amount in column B is greater.
(C) The two amounts are equal.
(D) The relationship cannot be determined from the information provided.

Data & Probability

Probability

1. A box contains 2 red markers, 5 blue markers, and 7 green markers. If one marker is chosen from the box at random, what is the probability that it will be green?

   (A) $\frac{1}{7}$

   (B) $\frac{2}{7}$

   (C) $\frac{1}{2}$

   (D) $\frac{7}{7}$

2. A standard American coin is flipped 100 times. What is the expected number of heads?

   (A) 25
   (B) 50
   (C) 55
   (D) 75

3. Of the 21 students in Ms. Klein's class, 7 were born in a month having exactly 30 days. If a student is chosen at random, what is the chance that he or she will be born in a month with either more or less than 30 days?

   (A) $\frac{1}{3}$

   (B) $\frac{1}{2}$

   (C) $\frac{2}{3}$

   (D) $\frac{4}{5}$

4. An elephant's diet consists of 10% grass, 20% leaves, 30% peanuts, and 40% bananas. What is the probability that for a certain meal, the elephant does NOT eat bananas?

   (A) $\frac{3}{5}$

   (B) $\frac{2}{5}$

   (C) $\frac{3}{10}$

   (D) $\frac{1}{5}$

5. There is a 3 out of 4 chance it will rain on Saturday this coming weekend, and also a 3 out of 4 chance it will rain on Sunday this coming weekend. What is the chance that it will NOT rain on either day?

   (A) 0.75
   (B) 0.5625
   (C) 0.25
   (D) 0.0625

6. There are 30 marbles in a box. The probability of picking a green marble is more than 20%, but less than 40%. What is the maximum number of green marbles in the box?

   (A) 9
   (B) 10
   (C) 11
   (D) 12

7. Jurvis and his friends are playing a board game that involves two standard, six-sided dice. Each side of each die is labeled with a number from 1 through 6. The only way for everyone to lose the game is for the combined value of Jurvis' next roll to be 2. What is the probability that everyone will lose the game on Jurvis' next roll?

(A) $\frac{1}{36}$

(B) $\frac{1}{12}$

(C) $\frac{1}{6}$

(D) $\frac{1}{3}$

8. A certain bag contains only white, dark, and milk chocolates. There are twice as many dark chocolates as white chocolates in that bag. There are three times as many milk chocolates as there are dark chocolates in that bag. What is the probability of picking a white chocolate out of the bag at random?

(A) $\frac{1}{9}$

(B) $\frac{1}{6}$

(C) $\frac{1}{4}$

(D) $\frac{1}{3}$

9. A soda company purchased six 60-second timeslots between the hours of 7 P.M. and 10 P.M. During these timeslots, the company will air a commercial it created. If Neba turns on her television during this time period, what is the probability that she will see the soda company's commercial?

(A) $\frac{1}{30}$

(B) $\frac{1}{60}$

(C) $\frac{1}{90}$

(D) $\frac{1}{900}$

10. Two six-sided number cubes, each numbered 1 through 6, are rolled together. What is the probability that the product of the numbers shown on the cubes is prime?

(A) 0

(B) $\frac{1}{12}$

(C) $\frac{1}{6}$

(D) $\frac{1}{2}$

11. Nguyen is rolling a 10-sided die. Each side has a different number on it, from 1 to 10. What is the probability that Nguyen's first two rolls both result in a number greater than 6?

(A) $\frac{3}{25}$

(B) $\frac{4}{25}$

(C) $\frac{2}{5}$

(D) $\frac{4}{5}$

12. Charice chooses a musical instrument to play from the music room. There are 2 flutes, 3 guitars, and 5 keyboards. If she chooses one instrument from the room at random, what is the probability that it will be a not be a keyboard?

(A) $\frac{3}{10}$

(B) $\frac{3}{5}$

(C) $\frac{1}{2}$

(D) $\frac{2}{3}$

13. There is a 3 out of 4 chance it will freeze on Friday, and a 1 out of 3 chance it will rain on Sunday. What is the chance that it will both NOT freeze on Friday, and NOT rain on Sunday?

(A) $\frac{1}{6}$

(B) $\frac{1}{4}$

(C) $\frac{1}{12}$

(D) $\frac{1}{2}$

14. A standard 6-sided number cube is rolled 60 times. What is the expected number of 4's?

(A) 4
(B) 6
(C) 10
(D) 24

15. A certain bag contains only gold, silver, and bronze coins. There are the same number of gold and silver coins in the bag. There are three times as many bronze coins as there are gold coins in that bag. What is the probability of picking a silver coin out of the bag at random?

(A) $\frac{1}{3}$

(B) $\frac{1}{4}$

(C) $\frac{1}{5}$

(D) $\frac{1}{6}$

16. Bryce is rolling a 8-sided die. Each side has a different number on it, from 1 to 8. What is the probability that Bryce's first two rolls both result in a number less than 5?

(A) $\frac{1}{8}$

(B) $\frac{1}{6}$

(C) $\frac{1}{2}$

(D) $\frac{1}{4}$

17. There are 10 tiles in a bag, numbered sequentially from 10-19. If Leo picks a tile, what is the probability that he will pick a prime number on his first try?

(A) 0.19
(B) 0.30
(C) 0.36
(D) 0.40

18. Two squares are drawn with the same center, one bigger than the other, as shown below.

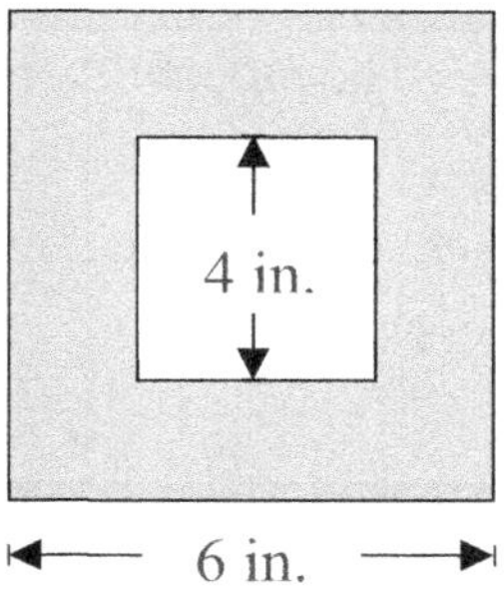

What is the probability that a point picked at random inside the bigger square will be in the shaded area?

(A) $\frac{1}{3}$

(B) $\frac{4}{9}$

(C) $\frac{5}{9}$

(D) $\frac{2}{3}$

19. A square is drawn on an xy-plane with vertices at (0,0), (0,5), (5,0), and (5,5). What is the probability that a point picked at random inside the square has an x **and** y-coordinate of 3 or greater?

(A) $\frac{3}{5}$

(B) $\frac{2}{5}$

(C) $\frac{9}{25}$

(D) $\frac{4}{25}$

Quantitative Comparison Practice

Answer Choices:

(A) The amount in column A is greater.
(B) The amount in column B is greater.
(C) The two amounts are equal.
(D) The relationship cannot be determined from the information provided.

Sarah's closet contains 2 pairs of rain boots, 1 pair of high heels, and 3 pairs of sneakers.

	Column A	Column B
20.	The probability of randomly choosing either rain boots or high heels	The probability of randomly choosing sneakers

Two positive integers, a and b, are picked at random from the set from 1 through 10, inclusive.

	Column A	Column B
21.	The chance that both a and b are odd	The chance that both a and b are multiples of 2

1 in 10 peppers is very hot, while the rest are very mild.

	Column A	Column B
22.	The chance of picking a hot pepper out of a pile of 20	The chance of picking a hot pepper out of a pile of 30

A card is picked from a standard, 52-card deck. This deck has 4 different suits, each of which contains 13 cards.

	Column A	Column B
23.	The probability of obtaining a spade	The probability of obtaining either a queen, king, or ace

Ollie has a jar full of equally-sized red, yellow, and green candies. The probability of picking out a red candy is $\frac{1}{8}$. There are twice as many yellow candies as red candies.

	Column A	Column B
24.	The number of green candies in the jar	The number of yellow and red candies in the jar

A class of students all put pieces of paper with their names on them into a hat. The probability of picking out a name that starts with the letter B is $\frac{2}{15}$. The probability of picking out a name that starts with B, replacing it into the hat, and then picking out a name that starts with C is $\frac{1}{45}$.

	Column A	Column B
25.	The probability of picking out a name that starts with C	$\frac{1}{6}$

Tim rolls two standard, six-sided dice, each of which is numbered from 1 through 6.

	Column A	Column B
26.	The probability that the sum of both rolls is 2	The probability that the sum of both rolls is 11

In a list of the first 25 positive integers, all the multiples of 3 are circled. All the multiples of 5 are shaded in purple. Joseph is thinking of a number in the set.

	Column A	Column B
27.	The probability that Joseph's number is neither circled nor shaded in purple	50%

Mean, Median, Mode, & Range

1. The bar graph shows the number of hours Natalie spent doing homework each day for one week.

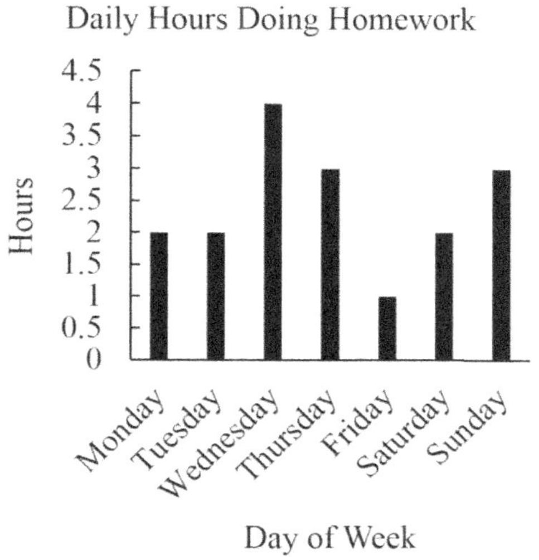

According to the graph, what is the mode number of hours Natalie spent doing homework each day last week?

(A) 1
(B) 2
(C) 3
(D) 4

2. Over the course of five soccer games, Ismail scored a total of 15 goals. What was the average number of goals he scored per game?

(A) 3
(B) 5
(C) 10
(D) 15

3. Horace took four exams. His average on these exams was 88. What was the total of all four exam scores?

(A) 22
(B) 88
(C) 176
(D) 352

4. Carly, a professional bowler, has 5 different bowling balls. Each ball is described in the table below:

Ball	Weight (kg)
A	5.0
B	5.5
C	6.0
D	6.5
E	7.0

What is the average weight of the bowling balls that Carly has?

(A) 1 kg
(B) 2 kg
(C) 5 kg
(D) 6 kg

5. Jermaine will take five quizzes in class this year. If he wants to end up with a quiz average of 90, what must the sum of all of the quiz scores be?

(A) 360
(B) 450
(C) 540
(D) 630

6. What is the median value of the set $\{1, 2, 2, 3, 3, 3\}$?

(A) 1.5
(B) 2.0
(C) 2.5
(D) 3.0

7. 5 different equilateral triangles with side lengths 3, 4, 5, 6, and 7 respectively are drawn. What is the average (arithmetic mean) of their perimeters?

(A) 5
(B) 15
(C) 21
(D) 25

8. The bar graph shows the number of customers in a restaurant at each hour one evening.

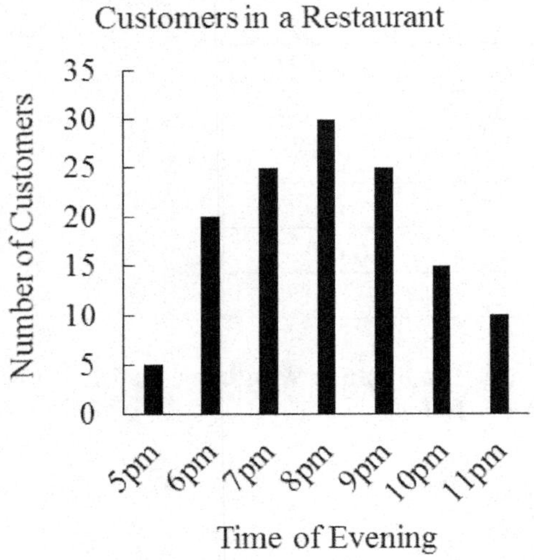

According to the graph, what is the sum of the median number of customers and the range of the number of customers who visit the restaurant in one evening?

(A) 20
(B) 25
(C) 35
(D) 45

9. The average height of seven students is x inches. In terms of x, what is the total height of all seven students, in inches?

(A) $7 + x$
(B) $x - 7$
(C) $7x$
(D) $\frac{7}{x}$

10. If the mean of $\{x, 3x, 5x\}$ is 45, what is the value of x?

(A) 3
(B) 5
(C) 9
(D) 15

11. Kassandra was trying to calculate the mean of her four test scores. She forgot what she had scored on each of the first three tests, but knew that the sum of those three scores was 274. If Kassandra scored an 86 on her fourth test, then what was the mean of all four scores?

(A) 69
(B) 86
(C) 90
(D) 91

12. A set of five numbers has an average of 13. If one more number is added to the set, the new average will be 18. What is the new number that is added to the set?

(A) 43
(B) 78
(C) 90
(D) 108

13. The mean of the set containing 3, 4, 5, 10, and x is equal to 5.6. What is the value of x?

(A) 9
(B) 8
(C) 7
(D) 6

14. According to the line plot below, which of the following statements is true?

QUIZ SCORES FOR 20 STUDENTS

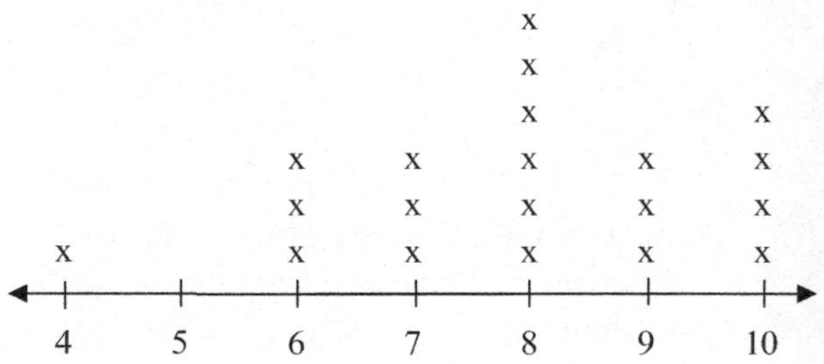

(A) The range of the quiz scores is greater than the median of the quiz scores.
(B) The mean of the quiz scores is less than the median of the quiz scores.
(C) The mode of the quiz scores is greater than the median of the quiz scores.
(D) The range of the quiz scores is greater than the mode of the quiz scores.

Quantitative Comparison Practice

Answer Choices:

(A) The amount in column A is greater.
(B) The amount in column B is greater.
(C) The two amounts are equal.
(D) The relationship cannot be determined from the information provided.

A class of 20 students collected an average of 15 box-tops before the beginning of the school year.

	Column A	Column B
15.	300	The total number of box-tops collected by the students

---

Four different brands of cereal are sold in a store. Brand A has 10% of the recommended daily value of iron per serving. Brands B, C, and D have 20%, 25%, and 45% of the recommended daily value of iron per serving, respectively.

	Column A	Column B
16.	The recommended daily value of iron in a serving of cereal C	The mean of the recommended daily values of iron for the four brands of cereal

---

Consider the following set of values: {5, 3, 1, 3, 5, 8, 10, 9, 8, 3, 4, 5}

	Column A	Column B
17.	The number of modes	The mean of all the modes

Parker scores an average of 11 points per game over four games.

	Column A	Column B
18.	Parker's new per game point average, if he scores 16 points in his fifth game	16

The first six digits of π are 3.14159.

	Column A	Column B
19.	The mode of the first six digits	The mean of the first six digits

---

The mean of a set of 6 values is 5. If x is added to the set, the mean becomes 6.

	Column A	Column B
20.	The value of x	The mode of the set

Set S contains the first 6 positive integer multiples of 4.

	Column A	Column B
21.	The range of values in S	The sum of the mean and median of S

$$\left\{\frac{1}{2}, \frac{1}{3}, \frac{1}{4}\right\}$$

	Column A	Column B
22.	The median value of the three fractions	The mean of the three fractions

Interpreting Data

1. Qi Fei kept track of her monthly expenses. She found out that she spent 35% of her income on rent, 20% on utilities, 15% on clothes, and 30% on food. Which of the following circle graphs represents Qi Fei's expenses?

(A)

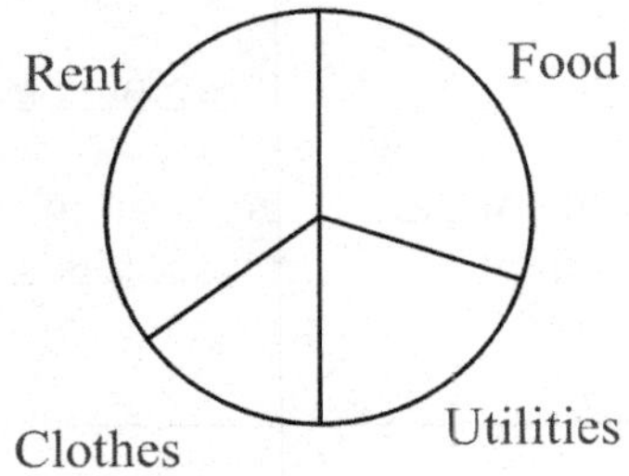

(B)

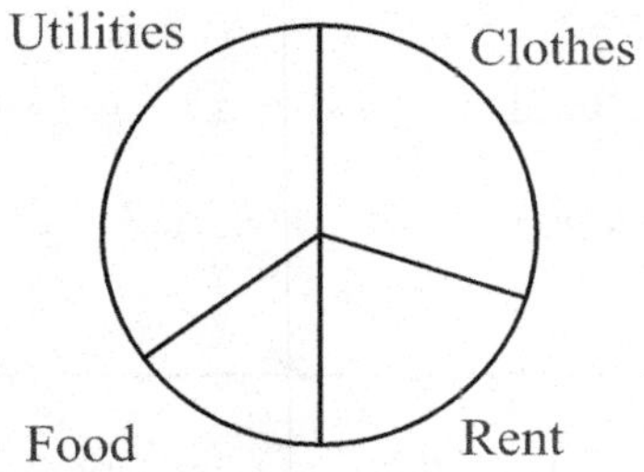

(C)

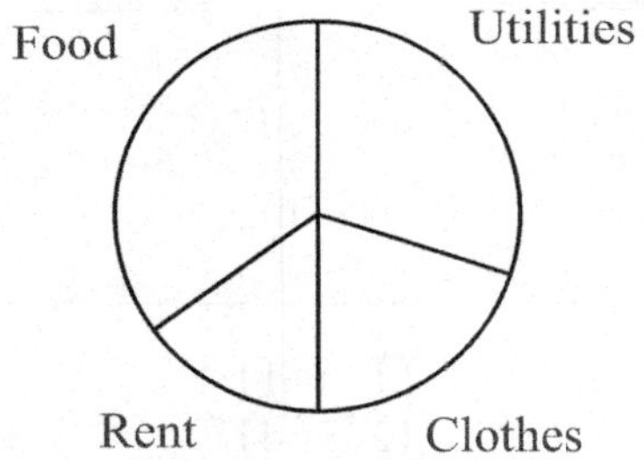

(D)

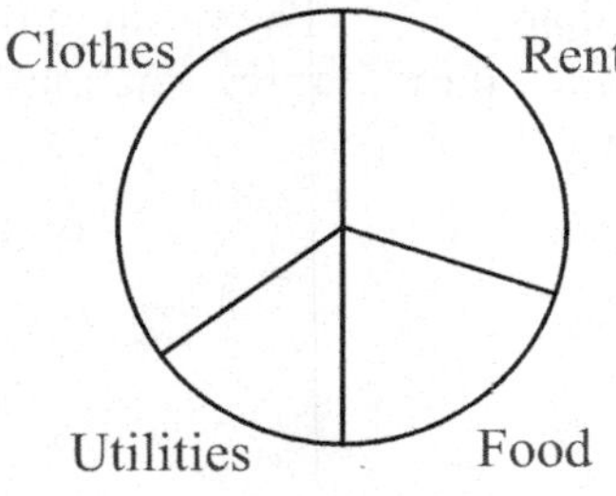

2. The circle graph shows a group of students' favorite day of the week.

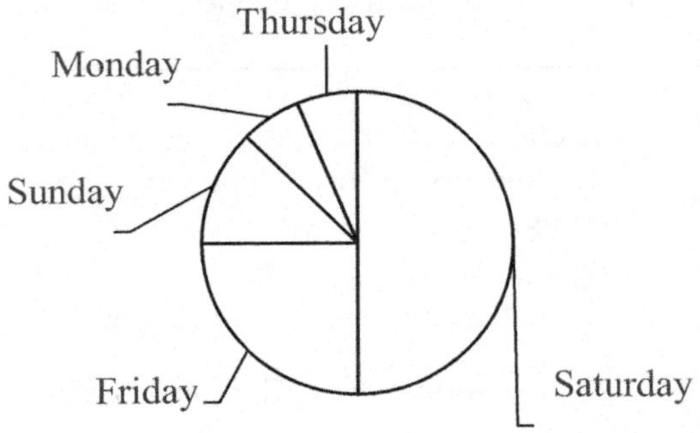

If 24 people chose Saturday, approximately how many people chose Sunday?

(A) 2
(B) 3
(C) 6
(D) 12

3. The circle graph shows the distribution of grades for a state-wide math test.

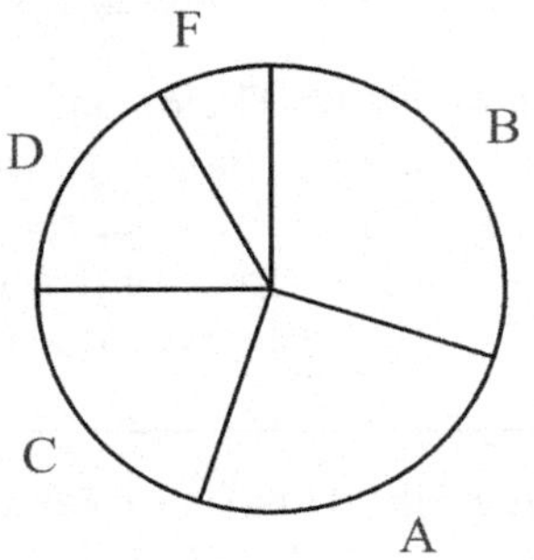

If 200 students earned a C, how many students could have taken the test in total?

(A) 400
(B) 600
(C) 800
(D) 1,000

Use the information below to answer the next 3 questions.

Ms. Dorphin surveyed the students in her class to see how much time they had spent studying for an exam. She plotted this information along with the score of each student on the scatter-plot below.

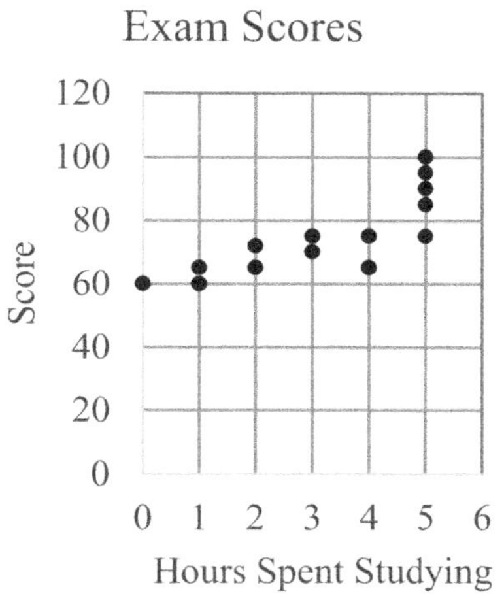

4. What does each point on the scatter-plot represent?

    (A) The data of an individual student.
    (B) The data of the entire class as a whole.
    (C) The total amount of time students spent studying for the exam.
    (D) The average score that students in the class earned on the exam.

5. According to the scatter-plot above, the student who scored a 100 on the exam studied for how many hours?

    (A) 2
    (B) 3
    (C) 4
    (D) 5

6. Based on the information shown in the scatter-plot, what could a student who studied for 30 minutes expect to score on the exam?

    (A) 45
    (B) 65
    (C) 75
    (D) 85

7. The graph below shows the relationship between the outside temperature and the dollar amount spent on oil for heat.

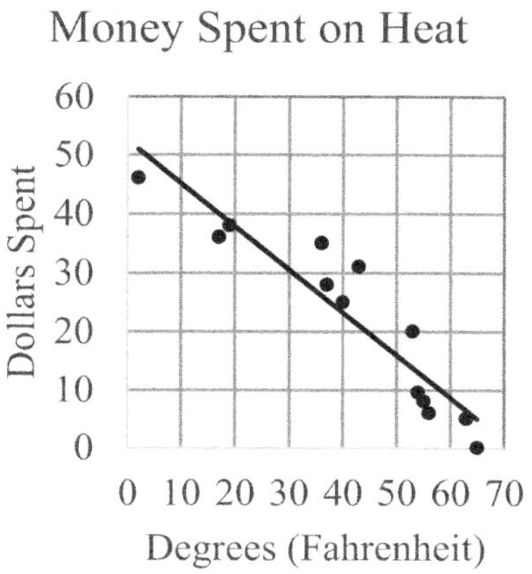

Using the line of best fit, how much money would a homeowner expect to spend on oil for heat when the temperature is 20°?

    (A) \$20
    (B) \$37
    (C) \$40
    (D) \$45

Use the information below to answer the next 3 questions.

A restaurant graphed the amount of money it made on Wednesday night on the scatter-plot below.

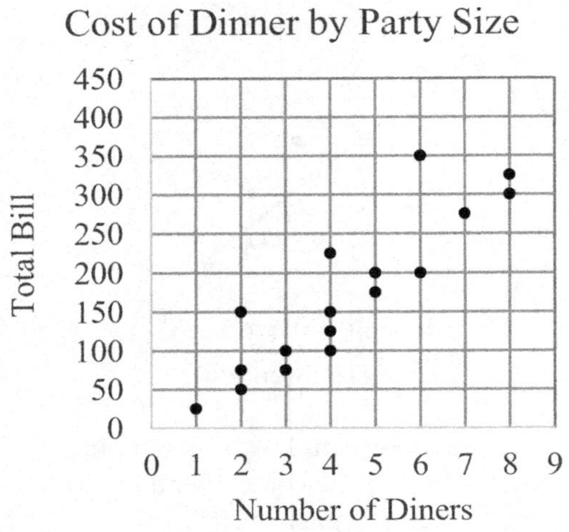

8. How many parties paid for dinner that Wednesday night?

(A) 8
(B) 16
(C) 17
(D) 74

9. What was the median cost of dinner, as determined by the size of the bill?

(A) 130
(B) 150
(C) 200
(D) 225

10. For a party of two diners, what was the average per-party price paid for dinner?

(A) $\dfrac{50+75+150}{2}$

(B) $\dfrac{50+75+150}{3}$

(C) $\dfrac{50+75+150}{2+2+2}$

(D) $\dfrac{50+75+150}{3+3+3}$

Use the information below to answer the next 3 questions.

The histogram below shows the weights of everyone who participated in an eating study.

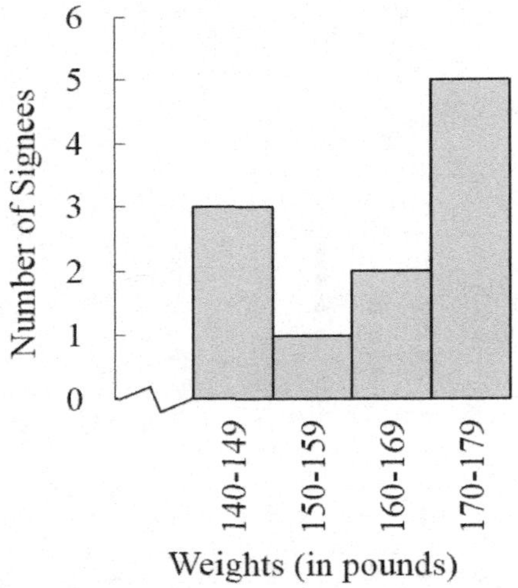

11. How many people weighed less than 170 pounds?

(A) 2
(B) 4
(C) 6
(D) 11

12. What is the median weight-range of the signees surveyed?

(A) 140-149 lbs.
(B) 150-159 lbs.
(C) 160-169 lbs.
(D) 170-179 lbs.

13. Based on the information in the histogram, which of the following statements is true?

(A) Each column represents the total weight of signees responding to a study.
(B) Each column represents the total number of signees responding to a study.
(C) Each column represents the total number of signees falling into a weight range.
(D) More signees fall into the 170-179 weight range than all other weight ranges combined.

14. The stem-and-leaf plot below shows the number of minutes Kenneth spent exercising each day, where 3 | 1 represents 31 minutes.

Stem	Leaf
3	1 2 5 5 6
4	1 2 3 5 6
5	1 2 3 3 5 7 7
6	1 2 2 3 6 6
7	4 7 8

For how many days did he keep track of his time spent exercising?

(A) 26
(B) 31
(C) 52
(D) 78

The stem-and-leaf plot below shows the grade each student in a class earned on a science test. Use this plot to answer the next 2 questions.

Stem	Leaf
7	2 6 8 9
8	1 3 4 6 7 7 8 9
9	2 3 7 8 9

15. What is the median score of the class?

(A) 81
(B) 86
(C) 87
(D) 88

16. What is the range of scores in the class?

(A) 10
(B) 17
(C) 20
(D) 27

17. A teacher needs to order pencils for her students. Each box costs $0.90, with a flat shipping fee added to each order. The table gives the total cost, including shipping, for three different order sizes. There is no sales tax.

COST OF PENCILS

Boxes Ordered	Total Order Cost
1	$3.89
5	$7.49
10	$11.99

What is the shipping charge per order?

(A) $1.19
(B) $1.99
(C) $2.49
(D) $2.99

18. A school's art department wanted to increase its budget by holding a fundraiser. It made the table shown to keep track of their total budget, including the fundraising income.

TOTAL BUDGET

Week	Number of Students
1	$1,000
2	$1,555
3	$1,710
4	$1,965
5	$2,220

After Week 3, how much did the fundraiser bring in each week?

(A) $55
(B) $155
(C) $255
(D) $555

Quantitative Comparison Practice

Answer Choices:

(A) The amount in column A is greater.
(B) The amount in column B is greater.
(C) The two amounts are equal.
(D) The relationship cannot be determined from the information provided.

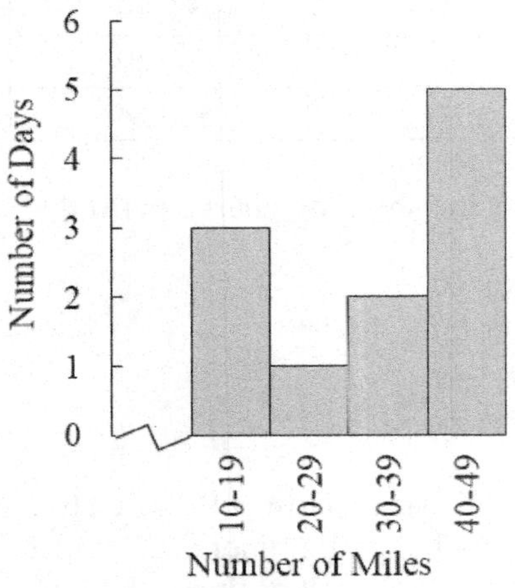

The histogram shows the number of miles travelled by a bus over several days.

	Column A	Column B
19.	The number of days it travelled fewer than 40 miles	The number of days it travelled more than 40 miles

The following table shows the price of tea at a local shop.

COST OF TEA

Ounces of Tea	Total Cost
8	\$8.80
16	\$16.00
24	\$21.60
32	\$25.60

	Column A	Column B
20.	The price per ounce of 8 ounces of tea	The price per ounce of 24 ounces of tea

Data & Probability Mixed Practice

1. Luna is drawing twice from a box that contains 7 blue, 8 red, and 9 green marbles. What is the probability that she will draw a green marble the first draw and a red marble the second draw without replacement?

   (A) $\frac{3}{23}$

   (B) $\frac{3}{24}$

   (C) $\frac{7}{72}$

   (D) $\frac{7}{69}$

2. Jennie is rolling a 10-sided dice two times. Each side has a different number on it, from 1 to 10. What is the probability that Jennie will roll a prime number both times?

   (A) $\frac{1}{4}$

   (B) $\frac{2}{15}$

   (C) $\frac{4}{25}$

   (D) $\frac{1}{5}$

3. Fifteen students in Mr. Smith's algebra class took an algebra quiz last Friday. Ben was sick that day, so he did not take the exam. He will do a make-up quiz today. The class average was 80. If Mr. Smith wants to have a class average of 82, what score does Ben need to get on his quiz?

(A) 80
(B) 82
(C) 100
(D) 112

4. The range of the set containing 2, 6, 8, 12, and x is equal to 16. What is the mean of the data set?

(A) 4.5
(B) 8.3
(C) 9.2
(D) 14

5. Which set has the mode with the smallest value?

(A) 4, 5, 4, 8, 4, 6, 2, 4, 5
(B) 10, 8, 9, 4, 4, 8, 8, 10
(C) 3, 6, 2, 5, 3, 7, 4, 3, 5
(D) 4, 4, 5, 6, 6, 6, 6, 7, 7

6. The pie graph shows the distribution of how Nam spent his time on a weekend.

How many hours did Nam spend sleeping?

(A) 10
(B) 12
(C) 20
(D) 25

7. 4 unique squares with side lengths 4, 5, 6, and 7 respectively are presented on the bulletin board. What is the average (arithmetic mean) of their area?

(A) 25.5
(B) 28.5
(C) 31.5
(D) 35.5

8. Lily's bakery shop sells different pastries. The chart below shows the number of each pastry sold on a Monday.

Pastry	**Number Sold**
Croissants	15
Brownies	10
Macarons	8
Cookies	20
Tarts	12
Cannolis	16
Doughnut	27

Which pastry corresponds to the **median** number of pastries sold?

(A) Macarons
(B) Brownies
(C) Croissants
(D) Tarts

The stem-and-leaf plot below shows the number of laptops each company owns in a neighborhood. Use this plot to answer the next 2 questions.

Stem	Leaf
3	0 1 2 2 7 8 8
4	2 4 5 8 8 8
5	1 3 3 4 5 5

9. What is the mode of the number of laptops owned by each company in the neighborhood?

(A) 42
(B) 48
(C) 53
(D) 55

10. What is the mean of number of median own by each company in the neighborhood?

(A) 44
(B) 45
(C) 48
(D) 50

11. Compare the following and choose the correct answer:

Laura rolls one standard, six-sided dice, each of which is numbered from 1 through 6.

Column A	Column B
The probability of rolling an even number.	The probability of rolling an odd number.

(A) The amount in column A is greater.
(B) The amount in column B is greater.
(C) The two amounts are equal.
(D) The relationship cannot be determined from the information provided.

12. Compare the following and choose the correct answer:

Total Students Per Class

Class	Number of Students
Math	35
ELA	25
Science	22
History	30
Gym	40

Column A	Column B
The mean of the number of students per class.	The median of the number of students per class.

(A) The amount in column A is greater.
(B) The amount in column B is greater.
(C) The two amounts are equal.
(D) The relationship cannot be determined from the information provided.

The Essay

Overview

The essay is the only section of the test that is not multiple-choice. It is also the only section that is not scored by the ERB. Instead, copies of your essay will be sent to every school to which you apply. The admissions departments will read your essay, and they will use it as part of your application. This means that even though it is not scored, the essay is still a very important part of the test.

You will have 30 minutes to complete your essay. Consider mapping out your time as follows:

> 3 minutes – PLAN. Brainstorm ideas and jot down notes. Organize your essay into five paragraphs (a brief introduction, three body paragraphs, and a brief conclusion).
>
> 25 minutes – WRITE. If you've planned well, the actual writing of the essay should not be difficult.
>
> 2 minutes – PROOFREAD. This is very important! You want to catch and fix all errors in punctuation, spelling and grammar. Never let anyone else read what you have written before you have read it to yourself carefully.

Every essay prompt will as you do the same thing – to talk about yourself in some way.

Below are 5 essay prompts for you to practice under a timed setting.

1. If you could go anywhere on earth you haven't been before, where would you go?
2. What would you do with one million dollars?
3. If you could change one thing about your school, what would it be?
4. Tell about someone who inspires you.
5. Tell about your favorite book. Why is it your favorite?

How to Use This Section

Choose one of the above 5 topics. Set a timer for 30 minutes, then make your notes and write your essay on a separate sheet of lined paper. Copy the prompt into the box at the top of the essay page and begin writing. You are limited to two pages for the essay, so plan accordingly. Remember to proofread!

Tutorverse Tips!

Remember that the essay has two purposes. Schools want to see how well you can write and also want to learn something about you as a person. Think of the essay as a written interview. If you are asked to describe the best birthday party you have ever attended, consider focusing on the experience itself and how it made you feel. Why was the birthday party special to you? How did the party make you feel? Instead of focusing only on describing the events that happened, ask yourself "So what?" – why were the events special?

Remember to plan thoroughly before you start writing and to proofread carefully when you are done. The planning is important because admissions directors can identify well organized essays versus those essays that lack structure. Proofreading is important because you want to remove careless mistakes – such as simple punctuation or spelling errors – that will reflect poorly on your writing skills.

Final Practice Test (Form B)

Overview

The practice test is designed to assess your understanding of key skills and concepts. It is important to take the final practice test after completing the diagnostic test and after you have spent time studying and practicing.

Though this practice test assesses your mastery of certain skills and concepts that you may see on the actual exam, there is one primary differences between this practice test and the actual exam. The practice test is scored differently from how the actual exam is scored. For example, though this test contains the same number of questions as the actual exam, a number of questions included will not be scored (and are included for analysis purposes only).

Lastly, note that a number of questions on the actual test will not be scored, as they are included for research purposes only. However, students will not know which questions on the actual test will not be scored. For practice purposes, this diagnostic test includes the same number of questions as the actual test, including the number of questions that will not be scored. This gives students a more realistic experience in terms of test taking.

Because of this, this practice test should be used to gauge your mastery over skills and concepts, *not* as a gauge of how you will score on the test.

Format

The format of the practice test is similar to that of the actual test, and includes the following sections:

Practice Test Section	**Questions**	**Time Limit**
Verbal Reasoning	40	20 minutes
Quantitative Reasoning	37	35 minutes
Break #1	N/A	5 minutes
Reading Comprehension	36	35 minutes
Mathematics Achievement	47	40 minutes
Break #2	N/A	5 minutes
Essay Prompt	1	30 minutes
Total	**161**	**170 minutes**

Answering

Use the answer sheet provided on the next several pages to record your answers. You may wish to tear these pages out of the workbook.

Practice Test Answer Sheet

Section 1: Verbal Reasoning

1. Ⓐ Ⓑ Ⓒ Ⓓ
2. Ⓐ Ⓑ Ⓒ Ⓓ
3. Ⓐ Ⓑ Ⓒ Ⓓ
4. Ⓐ Ⓑ Ⓒ Ⓓ
5. Ⓐ Ⓑ Ⓒ Ⓓ
6. Ⓐ Ⓑ Ⓒ Ⓓ
7. Ⓐ Ⓑ Ⓒ Ⓓ
8. Ⓐ Ⓑ Ⓒ Ⓓ
9. Ⓐ Ⓑ Ⓒ Ⓓ
10. Ⓐ Ⓑ Ⓒ Ⓓ
11. Ⓐ Ⓑ Ⓒ Ⓓ
12. Ⓐ Ⓑ Ⓒ Ⓓ
13. Ⓐ Ⓑ Ⓒ Ⓓ
14. Ⓐ Ⓑ Ⓒ Ⓓ
15. Ⓐ Ⓑ Ⓒ Ⓓ
16. Ⓐ Ⓑ Ⓒ Ⓓ
17. Ⓐ Ⓑ Ⓒ Ⓓ
18. Ⓐ Ⓑ Ⓒ Ⓓ
19. Ⓐ Ⓑ Ⓒ Ⓓ
20. Ⓐ Ⓑ Ⓒ Ⓓ
21. Ⓐ Ⓑ Ⓒ Ⓓ
22. Ⓐ Ⓑ Ⓒ Ⓓ
23. Ⓐ Ⓑ Ⓒ Ⓓ
24. Ⓐ Ⓑ Ⓒ Ⓓ
25. Ⓐ Ⓑ Ⓒ Ⓓ
26. Ⓐ Ⓑ Ⓒ Ⓓ
27. Ⓐ Ⓑ Ⓒ Ⓓ
28. Ⓐ Ⓑ Ⓒ Ⓓ
29. Ⓐ Ⓑ Ⓒ Ⓓ
30. Ⓐ Ⓑ Ⓒ Ⓓ
31. Ⓐ Ⓑ Ⓒ Ⓓ
32. Ⓐ Ⓑ Ⓒ Ⓓ
33. Ⓐ Ⓑ Ⓒ Ⓓ
34. Ⓐ Ⓑ Ⓒ Ⓓ
35. Ⓐ Ⓑ Ⓒ Ⓓ
36. Ⓐ Ⓑ Ⓒ Ⓓ
37. Ⓐ Ⓑ Ⓒ Ⓓ
38. Ⓐ Ⓑ Ⓒ Ⓓ
39. Ⓐ Ⓑ Ⓒ Ⓓ
40. Ⓐ Ⓑ Ⓒ Ⓓ

Section 2: Quantitative Reasoning

1. Ⓐ Ⓑ Ⓒ Ⓓ
2. Ⓐ Ⓑ Ⓒ Ⓓ
3. Ⓐ Ⓑ Ⓒ Ⓓ
4. Ⓐ Ⓑ Ⓒ Ⓓ
5. Ⓐ Ⓑ Ⓒ Ⓓ
6. Ⓐ Ⓑ Ⓒ Ⓓ
7. Ⓐ Ⓑ Ⓒ Ⓓ
8. Ⓐ Ⓑ Ⓒ Ⓓ
9. Ⓐ Ⓑ Ⓒ Ⓓ
10. Ⓐ Ⓑ Ⓒ Ⓓ
11. Ⓐ Ⓑ Ⓒ Ⓓ
12. Ⓐ Ⓑ Ⓒ Ⓓ
13. Ⓐ Ⓑ Ⓒ Ⓓ
14. Ⓐ Ⓑ Ⓒ Ⓓ
15. Ⓐ Ⓑ Ⓒ Ⓓ
16. Ⓐ Ⓑ Ⓒ Ⓓ
17. Ⓐ Ⓑ Ⓒ Ⓓ
18. Ⓐ Ⓑ Ⓒ Ⓓ
19. Ⓐ Ⓑ Ⓒ Ⓓ
20. Ⓐ Ⓑ Ⓒ Ⓓ
21. Ⓐ Ⓑ Ⓒ Ⓓ
22. Ⓐ Ⓑ Ⓒ Ⓓ
23. Ⓐ Ⓑ Ⓒ Ⓓ
24. Ⓐ Ⓑ Ⓒ Ⓓ
25. Ⓐ Ⓑ Ⓒ Ⓓ
26. Ⓐ Ⓑ Ⓒ Ⓓ
27. Ⓐ Ⓑ Ⓒ Ⓓ
28. Ⓐ Ⓑ Ⓒ Ⓓ
29. Ⓐ Ⓑ Ⓒ Ⓓ
30. Ⓐ Ⓑ Ⓒ Ⓓ
31. Ⓐ Ⓑ Ⓒ Ⓓ
32. Ⓐ Ⓑ Ⓒ Ⓓ
33. Ⓐ Ⓑ Ⓒ Ⓓ
34. Ⓐ Ⓑ Ⓒ Ⓓ
35. Ⓐ Ⓑ Ⓒ Ⓓ
36. Ⓐ Ⓑ Ⓒ Ⓓ
37. Ⓐ Ⓑ Ⓒ Ⓓ

Section 3: Reading Comprehension

1. Ⓐ Ⓑ Ⓒ Ⓓ	10. Ⓐ Ⓑ Ⓒ Ⓓ	19. Ⓐ Ⓑ Ⓒ Ⓓ	28. Ⓐ Ⓑ Ⓒ Ⓓ
2. Ⓐ Ⓑ Ⓒ Ⓓ	11. Ⓐ Ⓑ Ⓒ Ⓓ	20. Ⓐ Ⓑ Ⓒ Ⓓ	29. Ⓐ Ⓑ Ⓒ Ⓓ
3. Ⓐ Ⓑ Ⓒ Ⓓ	12. Ⓐ Ⓑ Ⓒ Ⓓ	21. Ⓐ Ⓑ Ⓒ Ⓓ	30. Ⓐ Ⓑ Ⓒ Ⓓ
4. Ⓐ Ⓑ Ⓒ Ⓓ	13. Ⓐ Ⓑ Ⓒ Ⓓ	22. Ⓐ Ⓑ Ⓒ Ⓓ	31. Ⓐ Ⓑ Ⓒ Ⓓ
5. Ⓐ Ⓑ Ⓒ Ⓓ	14. Ⓐ Ⓑ Ⓒ Ⓓ	23. Ⓐ Ⓑ Ⓒ Ⓓ	32. Ⓐ Ⓑ Ⓒ Ⓓ
6. Ⓐ Ⓑ Ⓒ Ⓓ	15. Ⓐ Ⓑ Ⓒ Ⓓ	24. Ⓐ Ⓑ Ⓒ Ⓓ	33. Ⓐ Ⓑ Ⓒ Ⓓ
7. Ⓐ Ⓑ Ⓒ Ⓓ	16. Ⓐ Ⓑ Ⓒ Ⓓ	25. Ⓐ Ⓑ Ⓒ Ⓓ	34. Ⓐ Ⓑ Ⓒ Ⓓ
8. Ⓐ Ⓑ Ⓒ Ⓓ	17. Ⓐ Ⓑ Ⓒ Ⓓ	26. Ⓐ Ⓑ Ⓒ Ⓓ	35. Ⓐ Ⓑ Ⓒ Ⓓ
9. Ⓐ Ⓑ Ⓒ Ⓓ	18. Ⓐ Ⓑ Ⓒ Ⓓ	27. Ⓐ Ⓑ Ⓒ Ⓓ	36. Ⓐ Ⓑ Ⓒ Ⓓ

Section 4: Mathematics Achievement

1. Ⓐ Ⓑ Ⓒ Ⓓ	13. Ⓐ Ⓑ Ⓒ Ⓓ	25. Ⓐ Ⓑ Ⓒ Ⓓ	37. Ⓐ Ⓑ Ⓒ Ⓓ
2. Ⓐ Ⓑ Ⓒ Ⓓ	14. Ⓐ Ⓑ Ⓒ Ⓓ	26. Ⓐ Ⓑ Ⓒ Ⓓ	38. Ⓐ Ⓑ Ⓒ Ⓓ
3. Ⓐ Ⓑ Ⓒ Ⓓ	15. Ⓐ Ⓑ Ⓒ Ⓓ	27. Ⓐ Ⓑ Ⓒ Ⓓ	39. Ⓐ Ⓑ Ⓒ Ⓓ
4. Ⓐ Ⓑ Ⓒ Ⓓ	16. Ⓐ Ⓑ Ⓒ Ⓓ	28. Ⓐ Ⓑ Ⓒ Ⓓ	40. Ⓐ Ⓑ Ⓒ Ⓓ
5. Ⓐ Ⓑ Ⓒ Ⓓ	17. Ⓐ Ⓑ Ⓒ Ⓓ	29. Ⓐ Ⓑ Ⓒ Ⓓ	41. Ⓐ Ⓑ Ⓒ Ⓓ
6. Ⓐ Ⓑ Ⓒ Ⓓ	18. Ⓐ Ⓑ Ⓒ Ⓓ	30. Ⓐ Ⓑ Ⓒ Ⓓ	42. Ⓐ Ⓑ Ⓒ Ⓓ
7. Ⓐ Ⓑ Ⓒ Ⓓ	19. Ⓐ Ⓑ Ⓒ Ⓓ	31. Ⓐ Ⓑ Ⓒ Ⓓ	43. Ⓐ Ⓑ Ⓒ Ⓓ
8. Ⓐ Ⓑ Ⓒ Ⓓ	20. Ⓐ Ⓑ Ⓒ Ⓓ	32. Ⓐ Ⓑ Ⓒ Ⓓ	44. Ⓐ Ⓑ Ⓒ Ⓓ
9. Ⓐ Ⓑ Ⓒ Ⓓ	21. Ⓐ Ⓑ Ⓒ Ⓓ	33. Ⓐ Ⓑ Ⓒ Ⓓ	45. Ⓐ Ⓑ Ⓒ Ⓓ
10. Ⓐ Ⓑ Ⓒ Ⓓ	22. Ⓐ Ⓑ Ⓒ Ⓓ	34. Ⓐ Ⓑ Ⓒ Ⓓ	46. Ⓐ Ⓑ Ⓒ Ⓓ
11. Ⓐ Ⓑ Ⓒ Ⓓ	23. Ⓐ Ⓑ Ⓒ Ⓓ	35. Ⓐ Ⓑ Ⓒ Ⓓ	47. Ⓐ Ⓑ Ⓒ Ⓓ
12. Ⓐ Ⓑ Ⓒ Ⓓ	24. Ⓐ Ⓑ Ⓒ Ⓓ	36. Ⓐ Ⓑ Ⓒ Ⓓ	

Section 5: Essay

Final Practice Test (Form B)

VR

Section 1
Verbal Reasoning

1

Questions: 40

Time Limit: 20 minutes

There are two different types of questions in this section. Each question has four answer choices. Record your answer choice on your answer sheet. Once you have finished work on Part One, you may continue to work on Part Two. Writing or taking notes in your test booklet is permitted.

Part One – Synonyms

In Part One, four possible answers follow a word written in capital letters. Choose one of the four possible answers that is most nearly the same meaning as the word in capital letters.

Sample Question:

BOON:

(A) benefit
(B) trouble
(C) vibration
(D) virtue

Sample Answer:

(A) B C D

Part Two – Sentence Completion

In Part Two, four possible answers follow a sentence with one missing word denoted by one blank. The correct answer is the single word that contextually completes the sentence.

Sample Question:

Joe forgot to bring his books to school and was ------- for class.

(A) absent
(B) ready
(C) unprepared
(D) waiting

Sample Answer:

A B (C) D

1

Part One – Synonyms

VR

Directions: Select the word that is most nearly the same in meaning as the word in capital letters.

1. AUTHENTIC:

    (A) basic
    (B) fake
    (C) genuine
    (D) written

2. SUPERIOR:

    (A) below
    (B) better
    (C) delicious
    (D) frequent

3. ACCURATE:

    (A) insincere
    (B) miserable
    (C) prized
    (D) true

4. ELIGIBLE:

    (A) allowed
    (B) barred
    (C) forced
    (D) required

5. CAPACITY:

    (A) amount
    (B) decision
    (C) envy
    (D) patience

6. NAVIGATE:

    (A) dominate
    (B) escape
    (C) prevent
    (D) steer

7. UNRULY:

    (A) broken
    (B) orderly
    (C) timid
    (D) wild

8. SUBTLE:

    (A) delicate
    (B) flooded
    (C) sunken
    (D) unbelievable

9. ABODE:

    (A) dwelling
    (B) homage
    (C) momentum
    (D) tolerance

10. MELANCHOLY:

    (A) affinity
    (B) fondness
    (C) leisure
    (D) sorrow

11. POTENTIAL:

    (A) conceivable
    (B) impossible
    (C) lavish
    (D) powerful

12. VOLUME:

    (A) figment
    (B) quantity
    (C) silence
    (D) siren

Go on to the next page. ➡

VR

1

13. AGILE:

(A) awkward
(B) curious
(C) nimble
(D) shy

14. ASSIMILATE:

(A) alleviate
(B) injure
(C) incorporate
(D) publicize

15. HAPHAZARD:

(A) dangerous
(B) fatal
(C) random
(D) unsafe

16. ORTHODOX:

(A) important
(B) impressive
(C) perfect
(D) traditional

17. PERSUASIVE:

(A) compelling
(B) stubborn
(C) sophisticated
(D) unconvincing

18. TIRADE:

(A) criticism
(B) ovation
(C) parade
(D) prodigy

19. VILIFY:

(A) consult
(B) criticize
(C) enable
(D) notice

20. GLUT:

(A) atrocity
(B) disorder
(C) instinct
(D) surplus

21. INUNDATE:

(A) bombard
(B) caress
(C) devastate
(D) estimate

Go on to the next page.

1

VR

Part Two – Sentence Completion

Directions: Select the word that best completes the meaning of the sentence.

22. Instead of running to ------- the stick, Caitlin's dog wagged its tail and looked blankly at her master.

    (A) incorporate
    (B) observe
    (C) release
    (D) retrieve

23. High taxes placed on gasoline have helped to ------- the number of cars on the road, as the rising cost of driving has encouraged carpooling.

    (A) accelerate
    (B) develop
    (C) diminish
    (D) restore

24. Divya could not understand why Evan was always so ------- toward her, especially since she had been nothing but nice to him.

    (A) hostile
    (B) sluggish
    (C) vibrant
    (D) welcoming

25. Many people can easily spot the difference between a ------- smile and a forced smile.

    (A) false
    (B) flexible
    (C) natural
    (D) widespread

26. Beavers, considered by many to be one of the most ------- creatures, can often be observed tirelessly felling trees and working on their dams.

    (A) content
    (B) industrious
    (C) private
    (D) useless

27. Friendly and liked by many, Ned's ------- grew among the rich and powerful, allowing him to control the outcome of many important decisions.

    (A) apprehension
    (B) discretion
    (C) influence
    (D) mistrust

28. In order to educate its visitors, the museum has focused on growing its collection by ------- new, rare, and significant artifacts.

    (A) acquiring
    (B) concealing
    (C) contaminating
    (D) demolishing

29. After the big storm, the government helped many families, whose homes and businesses had been completely destroyed, to ------- new houses and stores.

    (A) certify
    (B) construct
    (C) renovate
    (D) stifle

30. A(n) ------- change in the school's dismissal process surprised the parents.

    (A) abrupt
    (B) cautious
    (C) planned
    (D) unwilling

Go on to the next page. ➡

VR

1

31. Though he read for hours a day, Jeff eventually began to grow ------- as he realized he might not actually finish the thousand-page book before his book report was due.

(A) cautious
(B) glum
(C) heartened
(D) nonchalant

32. Kelly delivered such a passionate and convincing argument that even her critics and opponents ------- with her points.

(A) concurred
(B) coped
(C) feuded
(D) opposed

33. Because in the past I have often arrived at false conclusions, I no longer ------- to know a person before I have had a chance to speak with him at length.

(A) decline
(B) fail
(C) intervene
(D) presume

34. In the eyes of her fans, the athlete was a hero because she remained ------- in the face of many challenges and refused to give up on her goals.

(A) careful
(B) humane
(C) steadfast
(D) ungainly

35. Several hundred years ago, travelling between Europe and the United States in a matter of hours would not have seemed -------, as such a journey took many days.

(A) astounding
(B) difficult
(C) feasible
(D) impractical

36. It is important to ------- despite difficulties and setbacks, for short of getting lucky, hard work and persistence is the only way to achieve one's dreams and goals.

(A) abstain
(B) cooperate
(C) hover
(D) persevere

37. Because Jonas ------- many positive values, others see him as a role model worthy of emulating.

(A) disputes
(B) exemplifies
(C) recalls
(D) reject

38. The fact that Lewis and Clark still chose to embark on their famous expedition in spite of great risk and uncertainty is a ------- of the human spirit.

(A) fantasy
(B) guarantee
(C) shock
(D) testament

39. Because several days had already elapsed since the disaster, it was ------- that emergency supplies reach those in need as soon as possible.

(A) imminent
(B) imperative
(C) inconsequential
(D) virtuous

40. For many viewers, the one-sided game was neither fun nor entertaining, as the underdog was ------- by the top-ranked team.

(A) annihilated
(B) dumbfounded
(C) practiced
(D) transformed

STOP. Do not go on until instructed to do so.

STOP

2

Section 2
Quantitative Reasoning

QR

Questions: 37

Time Limit: 35 minutes

This section contains two parts. As soon as you finish Part One, continue on to Part Two. Remember to fill in the corresponding bubbles on your answer sheet. You may write in your test booklet.

Part One – Word Problems

Each question in this part is a word problem followed by four answer choices. Select the best answer from the four answer choices. You may write in your test booklet.

Example: A square has an area of 16 square inches. What is the perimeter, in inches?

(A) 4
(B) 8
(C) 16
(D) 64

Example Answer

A B (C) D

The correct answer is 16, so circle C is darkened.

Part Two – Quantitative Comparison

Part Two is comprised of quantitative comparisons between amounts shown in Column A and Column B. Using the given information, compare the two amounts and choose one of the answer choices below:

(A) The amount in Column A is greater.
(B) The amount in Column B is greater.
(C) The two amounts are equal.
(D) The relationship cannot be determined from the information provided.

Example:

$x < 0$

Column A	Column B
x^2	x^3

Example Answer

(A) B C D

Even though we don't know exactly what the value of x is, the given information states that x must be a negative number. Squaring a negative number results in a positive number. Raising a negative number to the third power results in a negative number, so the amount in Column A must be greater than the amount in Column B.

QR

Part One – Word Problems

2

Directions – Choose the best of the four possible answers.

1. The circle graph shows the favorite fruit of 360 shoppers at a farmer's market.

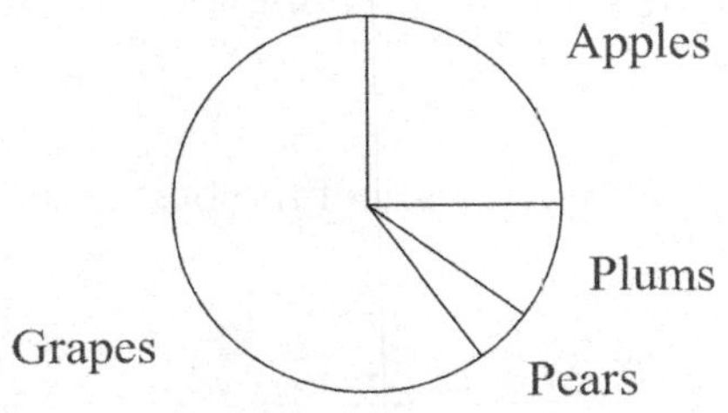

The portion labeled Apples has a central angle of 90°. How many of the shoppers chose a fruit other than apples as their favorite fruit?

(A) 45
(B) 90
(C) 180
(D) 270

2. Triangle *ABC* has been transformed to produce Triangle *A'B'C'*.

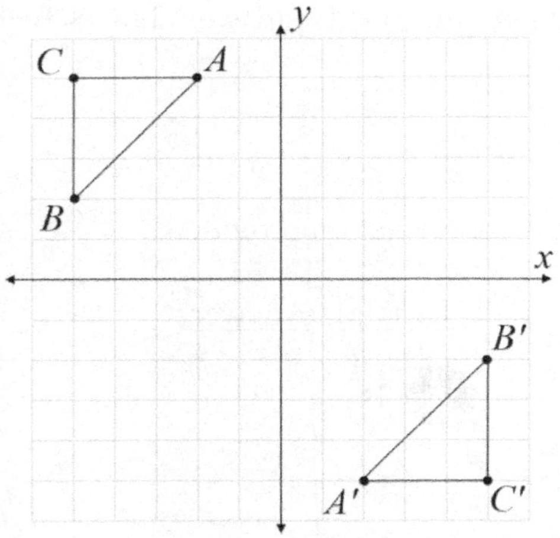

Which type of transformation was performed?

(A) translation
(B) rotation
(C) dilation
(D) reflection over the *x*-axis

3. Which value which most closely approximates the expression $81^2 \div 19^2$?

(A) 2
(B) 4
(C) 8
(D) 16

4. The bar graph shows the number of kilometers Ming Yu ran each day for one week.

Kilometers Run Each Day

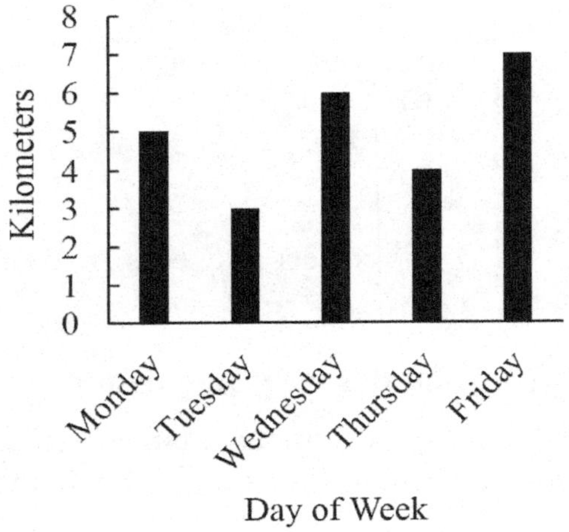

According to the graph, what is the median number of kilometers Ming Yu ran last week?

(A) 4
(B) 5
(C) 6
(D) 7

Go on to the next page. ➡

2

QR

5. Use the figure shown below to answer the question. All sides that appear parallel are parallel.

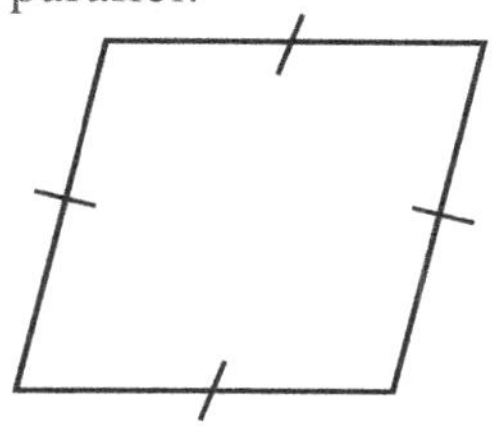

Which type of quadrilateral is shown above?

(A) square
(B) rhombus
(C) rectangle
(D) trapezoid

6. The below graph shows the relationship between the outside temperature and the number of ice cream cones a certain ice cream truck sells.

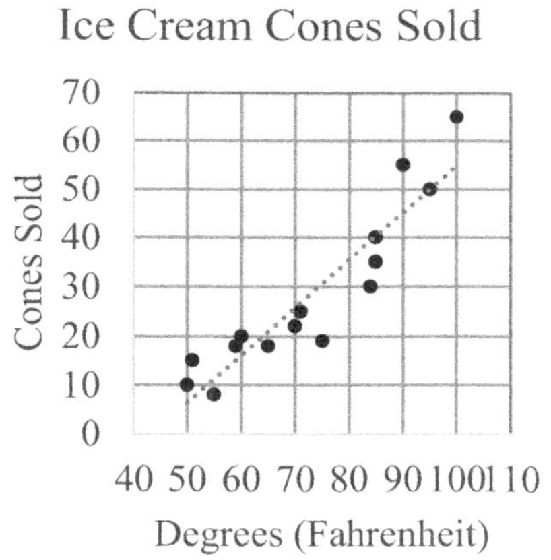

Using the line of best fit, how many ice cream cones would the truck expect to sell when the temperature is 65°?

(A) 15
(B) 20
(C) 45
(D) 105

7. The grid shows two vertices of a right triangle.

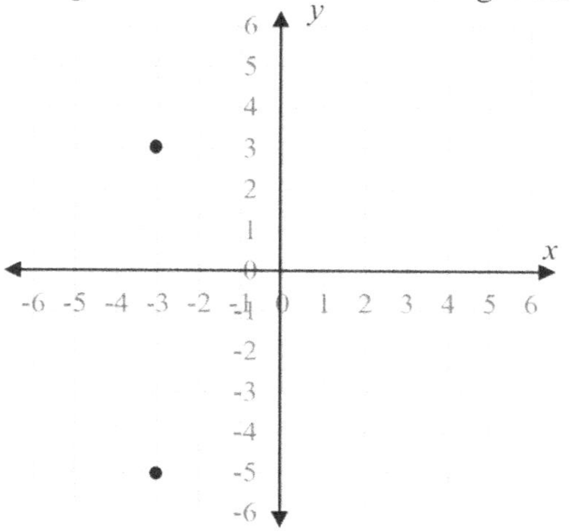

Which could be the coordinates of the third vertex of the right triangle?

(A) (0,4)
(B) (0,3)
(C) (5,0)
(D) (3,–3)

8. Jamie, Oscar, and Britney are all running at different speeds, as shown in the chart below.

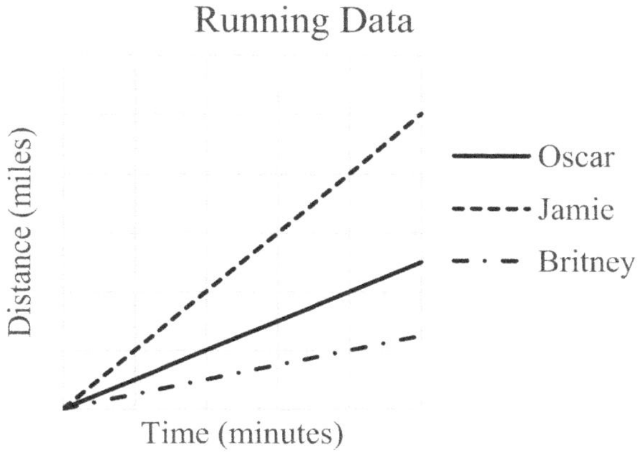

Which of the following lists their speeds in order from slowest to fastest?

(A) Jamie, Oscar, Britney
(B) Oscar, Britney, Jamie
(C) Britney, Oscar, Jamie
(D) Oscar, Jamie, Britney

Go on to the next page.

QR

2

9. $\sqrt{130}$ is closest to which of the following numbers?

(A) 11
(B) 12
(C) 60
(D) 70

10. Triangle *GHI* is similar to Triangle *JKL*.

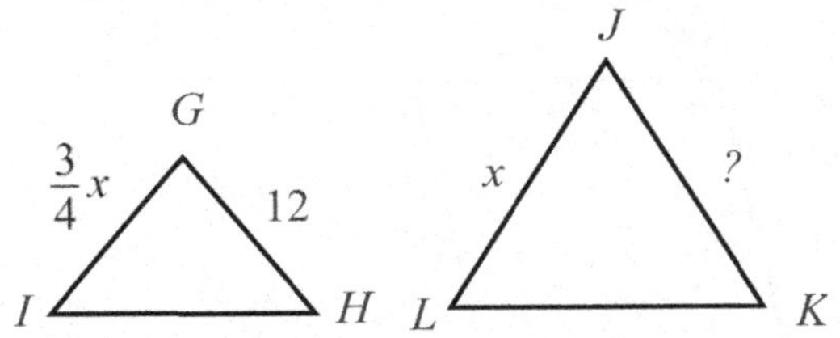

What is the length of side *JK*?

(A) 8
(B) 9
(C) 15
(D) 16

11. Which of the following graphs represents the equation $y = \frac{2}{3}x + 6$?

(A)

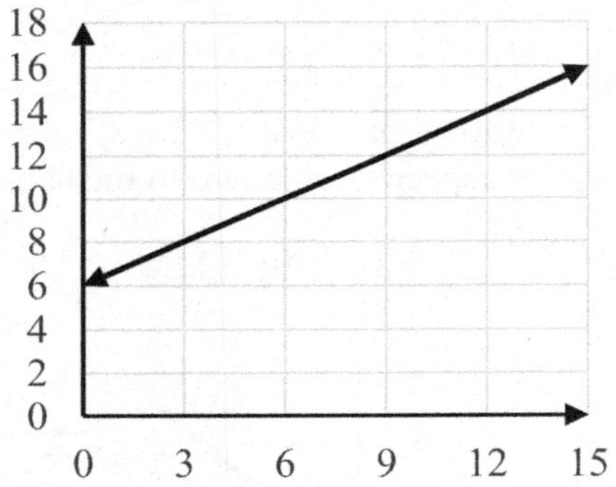

(C)

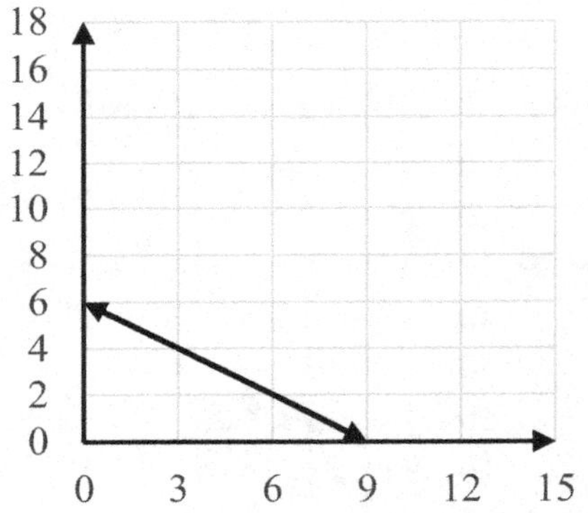

(B)

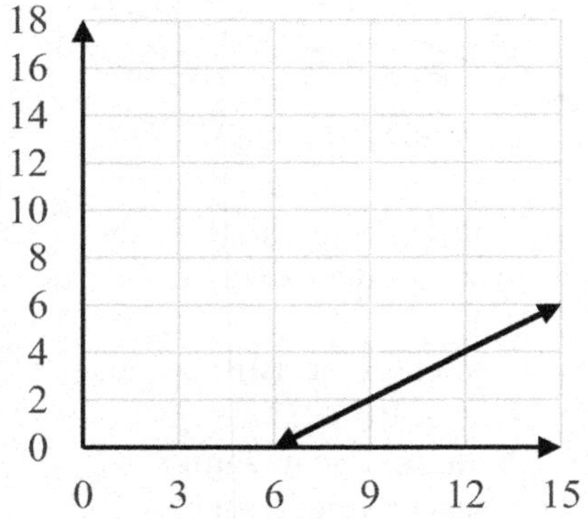

(D)

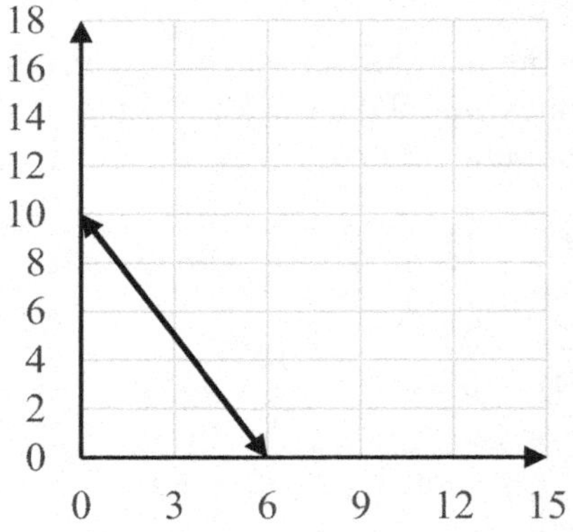

Go on to the next page.

2

QR

12. For her spring collection, Jackie's Jeans is spending between \$30,000 and \$50,000 producing different types of jeans. There are 10 weeks in the spring season. She plans to sell around 60-150 pairs of jeans per week. Profit is revenue minus cost. If she charges, on average, \$98 for a pair of jeans, approximately how much profit can she expect to make during the spring season, if profit is revenue minus cost?

(A) \$30,000
(B) \$40,000
(C) \$65,000
(D) \$105,000

13. In the figure shown below, angle x has a measure greater than 90°.

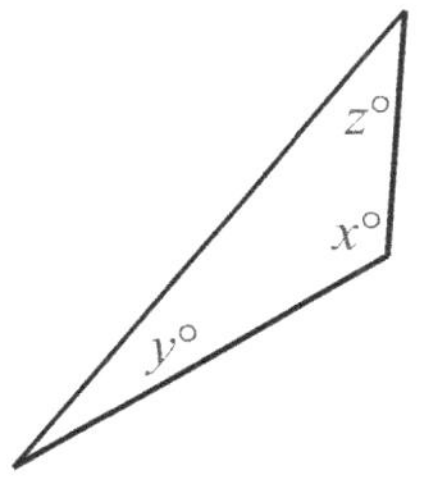

Which of the following could be the sum of $y + z$?

(A) 85
(B) 90
(C) 95
(D) 180

14. If x and y are different positive integers, and $7^x \times 7^y = 343$, what is the value of xy?

(A) 1
(B) 2
(C) 3
(D) 4

15. The graph shows Zhe's speed one day while driving to work.

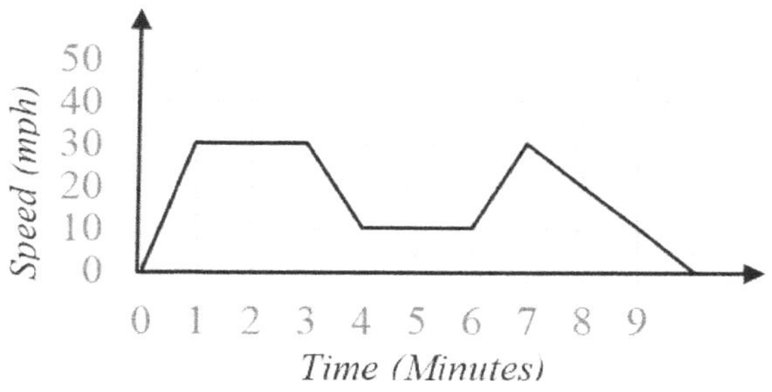

Which of the following **must** have happened between minutes 7 and 9?

(A) Zhe slowed her car to a stop.
(B) Zhe started driving downhill.
(C) Zhe slowed down but didn't stop.
(D) Zhe turned around and headed back towards home.

16. Chui is paid \$0.25 for each newspaper she delivers, plus a flat rate of \$20 per day. Which of the following expressions represents the total dollar amount Chui receives for a day when she delivers n newspapers?

(A) $5n$
(B) $20.25n$
(C) $20 + 0.25n$
(D) $20n + 0.25$

17. On a coordinate-plane, the center of a certain circle is located at the origin. A line segment is drawn from one side of the circle to the other, through its center, and represents the circle's diameter. If the line segment begins at point (–2,3), what are the coordinates of the other end of the line?

(A) (–2,–3)
(B) (–2,3)
(C) (2,–3)
(D) (2,3)

Go on to the next page. ➡

QR

2

18. Which fraction is closest to $1 \div 5$?

(A) $\frac{1}{3}$

(B) $\frac{1}{4}$

(C) $\frac{1}{6}$

(D) $\frac{3}{20}$

19. The table below shows the favorite flavor of ice cream of 7th graders in Erica's school.

FAVORITE FLAVOR OF ICE CREAM

Flavor	Number of Students
Chocolate	20
Vanilla	10
Mint	5
Cookies & Cream	10
Neapolitan	5

If a circle graph is made from the data, what will be the central angle of the portion of the graph that represents the number of 7th graders who like either chocolate or mint?

(A) 36°
(B) 108°
(C) 144°
(D) 180°

20. Mary has twice as much U.S. currency as Carol. Carol has 4 times as much U.S. currency as Susan. Which amount of U.S. currency can Mary NOT have?

(A) \$2
(B) \$4
(C) \$7
(D) \$10

21. The figure shows the first five elements of a pattern.

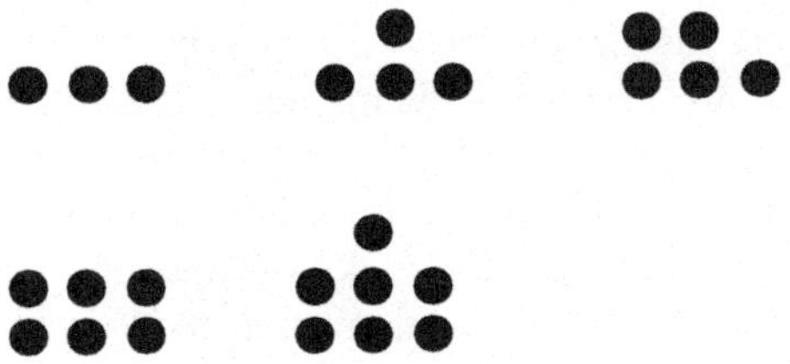

What is the sixth element of this pattern?

(A)

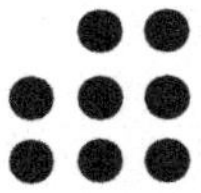

(B)

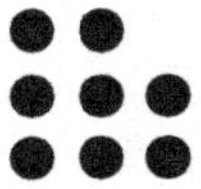

(C)

(D)

22. Allan drank $\frac{2}{3}$ of a full bottle of lemonade, which initially contained 96 fluid ounces of lemonade. He then mixed $\frac{1}{4}$ of what remained of the lemonade with 16 fluid ounces of water. What fraction of the resulting mixture was lemonade?

(A) $\frac{1}{3}$

(B) $\frac{1}{2}$

(C) $\frac{2}{3}$

(D) $\frac{3}{4}$

Go on to the next page.

2

Part Two – Quantitative Comparisons

QR

Directions – Compare the amount in Column A to the amount in Column B using the information provided in each question. All questions in this part have the following answer choices:

(A) The amount in column A is greater.
(B) The amount in column B is greater.
(C) The two amounts are equal.
(D) The relationship cannot be determined from the information provided.

	Column A	Column B
23.	2	The reciprocal of $\frac{1}{6}+\frac{1}{3}$

	Column A	Column B
24.	In a coordinate plane, the sum of the *x*-coordinate and *y*-coordinate of a point in the first quadrant	In a coordinate plane, the sum of the *x*-coordinate and *y*-coordinate of a point in the third quadrant

Line *AC* is shown below:

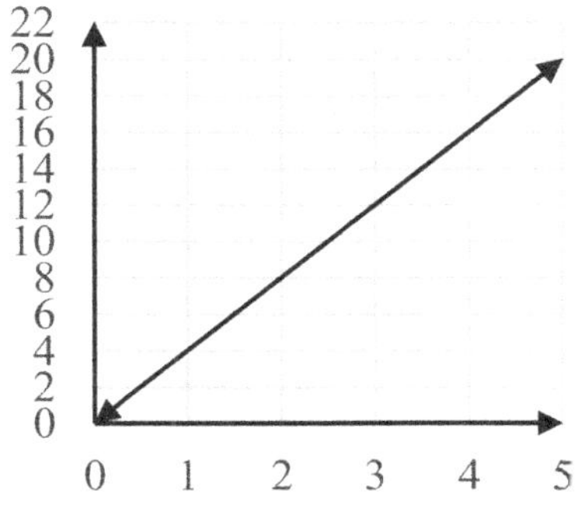

	Column A	Column B
25.	$\frac{1}{4}$	The slope of a line perpendicular to *AC*

	Column A	Column B
26.	$\sqrt{4.9}$	0.7

Rectangle *PQRS* is similar to Rectangle *TUVW*.

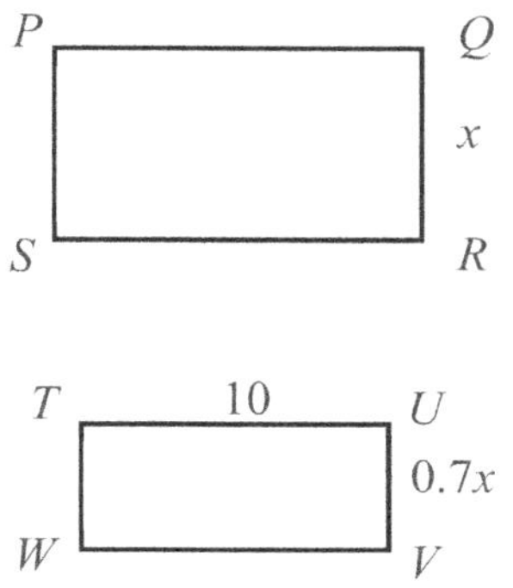

Note: Figures not drawn to scale.

	Column A	Column B
27.	The length of side *SR*	7

In a closet, there are three pairs of shoes: a red pair, a white pair, and a black pair. First, one shoe is chosen at random. Then, a second shoe is chosen at random, without replacement.

	Column A	Column B
28.	The probability of getting a matching pair	$\frac{1}{4}$

Go on to the next page.

QR

2

All questions in this part have the following answer choices:

(A) The amount in column A is greater.
(B) The amount in column B is greater.
(C) The two amounts are equal.
(D) The relationship cannot be determined from the information provided.

Casey lives 2 miles away from school. It takes Casey 15 minutes to bike home from school, but 40 minutes to walk home from school. Casey always bikes and walks at the same speed, no matter where he goes.

	Column A	Column B
29.	The time it takes Casey to bike 6 miles to the mall	The time it takes Casey to walk 3 miles to his friend's house

---

$$\frac{x}{5} + 3 = 28$$

$$7y - 4 = 31$$

	Column A	Column B
30.	x	$25y$

A swimming pool has a 3-foot-wide path around it as shown by the shaded area.

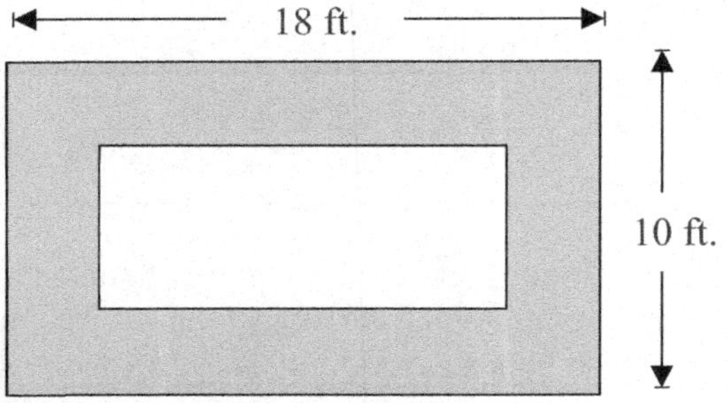

Note: Figures are not drawn to scale.

	Column A	Column B
31.	The area of the pool	The area of the path

To drive to the supermarket from home, Jerry takes Main Street for 5 miles and drives at an average speed of 20 miles per hour. To drive from the supermarket to the hardware store, Jerry takes Broadway for 1 mile at an average speed of 10 miles per hour.

	Column A	Column B
32.	The average amount of time it takes Jerry to drive from home to the supermarket	The amount of time it takes Jerry to drive from the supermarket to the hardware store

---

Percy is a contestant on a game show. There are 5 doors in front of him. Behind one of these doors is a boat, which he will win if he opens the correct door. He must open exactly 2 of the doors.

	Column A	Column B
33.	The probability that Percy will win the boat	$\frac{1}{25}$

	Column A	Column B
34.	x, if x, $x + 2$, and $x + 4$ are all prime	A prime factor of 64

Go on to the next page.

2

QR

All questions in this part have the following answer choices:
(A) The amount in column A is greater.
(B) The amount in column B is greater.
(C) The two amounts are equal.
(D) The relationship cannot be determined from the information provided.

There are more pennies than nickels in a collection of coins. There are more nickels than dimes. There are more dimes than quarters. The value of the pennies totals 4 cents.

	Column A	Column B
35.	10%	The percentage of the total amount of money in quarters

	Column A	Column B
36.	The units digit of $11 \times 12 \times 13 \times 14 \times 15$	The tens digit of $21 \times 22 \times 23 \times 24 \times 25$

The town council decided to survey a group of men and a group of women to see if they were FOR or AGAINST a planned renovation to the town hall. To estimate how both groups would vote, Maggie decided to ask a small sample of each group to see how they would vote. The results of Maggie's findings are shown in the table below.

Group	Men	Women
VOTE: FOR	5	20
VOTE: AGAINST	10	10
% of Group Sampled	20%	40%

	Column A	Column B
37.	The number of men who are expected to vote AGAINST	The number of women who are expected to vote FOR

STOP. Do not go on until instructed to do so.

STOP

RC

Section 3

Reading Comprehension

3

Questions: 36

Time Limit: 35 minutes

There are six passages in this section. There are six questions associated with each passage, for a total of 36 questions. The correct answer for each question will be based on what is either stated or implied in the related passage. You may take notes in your test pamphlet.

Questions 1-6

A tipi (also: tepee, or teepee), is a cone shaped tent. Unlike other cone shaped tents, tipis have an opening at the point of the cone that vents smoke. Tipis were used by many groups of people because they were durable, maintained a comfortable temperature in all seasons, and kept people dry during rain or snow. Other positive attributes that contributed to the popularity of the tipi were its portability and simplicity.

To build a tipi, a builder first tied together the ends of several wooden poles with a long rope, leaving the opposite ends of the poles untied. The number of poles varied by region and by custom, as did the type of wood used. The basic frame would then be stood upright, with the untied ends planted into the ground to form the base of the cone. The tied ends of the poles formed the tip of the cone, from which extra rope would hang.

After the frame was raised, the builder would place supporting poles between each of the primary poles. Holding the length of extra rope that hung from the point of the cone, the builder would walk around the base of the tipi several times, winding the rope across all of the poles of the frame. By pulling tight and tying down the rope, the supporting poles were secured to the primary poles, forming a completed frame.

Once completed, the builder would then proceed to encase the frame of poles with animal hide – typically buffalo skins – or canvas. The material would be raised to the crown of the tipi and rested on the tip of the frame. It was then stretched down and wrapped around the completed frame such that the ends of the covering would meet at a seam. This seam was usually covered by a smaller animal hide or cloth, forming a door. At the base of the tipi, the skin was pegged to the ground, which created a stable shell around the entire tipi.

The builders and users of tipis were masters of both construction and deconstruction. It is estimated that a small team of experienced builders could erect a tipi in less than an hour and have it taken down in about the same time. The speed with which the tipis could be set up and taken down allowed the users to move quickly and efficiently. Because many of the users of the tipi did not settle in permanent locations, often traveling with animal herds or with the seasons, the portability, simplicity, and durability of the tipi was prized and widely used.

Go on to the next page. ➡

3

RC

1. One of the main points of the passage is to

   (A) detail different types of portable shelters.
   (B) explain how different groups of people used shelters differently.
   (C) describe how a certain type of shelter can built up and taken apart.
   (D) compare and contrast the benefits and challenges of portable shelters.

2. In line 48, the word "efficiently" most nearly means

   (A) without any experience.
   (B) without much difficulty.
   (C) with a great deal of effort.
   (D) with the help of many people.

3. The phrase "construction and deconstruction" (line 42), refers to

   (A) pegging and unpegging seams.
   (B) setting up and taking down tents.
   (C) building and breaking down doors.
   (D) building permanent settlements and towns.

4. Which of the following best describes the organization of the second, third, and fourth paragraphs?

   (A) a series of steps and actions
   (B) opinions supported by facts
   (C) a number of different opinions
   (D) details related to a specific event

5. According to the author, all of the following qualities contributed to the tipi's popularity EXCEPT

   (A) comfort.
   (B) durability.
   (C) simplicity.
   (D) inexpensiveness.

6. The passage's style is most similar to the style of a(n)

   (A) fairytale.
   (B) autobiography.
   (C) encyclopedia entry.
   (D) magazine advertisement.

Go on to the next page. ➡

RC

3

Questions 7 – 12

The Metropolitan Museum of Art in New York City, commonly known as the Met, is home to one of the world's greatest collections of art. Occupying nearly four square blocks on the eastern edge of Central Park, the Met is a grand example of the Beaux-Arts architectural style. Both the exterior and the interior are heavily influenced by classical designs, such as long rows of elegant columns, soaring domes, massive arched windows, and grand staircases.

Endless halls and rooms filled with paintings, sculptures, and other antiques entice visitors to wander for hours, or even days. The collection is so large that return visitors are often greeted with new displays and exhibits, as artifacts are rotated in and out of shelves and display cases.

The museum has the ability to transport visitors to a different time and place. Down one hall are heroes and gods of Greek and Roman mythology immortalized in marble; down another are vases, jewelry, and scrolls from the Chinese Ming dynasty; in yet another are medieval European swords, crossbows, and spears. Interested in Micronesian tribal carvings? The Met has a room for that. Want to learn more about Aztec sculptures from the 16th century? The Met has a wing dedicated to art in the Americas.

Gallery after gallery honeycombs each floor. Many galleries are filled with glass cases protecting pottery, coins, and clothing. However, not all of the art hides behind glass. The Met itself is a work of art. Sometimes, an entire room is an exhibit, as is the case of gallery 534, which displays a 16th-century patio from the Castle of Vélez Blanco. The original marble fittings from the patio were sold to a private collector in the early 20th century. Nearly two thousand blocks of the original marble were later reassembled at the Met in the mid-20th century.

Whether one chooses to admire a wrought iron staircase, read about an African tribal mask, or walk through the Egyptian Temple of Dendur, the Met houses enough culture to satisfy a lifetime of learning and curiosity. In addition, the Met itself speaks to us through its own artful features.

Go on to the next page. ➡

3

RC

7. Which sentence best expresses the passage's main idea?

 (A) Art has a strict and narrow definition.
 (B) Curiosity is an important trait to possess.
 (C) The greatest museum in the world is the Met.
 (D) A museum can be as much art as the collection of art it contains.

8. The main purpose of the first paragraph (lines 1-10) is to

 (A) explain why the Met was created.
 (B) describe the appearance of the Met.
 (C) compare different styles of architecture.
 (D) detail the extent of the Met's art collection.

9. In line 12, "entice" most nearly means

 (A) attract.
 (B) confuse.
 (C) impress.
 (D) repel.

10. The phrase "the ability to transport visitors to a different time" (lines 18-19), refers to

 (A) the superiority of classical art.
 (B) the ability of visitors to relate to all art.
 (C) the large amount and wide variety of art housed at the Met.
 (D) certain parts of the museum that allow visitors to actually time travel.

11. The patio from the Castle of Vélez Blanco mentioned in lines 34-41 can best be interpreted as an example where

 (A) the museum itself is art.
 (B) art can be admired by everyone.
 (C) visitors must observe the art through glass.
 (D) the art should be returned to its original owner.

12. The author would support which of the following statements about art?

 (A) Art is often all around us.
 (B) Architecture is not a form of art.
 (C) Classical art is the most deeply respected type of art.
 (D) The only art is that which is displayed inside museums.

Go on to the next page. ➡

RC

3

Questions 13 – 18

Of all the holidays that my family celebrates, Thanksgiving is my absolute favorite.

My extended family only gets together during two holidays: Thanksgiving and Christmas. Because of this, Thanksgiving is usually the first and one of the only times I get to see my whole family. Our family is scattered across the country – some live in the southwest, some live in the northwest, and others, like me and my immediate family, live in the northeast. With everyone taking the same day off from school or work, Thanksgiving is a great opportunity for me to catch up with my cousins, aunts, and uncles.

Everyone travels to our house for Thanksgiving. I'm not sure how it was decided that we would host Thanksgiving, but I don't mind one bit. While it makes sense to me that Thanksgiving be celebrated only a few miles away from where the pilgrims landed, perhaps the weather has more to do with it than anything else. Where I live, the winters are very cold, and since nobody in my family particularly cares for the cold, we go to my Aunt Helen's home in California to celebrate Christmas.

While my cousins and I play video games all day, the house fills quickly with the delicious, warm aromas of Thanksgiving dinner. Every hour or so, we'll take a break to run into the kitchen, drawn by the sweet tang of baking fruit, the warm smell of spices, or the hearty and unmistakable scents of roasting meats. Our parents, chiding us beneath half-stifled smiles, send us out with a little snack and a warning not to return until dinner.

And what a dinner it will be! While I don't particularly care for the turkey that we always have, I'm a huge fan of the side dishes. I'll usually have a second (and sometimes even a third!) helping of each side: mashed potatoes and gravy, sweet potatoes with candied pecans, baked green beans with crunchy onions on top, pineapple bake, and, of course, stuffing. By the end, though I'm too full to eat anymore, I'll suffer through a slice (or two or three) of pumpkin, apple, or pecan pie.

Between the days off from school, the family, and the food, there's really nothing quite like Thanksgiving.

Go on to the next page. ➡

3

RC

13. Which of the following sentences best expresses the main idea of the passage?

    (A) Different holidays are compared.
    (B) Customary holiday foods are listed.
    (C) A personal memory and preference is portrayed.
    (D) Weather in different parts of the country is described.

14. In line 33, the word "chiding" most nearly means

    (A) praising.
    (B) reminding.
    (C) scolding.
    (D) teaching.

15. It can be inferred from the passage that the author would agree with which of the following statements?

    (A) Food is the most important part of any holiday.
    (B) Christmas is a better holiday than Thanksgiving.
    (C) Spending time with family is an important part of a holiday.
    (D) Video games should only be played on days when there is no school.

16. All of the following are reasons why the author enjoys Thanksgiving EXCEPT

    (A) that his family hosts the holiday.
    (B) that he spends time with his friends.
    (C) that the traditional food is delicious.
    (D) that family visits from around the country.

17. The author's tone when describing how he will "suffer through…pie" (line 45) can best be described as

    (A) sarcastic.
    (B) serious.
    (C) shocked.
    (D) sympathetic.

18. Which of the following best describes the organization of the passage?

    (A) A process is presented and later clarified.
    (B) An initial theory is described and later changed.
    (C) Reasons for a preference are followed by detailed examples.
    (D) A guess is ventured, considered, and proven to be incorrect.

Go on to the next page. ➡

RC

3

Questions 19 – 24

More and more, people rely on machines, such as computers and televisions, for both work and entertainment. As a result, people are spending more time sitting. According to many studies, sitting for extended periods of time can lead to a number of health issues. Despite the host of health problems associated with sitting, there are several ways to mitigate the negative results of sitting for a long time.

During a long sit, muscles burn less fat and blood flows more slowly than when the body is active. This allows fatty materials to more easily clog blood vessels. Sitting for a long time has been shown to lead to high blood pressure and cholesterol levels. In addition to being bad for the heart, sitting also causes the pancreas to produce more insulin, which can lead to diabetes.

While changes to the organs such as the heart and pancreas happen over time, many people can feel the immediate effects of prolonged sitting in their muscles and bones. People who sit for long periods of time often complain of inflexibility and soreness. Especially in the back and neck, collagen can harden around the tendons and ligaments that support the spine, resulting in stiffness. People who sit for extended periods of time are at a greater risk of damaging the discs in their spine than those who move around regularly. In addition, when it comes to bone strength, sitting has the opposite effect of exercise: lack of activity associated with sitting results in soft bones that are more easily broken.

Even if people wanted to move around more and sit less, the reality of many jobs and forms of entertainment is that people experience them in a seated position. Are people supposed to quit their jobs and stop watching movies?

Not necessarily. If sitting for a prolonged period of time is absolutely necessary – for instance, as a job requirement – proper posture can help prevent many of the negative effects of sitting. Proper posture means sitting up straight and not slouching, relaxing the shoulders, keeping the arms close to the sides at right angles, and planting the feet firmly on the floor.

While proper posture might help arrest or prevent some of the health issues associated with prolonged sitting, stretching and exercise can help to reduce the negative effects of some of these issues. Simple stretches that loosen the muscles, tendons, and ligaments in the hips and back can be effective in soothing soreness and releasing tightness.

While correcting posture and performing stretches both help to relieve the symptoms of long and frequent sitting, exercising remains the best way to stay healthy. While regular and vigorous exercise is best, even going for an occasional walk is better than nothing.

Go on to the next page. ➡

3

RC

19. The author would most likely agree with which statement about health?

    (A) Sitting for a long time will result in permanent health problems.
    (B) An active lifestyle can help prevent many problems related to sitting.
    (C) When it comes to sitting, some resulting problems are worse than others.
    (D) Any negative results of sitting for a long time have not yet been proven.

20. Which of the following sentences best expresses the main idea of the second paragraph (lines 10-17)?

    (A) Performing stretches can help regulate insulin levels.
    (B) Sitting for a long time can have long-term consequences.
    (C) There are many immediate side-effects resulting from prolonged sitting.
    (D) People should stop watching movies and television in order to spend less time sitting.

21. The passage suggests that

    (A) stretching is the only way to reduce soreness.
    (B) proper posture can permanently fix all health concerns.
    (C) the primary cause of diabetes is sitting for long periods of time.
    (D) there is a link between some health issues and relying heavily on machines.

22. The passage implies that exercise can have which of the following effects?

    (A) Exercise can help increase bone strength.
    (B) Sitting is a legitimate form of exercise.
    (C) Stretching is the most effective form of exercise.
    (D) Too much exercise can be as damaging to the body as not exercising enough.

23. In line 49, "reduce the negative effects of" most nearly means

    (A) alleviate.
    (B) deteriorate.
    (C) impair.
    (D) migrate.

24. Which of the following best describes the organization of the passage?

    (A) A procedure is described in order.
    (B) A memory is fondly recalled and described in great detail.
    (C) Terms are defined and explained using examples and stories.
    (D) A theory is put forward and possible solutions are discussed.

Go on to the next page. ➡

RC

3

Questions 25 – 30

The designation of national parks and protected wilderness areas is one of the greatest accomplishments of governments around the world. Governments and their people recognize the importance of setting aside land for recreational enjoyment and preservation. The laws that protect some of the world's most beautiful and often fragile ecosystems often run against the interests of businesses. However, national parks are proof that making money does not require the destruction and exploitation of natural resources. In fact, the preservation of unique environments can lead to its own economic benefits.

Yellowstone National Park in the United States was established in 1872 as the world's first national park. Ferdinand Hayden, explorer and conservationist, is widely credited with helping to convince the United States Congress to withdraw the region from public auction. He stated that the country should "set aside the area as a pleasure ground for the benefit and enjoyment of the people." He warned that otherwise, people would "make merchandise of these beautiful specimens." Hayden cited Niagara Falls as an example, which had been taken advantage of by businesses and money-making schemes. Hayden went on to say that "vandals who are now waiting to enter into this wonder-land, will in a single season despoil, beyond recovery, these remarkable curiosities, which have required all the cunning skill of nature thousands of years to prepare."

At the time, many countries had already afforded certain areas national protection and reserve status. Still, the widespread classification of national parks in other countries did not occur until after the creation of Yellowstone. Royal National Park was established in Australia in 1879; Rocky Mountain National Park was established in Canada in 1885. The first national parks in Europe were established in Sweden in 1909, followed by the Albert National Park in the Congo in 1925.

At the time, many businesses complained about the loss of economic opportunity. This is because the national park designation kept businesses away from many natural resources. For example, businesses could make a lot of money very quickly by cutting down trees to sell as lumber. However, businesses gained a long-term opportunity to make money in the form of ecotourism. Today, domestic and international tourists flock to national parks around the world, increasing tourism and encouraging environmentally friendly development. Countries such as Costa Rica have seen, over the past two decades, a significant increase in their tourism rates.

Surviving two world wars and countless other threats, national parks are a treasure for all humanity. These lands are worthy of preservation for future generations. Natural wonders are so easily destroyed, yet take so long to develop. It would be a shame to see works of nature destroyed forever just to make money.

Go on to the next page. ➡

3

RC

25. One of the main purposes of the passage is to

    (A) provide a list of national parks.
    (B) describe prominent features of national parks.
    (C) highlight the importance of tourism to the economy.
    (D) convince the reader that national parks are valuable in many different ways.

26. In line 24, the phrase "make merchandise of" most nearly means

    (A) exploit.
    (B) package.
    (C) pollute.
    (D) steal.

27. The author uses the direct quotations from Ferdinand Hayden (lines 29-33) in order to

    (A) describe laws that protect fragile ecosystems.
    (B) question the motivations of conservationists.
    (C) emphasize the urgency behind environmental preservation.
    (D) explain the events behind the establishment of Rocky Mountain National Park.

28. It can be inferred from the passage that the author would agree with which of the following statements?

    (A) All businesses are greedy and short-sighted.
    (B) Governments do not do enough to protect wilderness areas and national parks.
    (C) Many businesses prefer making money in the short-term over the long-term.
    (D) Other countries are better at conserving nature than the United States.

29. According to the passage, some businesses did not support national parks because

    (A) it was necessary to use resources in those areas to support wars.
    (B) the most important thing is not making money, but enjoying nature.
    (C) they wanted to make money selling natural resources in many of those areas.
    (D) they were concerned about preserving land for their children and grandchildren.

30. According to the author, which statement helps to justify environmental preservation?

    (A) Nature is resilient and does not need any help from people.
    (B) Niagara Falls is an example of a beautiful wilderness area.
    (C) Yellowstone National Park is one of the first national parks in the world.
    (D) Some countries have been able to make money while at the same time protecting nature.

Go on to the next page. ➡

RC

3

Questions 31 – 36

Many schools look at participation in extracurricular activities as a sign that students are "well-rounded." As a result, many students and parents have begun to see extracurricular activities not as hobbies or as places to make friends, but as boxes on an application to be checked. However, there are many other reasons for students to participate in extracurricular activities. Parents and students often lose sight of the fact that involvement in extracurricular activities can help to improve social skills and physical fitness. Extracurricular activities can also develop interests and hobbies that can last a lifetime.

In ancient Athens, physical and intellectual education was linked with activity. While bodies were trained in gyms, minds were trained both in school and through observation of the world itself. In today's society, education is often viewed as a purely intellectual pursuit. Many believe that learning is best conducted in a classroom or behind a desk.

However, extracurricular activities offer an opportunity for students to see ideas learned from a book take life in the real world. In fact, many of the principles that students learn about in books had their origins in everyday observation! For example, it was through observation of the stars that Copernicus, Galileo, and Kepler developed mathematical models describing the orbits of the planets around the Sun. Classroom learning has its merits. But educators, parents, and students should not discount the value of hands-on experiences and observations such as those that might be gained from involvement in a science club.

Sharing these experiences and observations with others can help students to develop friendships and meaningful relationships. Students who find that they have a shared interest can join together and learn from one another on a regular basis. A friendship forged by a shared experience can be many times stronger than a friendship between students who simply happen to sit near each other in class.

Perhaps some of the strongest friendships are those established by people who work together toward a common goal. Athletics can often provide participants with a sense of belonging. It can also help students learn the value of perseverance and hard work. It also teaches things that are not readily learned in books or in the classroom – things like teamwork, humility, and healthy competition. In addition to these less tangible benefits, athletic extracurricular activities help to keep the body active and healthy.

While students and parents may see extracurricular activities as an obligation, it may be more beneficial in the long-run to think of extracurricular activities more simply: as a way to grow and develop outside of the classroom. Clubs, groups, and athletics offer students a way to learn things that are not easily learned from books. They also allow students to learn about the world through their own eyes and with their own hands. Extracurricular activities are an important supplement to a classroom education.

Go on to the next page. ➡

3

RC

31. Which of the following sentences best expresses the main idea of the passage?

    (A) Learning is best pursued in a classroom with teachers.
    (B) There are many reasons to participate in extracurricular activities.
    (C) Modern education should model itself after ancient practices.
    (D) Today, students are too busy, and do not have time for extracurricular activities.

32. The phrase "boxes on an application to be checked" (lines 6-7) refers to the view that

    (A) extracurricular activities are like a chore or obligation.
    (B) students enjoy participating in extracurricular activities.
    (C) extracurricular activities benefit students in many different ways.
    (D) parents are only interested in the long-term benefits of extracurricular activities.

33. According to the author, an ancient Athenian would likely support which of the following statements about modern education?

    (A) Books alone are enough for a complete education.
    (B) Classroom learning is sufficient for most students.
    (C) Physical training is something to be pursued on a student's own time.
    (D) Modern education does not focus enough on learning outside of the classroom.

34. In line 34, "discount" most nearly means

    (A) count on.
    (B) pay less than.
    (C) think more of.
    (D) write off.

35. The main purpose of the fourth and fifth paragraphs (lines 37-57) is to

    (A) show how athletics are more important than other types of activities.
    (B) explain the importance of extracurricular activities on school applications.
    (C) describe both intangible and physical benefits of extracurricular activities.
    (D) illustrate how extracurricular activities are more valuable than classroom learning.

36. Which of the following best describes the organization of the passage?

    (A) Scientific principles are discussed and compared.
    (B) A personal experience is analyzed piece by piece.
    (C) A point of view is shared and supported by various ideas and examples.
    (D) Different types of extracurricular activities are listed and described.

STOP. Do not go on until instructed to do so.

STOP

MA

Section 4
Mathematics Achievement

4

Questions: 47

Time Limit: 40 minutes

Each question in this section is followed by four answer choices. Select the best answer from the four answer choices. You may write in your test booklet. Remember to fill in the corresponding bubbles on your answer sheet.

Example: Ann has twice as many books as Bob. Bob has twice as many books as Cindy. If Cindy has 20 books, how many books does Ann have?

(A) 5
(B) 10
(C) 40
(D) 80

Example Answer

A B C D

The correct answer is 80, so circle D is darkened.

4

MA

1. Area of a parallelogram = $b \times h$.

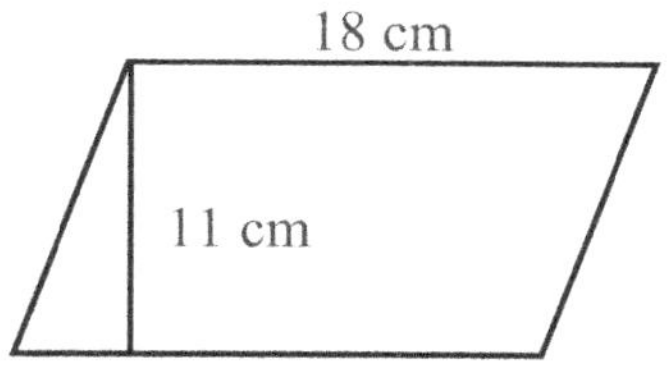

What is the area of the parallelogram shown above?

(A) 121 cm^2
(B) 198 cm^2
(C) 297 cm^2
(D) 324 cm^2

2. Which of the following answer choices is equivalent to the equation $4x - 4 = 5y + y$?

(A) $4(x - 1) = y(5 - 1)$
(B) $4(x - 1) = y(5 + 1)$
(C) $-4(x + 1) = y(5 + 1)$
(D) $-4(x - 1) = y(5 + 1)$

3. The diagram below represents a bathroom that will be covered in square stone tiles, which are shown by the dotted lines.

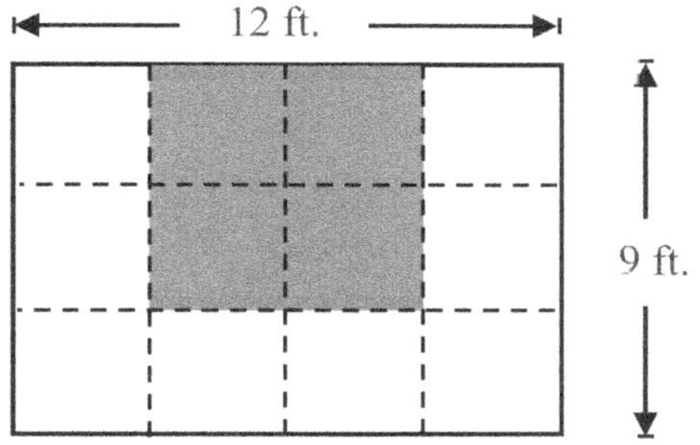

The shaded region represents the area of the shower that will be placed in the bathroom. About how many square feet of marble will **not** be covered by the shower?

(A) 12 square feet
(B) 24 square feet
(C) 36 square feet
(D) 72 square feet

4. A standard American coin is tossed into the air three times in a row. What is the probability that it will land on heads all three times?

(A) $\frac{1}{2}$

(B) $\frac{1}{3}$

(C) $\frac{1}{6}$

(D) $\frac{1}{8}$

5. 1 apple = 3 bananas
1 apple = 6 grapes
Using the conversions above, how many bananas are equivalent to 1 grape?

(A) 0.5
(B) 1.0
(C) 2.0
(D) 3.0

6. Joe has a water bottle filled with 4 liters of water. If he drinks half of the water, how many milliliters (mL) of water does he have left?

(A) 2 mL
(B) 20 mL
(C) 200 mL
(D) 2,000 mL

7. A square (not shown) has an area of 36 in^2. What is the perimeter of this square?

(A) 6 inches
(B) 12 inches
(C) 24 inches
(D) 36 inches

Go on to the next page. ➡

MA

4

8. From the time of his 2nd birthday to his 6th birthday, Frederick grew 3 inches per year. During this time, how many feet did Frederick grow? *Note: 1 foot = 12 inches*

(A) 0.50 feet
(B) 0.75 feet
(C) 1.00 foot
(D) 1.25 feet

9. Which of the following choices is equivalent to the expression $3(9x + y)$?

(A) $3x + \frac{y}{3}$
(B) $9x + \frac{y}{3}$
(C) $27x + 3y$
(D) $3x + 3y$

10. Professional sandcastle builders create a pyramid with a square base. The pyramid's volume is 18 ft^3, and stands 6 feet high. What is the area of the pyramid's base?

(A) 1 sq. ft.
(B) 3 sq. ft.
(C) 9 sq. ft.
(D) 18 sq. ft.

11. Henry read 50 pages of his book last night. This morning, Henry read 75 pages of his book. What was the percentage increase in the number of pages he read?

(A) 25%
(B) 33%
(C) 50%
(D) 66%

12. What is the value of x in the equation $63 = 5x + 8$?

(A) 5
(B) 11
(C) 21
(D) 55

13. The numerical expression 5,283 – 9,515 has a value of

(A) –4,232
(B) –4,332
(C) 4,332
(D) 4,232

14. Which of the following choices is equal to the expression 1.5 – 0.24 + 10.261?

(A) 10.521
(B) 10.837
(C) 11.521
(D) 11.737

15. Bartholomew is 6 feet tall. At 5pm, his shadow is 20 feet long, as shown in the diagram.

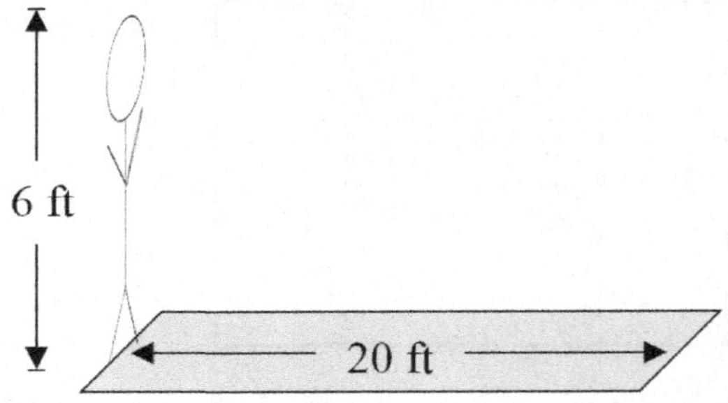

At the same time, the shadow of a flagpole is 60 feet long. What is the height of the flagpole?

(A) 6 ft.
(B) 12 ft.
(C) 18 ft.
(D) 24 ft.

Go on to the next page.

4

MA

16. If $3x - 2 = 4$, then which of the following choices must $15x - 10$ equal?

    (A) 2
    (B) 4
    (C) 20
    (D) 30

17. Rectangle *PQRS* (not shown) has a width of 4 and a length of 8. What is the area of a rectangle similar to rectangle *PQRS* with a scale factor of $\frac{3}{2}$?

    (A) 32
    (B) 36
    (C) 48
    (D) 72

18. What is the least common multiple of 15 and 36?

    (A) 3
    (B) 9
    (C) 180
    (D) 540

19. What is the value of q in the equation $2\frac{1}{6} + 4\frac{2}{3} = q$?

    (A) $6\frac{1}{3}$
    (B) $6\frac{1}{9}$
    (C) $6\frac{5}{6}$
    (D) $10\frac{5}{6}$

20. A farmer has 5 goats that can eat all the grass in a field in exactly 7 days. If the farmer sells 1 goat, what fraction of the field can the remaining goats eat in the same amount of time?

    (A) $\frac{4}{7}$
    (B) $\frac{5}{7}$
    (C) $\frac{4}{5}$
    (D) $\frac{5}{4}$

21. Which of the following choices is equivalent to $0.\overline{33} + 0.8$?

    (A) $\frac{41}{100}$
    (B) $\frac{11}{24}$
    (C) $1\frac{2}{15}$
    (D) $1\frac{4}{15}$

22. x represents an integer less than -1. Which choice represents the least quantity?

    (A) x
    (B) x^2
    (C) x^3
    (D) x^4

23. To make toothpicks, 25% of the 200 trees in a jungle were cut down during 2014. During 2015, 30% of the remaining trees were cut down. How many trees remained at the beginning of 2016?

    (A) 90
    (B) 105
    (C) 110
    (D) 120

Go on to the next page. ➡

MA

4

24. A right triangle has 5-inch legs. Which of the following choices is closest to the length of the triangle's hypotenuse? *Note: the lengths of a right triangle's sides is* $c^2 = a^2 + b^2$.

(A) 5 in.
(B) 7 in.
(C) 10 in.
(D) 12 in.

25. If $\sqrt{n+2} = m$, then which expression is equal to n?

(A) $2(m - 1)$
(B) $m^2 - 2$
(C) $(m - 2)^2$
(D) $\sqrt{m} + 2$

26. Maria's pocket contains q quarters, n nickels, and nothing else. If a coin is picked at random from her pocket, the probability that a quarter is picked is $\frac{3}{5}$. What is the value of $\frac{n}{q}$?

(A) $\frac{2}{3}$
(B) $\frac{3}{5}$
(C) $\frac{2}{5}$
(D) $\frac{1}{3}$

27. A man that weighs 2 kilograms on Mars would weigh 6 kilograms on Neptune. If an object weighs 7.5 kilograms on Neptune, how much would it weigh on Mars?

(A) 2.5 g
(B) 22.5 g
(C) 225 g
(D) 2,500 g

28. The following table shows the relationship between the value of x and the value of y:

x	1	2	3	4	5
y	1.25	2.5		5	6.25

Based on the relationship between x and y shown above, what is the value of y when x is 3?

(A) 2.25
(B) 2.75
(C) 3.25
(D) 3.75

29. The temperature at 6 A.M. was –8°C. By noon, the temperature was 14°C higher. What was the temperature at noon?

(A) –22°C
(B) 6°C
(C) 14°C
(D) 22°C

30. In the expression below, $y \neq 0$. Which of the following choices is NOT equivalent to the expression $y + \frac{y^2}{2y}$?

(A) $2y$
(B) $y + \frac{y}{2}$
(C) $y + \frac{y \times y}{y + y}$
(D) $y + (y^2 \div 2y)$

Go on to the next page. ➡

4

MA

31. Lamilla's purse contains 7 black hair-ties, 3 pink hair-ties, and 5 blue hair-ties. She loses 5 hair-ties, 3 of which are black. If she then reaches into her purse and picks out a hair-tie at random, what is the probability that it will be black?

(A) $\frac{2}{5}$

(B) $\frac{7}{10}$

(C) $\frac{4}{15}$

(D) $\frac{7}{15}$

32. One of a trapezoid's bases is 6 inches. Its height is 4 inches and its area is 36 inches. What is the length of the other base? *Note: area of a trapezoid* = $h\left(\frac{b_1 + b_2}{2}\right)$.

(A) 4 in.
(B) 6 in.
(C) 12 in.
(D) 18 in.

33. A circle is inscribed in a square, as shown.

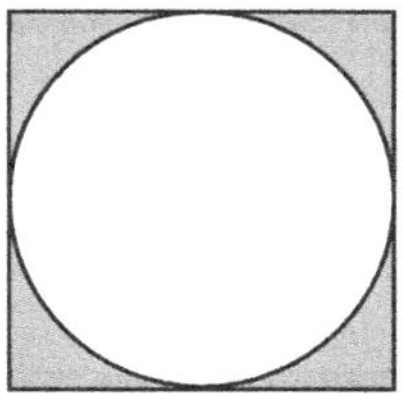

If the side length of the square is 4 inches, what is the area of the shaded region, in square inches?

(A) 8 sq. in.
(B) 16 sq. in.
(C) $4 - \pi$ sq. in.
(D) $16 - 4\pi$ sq. in.

34. The original cost of a DVD was $50. On Monday, the DVD was placed on sale for 10% off. On Tuesday, the DVD was marked up 10% from its sale price. What was the price of the DVD on Tuesday?

(A) $45.00
(B) $49.50
(C) $50.00
(D) $55.00

35. A pizza shop charges $10 for a pizza with one topping. Customers may buy additional toppings for $1.25 per topping. Which expression represents the cost, in dollars, of a pizza with x toppings?

(A) $8.75x$
(B) $11.25x$
(C) $10 + 1.25x$
(D) $10 + 1.25(x - 1)$

36. A newspaper editor can proofread an average of 150 words every 9 minutes. At this rate, how long will it take the editor to proofread 500 words?

(A) 15 minutes
(B) 30 minutes
(C) 45 minutes
(D) 60 minutes

37. In a standard deck of 52 playing cards, there are 4 aces and 4 kings. If one card is chosen at random, and then returned to the deck, and a second card is chosen at random, what is the probability that the first card will be an ace and the second card will be a king?

(A) $\frac{2}{52}$

(B) $\frac{4}{52} \times \frac{3}{52}$

(C) $\frac{1}{13} \times \frac{1}{13}$

(D) $\frac{1}{13} \times \frac{3}{52}$

Go on to the next page.

MA

4

38. The table below shows the number of times a certain value occurs in a set of values.

Value	Number of Times Appearing in Set
1	4
2	3
3	2
4	1

What is the mean of the values in the set?

(A) 2
(B) 3
(C) 4
(D) 5

39. A designer is ordering t-shirts for \$10.00 each, with an additional tax added per shirt. There is also a flat shipping fee added to each order. The table gives the total cost, including the shipping cost of \$10.00 per order, for four different order sizes.

COST OF T-SHIRTS

T-Shirts Ordered	Total Order Cost
2	\$32.00
4	\$54.00
6	\$76.00
8	\$98.00

What is the percentage of sales tax charged per shirt?

(A) 2%
(B) 10%
(C) 20%
(D) 50%

40. If Fiona has x pennies, and she has 8 fewer quarters than pennies, which expression represents the amount of money, in dollars, that Fiona has?

(A) $0.26x - 2$
(B) $0.26x + 2$
(C) $0.01x + 2x$
(D) $0.01x - 2x$

41. While measuring the door, Jon accidentally used centimeters instead of meters and got an unusually large area: 18,473 cm^2. What would the area have been if Jon measured the door to the nearest tenth of a meter?

(A) 0.2 m^2
(B) 1.8 m^2
(C) 18.5 m^2
(D) 184.7 m^2

42. What is the median of the first six prime numbers?

(A) 4
(B) 5
(C) 6
(D) 7

43. Store A sells a certain magazine for \$60. Store B sells the same magazine for 20% less than Store A. Store C sells that magazine for 10% more than Store B. How much does that magazine cost at store C?

(A) \$43.20
(B) \$52.80
(C) \$66.00
(D) \$72.00

Go on to the next page.

4

MA

44. Over the course of the year, Joe won a certain number of tennis matches. Kevin won 0.7 times as many tennis matches as Joe. Larry won 1.3 times as many as Kevin. Who won the most matches?

(A) Joe
(B) Kevin
(C) Larry
(D) Joe and Larry tied for most matches won.

45. Sam got a jar of marbles for his birthday. $\frac{1}{4}$ of the marbles were green, $\frac{1}{3}$ of them were red, and the rest were orange. If there were 10 orange marbles, how many total marbles were in the jar?

(A) 17
(B) 22
(C) 24
(D) 35

46. Two cars, one red and one blue, are driving down a straight raceway. Both cars started driving at the same time and place. The red car drives at a speed that is 4 times as fast as the blue car's speed (B). After 20 minutes, they are 2,000 feet apart. Which equation, when solved for B, would give the speed of the blue car, in feet per minute?

(A) $20(B + 4B) = 2{,}000$
(B) $80B - 20B = 2{,}000$
(C) $8B - 2B = 2{,}000$
(D) $80B + 20B = 2{,}000$

47. Lorna has taken three tests so far in her science class. Her scores on these tests are 94, 72, and 88. The score on her final exam will be counted twice in her mean. What is the lowest score she can get on her final exam and have a mean score of no less than 86?

(A) 45
(B) 86
(C) 88
(D) 90

good leader and good follower part
okay to fail, to learn from mistakes
better to try something new, grow confidence, new talent
kids should to have phones in emergency, rules, only after school passion

STOP. Do not go on until instructed to do so.

STOP

Essay Topic Sheet

Use the pre-lined pages in the answer sheet of this practice test to answer the essay topic.

You have 30 minutes to complete the essay. This includes planning and writing time. You are **only** to write on the topic written on the other side of this page. You **may not** write on another topic. No other topic will be acceptable.

This essay is an opportunity for you to show how you write. You should try to express your thoughts clearly enough for a reader to understand what you mean. However, how well you write is more important than how much you write.

You may want to write more than a brief paragraph. A copy of this essay will be sent to each school that is receiving your test results. You may only write on the pre-lined pages in the answer sheet. Print or write in cursive legibly, so that someone who has not seen your handwriting before can read your writing.

You may plan and take notes on the next page. However, only the writing on the pre-lined pages of your answer sheet will be accepted.

You may write only in black or blue ink.

There are additional directions on the other side of this page.

success meant doing best growing learning right thing
New students, open up, help her translate to english, she knew ideas good
part of team, people had different ideas, play crew, feel team
good friend, loyal, kind creativity
better to be kind than honest, truth may hurt, can say truth wrong don't hurt
We should chose the people we work with sometimes, new people
New class - life skill, useful, fun, baking, budget confident
I enjoy learning hands on than books, see results, see how it works
Meet leonardo de vinci, how he came up with ideas inspire curious
Superpower teleport, visit friends, help others, visit good places, explore observing
I would invent a mood miror, advice, hard time expresing feelings understand
I would live in paris 1920s, cafe, time of art, meet chanel, inspirer
I would go to Greece it has beaches, history gods, food, islands, culture
Perfect school, kind, handson

Essay Topic

Tell about a time you did something nice for someone else.

You may only write on this essay question.

Write down the topic below on the first few lines of your answer sheet.

Only the pre-lined pages of the answer sheet will be sent to schools.

Only write in black or blue ink.

Notes

- Interview a person: J.K. Rowling how she came up with idea
- Change one thing about school: flexible schedule less stress
- Fav. book: Sinclair's mysteries - braveness, normal people can do good
- important lesson never lie, honesty trust
- New skill - different languages, travel, book, help people, cultures connect
- Struggle - succeed - public speaking practice proud its okay to be scared
- President of US - better schools, art, creative learning to be happy then a better future
- Time failed at something - dance team no failure, feedback of growing
- fave teacher. Ms Lopez, brought dog, food, funny help learn
- good friends better happiness, [illegible] friends know who you are
- Character from book Sinclair, thoughtful, friendship calm, think, dont need to be loud to make difference
- Free speech protected, environment, people can be afraid to talk, no hate
- learn from mistakes. We dont grab attention when we succeed, but mistake resilient
- no good deed goes unpunished, sometimes backfire, comes from heart
- fondest memory = summer in france, bday w/ family, simple
- tech make world smaller tech bring people together
- field trip paris art cuz learn, history culture creativity exciting story, details
- community engagment proud, needs, meet people, responsibility

Scoring the Final Practice Test (Form B)

Using your answer sheet and referring to the answer key at the back of the book, calculate the percentage of questions you answered correctly in each section by taking the number of questions you answered correctly in that section and dividing it by the number of questions in that section. Multiply this number by 100 to determine your percentage score. The higher the percentage, the stronger your performance in that section.

Note that the actual test will not evaluate your score based on percentage correct or incorrect. Instead, it will evaluate your performance relative to all other students in your grade who took the test.

Record your results here:

Section	Questions Correct	Total Questions	Percent Questions Correct
Verbal Reasoning	_____	40	_____%
Quantitative Reasoning	_____	37	_____%
Reading Comprehension	_____	36	_____%
Mathematics Achievement	_____	47	_____%

Carefully consider the results from your practice test. If you're not happy with any of the results, take another look through the related section's practice questions to see if there is any more studying and preparing you can do. If necessary, revise your study plan based on these results.

Remember, the Middle Level ISEE is given to students in grades 6-7. When you take the actual test, your scores will only be compared with other scores of students in your grade.

Unless you've finished 7th grade, chances are that there is material on this test that you have not yet been taught. If this is the case, and you would like to improve your score beyond what is expected of your grade, consider outside help – such as a tutor or teacher – who can help you learn more about the topics that are new to you.

Answer Keys

The answer key to this practice test can be found at the back of the book in the Answer Key section. The keys are organized by section, and each question has an answer associated with it. Visit www.thetutorverse.com for detailed answer explanations.

The answer explanations for the practice test also describe the content area tested by each question. Use this information to help identify which sections of the book to revisit. Students should ask a parent or guardian's permission before going online. Note that there are no answers provided to the essay sections. Instead, consider having a tutor, teacher, or other educator review your writing and give you constructive feedback.

Get a Scaled Score Report @ thetutorverse.com/digital

Looking for an estimated Scaled Score Report? First, save your printed bubble sheet!

Then, navigate to thetutorverse.com/digital. Scroll to the "Get a Score Report" feature and follow the on-screen instructions. You'll be prompted to create or log in to your account on thetutorverse.com.

More Practice Tests Available Online

Need to take more practice tests? Want to work through more practice sections? Check out our computer-based practice on thetutorverse.com/digital. Take a fully-timed, automated practice test. Or, work through thousands of additional practice questions. Get this workbook for FREE using the code at the front of this workbook.

Answer Keys

This section provides the answer solutions to the practice questions in each section of the workbook except for the diagnostic test, practice test, and essay sections. The answers to the diagnostic and practice tests immediately follow their respective tests. There are no answers provided to the essay sections. Instead, consider having a tutor, teacher, or other educator review your writing and give you constructive feedback.

Remember: detailed answer explanations are available online at http://www.thetutorverse.com/. Students should ask a parent or guardian's permission before going online.

Diagnostic Practice Test (Form A)

Verbal Reasoning

1. B	6. B	11. B	16. C	21. A	26. B	31. B	36. D
2. B	7. C	12. B	17. C	22. D	27. B	32. B	37. A
3. C	8. D	13. C	18. B	23. A	28. C	33. A	38. B
4. C	9. D	14. B	19. B	24. B	29. A	34. B	39. D
5. B	10. A	15. B	20. A	25. A	30. A	35. C	40. B

Quantitative Reasoning

1. A	6. B	11. B	16. B	21. D	26. D	31. B	36. C
2. D	7. D	12. C	17. B	22. C	27. A	32. A	37. A
3. D	8. D	13. B	18. B	23. C	28. D	33. C	
4. B	9. A	14. B	19. B	24. D	29. B	34. C	
5. A	10. C	15. D	20. D	25. A	30. C	35. A	

Reading Comprehension

1. A	6. B	11. D	16. A	21. A	26. C	31. B	36. C
2. D	7. C	12. D	17. C	22. C	27. A	32. D	
3. C	8. C	13. B	18. C	23. B	28. C	33. C	
4. D	9. C	14. C	19. C	24. D	29. D	34. C	
5. B	10. A	15. B	20. A	25. D	30. B	35. B	

Mathematics Achievement

1. D	7. D	13. B	19. C	25. B	31. C	37. A	43. A
2. B	8. B	14. A	20. D	26. C	32. A	38. D	44. A
3. C	9. B	15. B	21. A	27. D	33. D	39. B	45. B
4. D	10. A	16. B	22. B	28. C	34. C	40. C	46. C
5. A	11. B	17. C	23. A	29. B	35. C	41. C	47. D
6. A	12. B	18. A	24. A	30. C	36. A	42. B	

Verbal Reasoning

Synonyms

Introductory

1. B	6. B	11. A	16. A	21. D	26. B	31. D
2. D	7. A	12. D	17. D	22. C	27. B	32. A
3. D	8. D	13. C	18. D	23. C	28. C	33. C
4. A	9. A	14. B	19. D	24. D	29. B	
5. B	10. D	15. A	20. A	25. B	30. D	

Intermediate

1. B	6. A	11. A	16. B	21. D	26. D	31. D
2. B	7. D	12. B	17. A	22. C	27. A	32. A
3. A	8. A	13. C	18. A	23. D	28. A	33. C
4. A	9. D	14. C	19. B	24. A	29. A	
5. D	10. D	15. B	20. D	25. B	30. A	

Advanced

1. C	6. C	11. C	16. A	21. C	26. C	31. D
2. D	7. B	12. D	17. A	22. B	27. A	32. C
3. D	8. C	13. C	18. B	23. D	28. A	33. A
4. A	9. B	14. D	19. C	24. A	29. B	
5. D	10. C	15. D	20. A	25. A	30. A	

Sentence Completion

Introductory

1. A	6. B	11. C	16. B	21. B	26. A	31. A
2. B	7. D	12. C	17. D	22. A	27. C	32. C
3. D	8. A	13. A	18. A	23. C	28. D	33. C
4. D	9. B	14. B	19. D	24. A	29. C	
5. C	10. A	15. D	20. D	25. C	30. B	

Intermediate

1. B	6. C	11. B	16. A	21. B	26. B	31. C
2. A	7. D	12. B	17. D	22. C	27. B	32. B
3. C	8. B	13. A	18. A	23. B	28. A	33. A
4. B	9. C	14. B	19. D	24. C	29. B	
5. A	10. C	15. A	20. D	25. C	30. B	

Advanced

1. B	6. D	11. B	16. A	21. B	26. C	31. D
2. D	7. B	12. C	17. A	22. C	27. C	32. D
3. A	8. D	13. A	18. C	23. B	28. C	33. B
4. C	9. B	14. C	19. D	24. D	29. A	
5. D	10. A	15. A	20. C	25. B	30. A	

Reading Comprehension

Passage 1	Passage 5	Passage 9	Passage 13	Passage 17	Passage 21	Passage 25	Passage 29
1. B	1. A	1. D	1. A	1. B	1. A	1. C	1. C
2. B	2. D	2. B	2. D	2. C	2. C	2. B	2. B
3. D	3. B	3. A	3. A	3. D	3. A	3. A	3. B
4. D	4. D	4. A	4. D	4. A	4. A	4. C	4. B
5. D	5. C	5. C	5. C	5. D	5. B	5. D	5. B
6. D	6. C	6. A	6. D	6. D	6. C	6. A	6. D

Passage 2	Passage 6	Passage 10	Passage 14	Passage 18	Passage 22	Passage 26	Passage 30
1. D	1. C	1. A	1. D	1. C	1. C	1. D	1. C
2. D	2. D	2. B	2. A	2. D	2. A	2. B	2. A
3. A	3. C	3. D	3. D	3. D	3. D	3. B	3. A
4. A	4. D	4. C	4. A	4. A	4. B	4. A	4. D
5. C	5. D	5. B	5. C	5. D	5. A	5. D	5. D
6. A	6. B	6. C	6. A	6. D	6. C	6. C	6. C

Passage 3	Passage 7	Passage 11	Passage 15	Passage 19	Passage 23	Passage 27
1. C	1. D	1. D	1. D	1. B	1. B	1. D
2. A	2. B	2. A	2. A	2. A	2. A	2. D
3. C	3. A	3. A	3. B	3. C	3. B	3. A
4. D	4. A	4. A	4. A	4. A	4. A	4. D
5. C	5. B	5. C	5. A	5. B	5. D	5. B
6. A	6. C	6. C	6. B	6. D	6. C	6. D

Passage 4	Passage 8	Passage 12	Passage 16	Passage 20	Passage 24	Passage 28
1. B	1. A	1. A	1. C	1. A	1. D	1. C
2. B	2. B	2. B	2. A	2. B	2. B	2. A
3. C	3. A	3. C	3. C	3. A	3. B	3. C
4. C	4. A	4. D	4. D	4. C	4. A	4. A
5. A	5. C	5. B	5. A	5. D	5. C	5. C
6. B	6. D	6. A	6. B	6. A	6. D	6. D

Quantitative Reasoning & Mathematics Achievement

Integers

1. C	3. C	5. A	7. D	9. C	11. A
2. B	4. C	6. B	8. C	10. D	12. B

Fractions

1. A	4. C	7. D	10. B	13. A	16. C	19. D
2. B	5. A	8. A	11. A	14. C	17. A	20. A
3. D	6. D	9. D	12. C	15. C	18. A	21. B

Decimals

1. B	4. C	7. D	10. D	13. B	16. A	19. A
2. A	5. C	8. C	11. B	14. B	17. A	
3. B	6. D	9. B	12. C	15. A	18. D	

Percents

1. A	4. D	7. C	10. C	13. A	16. B	19. C	22. A
2. B	5. B	8. A	11. C	14. C	17. B	20. B	23. C
3. C	6. B	9. B	12. D	15. A	18. C	21. B	24. A

Factors, Multiples, Primes

1. A	4. D	7. B	10. D	13. C	16. C	19. B
2. A	5. A	8. A	11. B	14. B	17. C	20. D
3. D	6. D	9. C	12. A	15. B	18. A	

Estimation

1. A	4. D	7. C	10. C	13. B	16. B	19. C
2. D	5. A	8. A	11. D	14. B	17. A	
3. B	6. C	9. B	12. C	15. C	18. B	

Numbers & Operations Mixed Practice

1. B	4. D	7. D	10. C	13. D	16. B
2. D	5. C	8. C	11. C	14. A	17. A
3. B	6. C	9. D	12. C	15. A	18. C

Solving Algebraic Equations

1. C	5. D	9. C	13. A	17. D	21. A	25. A
2. A	6. A	10. A	14. C	18. D	22. B	26. C
3. B	7. A	11. C	15. A	19. A	23. A	27. D
4. D	8. C	12. B	16. C	20. B	24. B	

Ratios, Proportions, & Scale Factor

1. D	5. B	9. C	13. A	17. A	21. A	25. A
2. C	6. D	10. B	14. A	18. A	22. C	
3. C	7. D	11. B	15. A	19. C	23. B	
4. D	8. A	12. A	16. B	20. A	24. B	

Functions & Patterns

1. B	5. B	9. B	13. D	17. B	21. D	25. C
2. A	6. D	10. C	14. B	18. C	22. B	
3. C	7. A	11. D	15. A	19. C	23. C	
4. B	8. C	12. C	16. C	20. D	24. D	

Slope

1. C	3. b	5. B	7. C	9. D	11. C	13. D	15. A
2. B	4. C	6. A	8. C	10. C	12. A	14. C	16. C

Algebraic Concepts Mixed Practice

1. C	3. B	5. B	7. D	9. D	11. B	13. B	15. C
2. B	4. A	6. B	8. A	10. C	12. B	14. B	16. D

Formulas

1. D	3. C	5. A	7. C	9. A	11. D	13. D	15. A
2. C	4. D	6. B	8. A	10. D	12. A	14. A	

Units

1. A	3. B	5. A	7. A	9. A	11. A
2. B	4. D	6. D	8. B	10. C	12. C

Geometric Objects

1. B	4. C	7. D	10. D	13. A	16. D	19. C
2. D	5. A	8. C	11. D	14. D	17. C	20. C
3. D	6. D	9. D	12. B	15. D	18. B	

Coordinates

1. A	3. D	5. A	7. A	9. D	11. A
2. C	4. D	6. D	8. D	10. D	12. D

Measurements & Geometry Mixed Practice

1. D	3. C	5. B	7. C	9. B	11. C	13. C
2. C	4. B	6. D	8. D	10. A	12. B	

Probability

1. C	5. D	9. A	13. A	17. D	21. C	25. C
2. B	6. C	10. C	14. C	18. C	22. C	26. B
3. C	7. A	11. B	15. C	19. D	23. A	27. A
4. A	8. A	12. C	16. D	20. C	24. A	

Mean, Median, Mode, & Range

1. B	4. D	7. B	10. D	13. D	16. C	19. B	22. B
2. A	5. B	8. D	11. C	14. B	17. B	20. D	
3. D	6. C	9. C	12. A	15. C	18. B	21. B	

Interpreting Data

1. A	4. A	7. B	10. B	13. C	16. D	19. D
2. C	5. D	8. C	11. C	14. A	17. D	20. A
3. D	6. B	9. B	12. C	15. C	18. C	

Data & Probability Mixed Practice

1. A	3. D	5. C	7. C	9. B	11. C
2. C	4. C	6. B	8. C	10. B	12. A

Final Practice Test (Form B)

Verbal Reasoning

1. C	6. D	11. A	16. D	21. A	26. B	31. B	36. D
2. B	7. D	12. B	17. A	22. D	27. C	32. A	37. B
3. D	8. A	13. C	18. A	23. C	28. A	33. D	38. D
4. A	9. A	14. C	19. B	24. A	29. B	34. C	39. B
5. A	10. D	15. C	20. D	25. C	30. A	35. C	40. A

Quantitative Reasoning

1. D	6. B	11. A	16. C	21. B	26. A	31. B	36. C
2. B	7. B	12. C	17. C	22. A	27. A	32. A	37. C
3. D	8. C	13. A	18. C	23. C	28. B	33. A	
4. B	9. A	14. B	19. D	24. A	29. B	34. A	
5. B	10. D	15. C	20. C	25. A	30. C	35. B	

Reading Comprehension

1. C	6. C	11. A	16. B	21. D	26. A	31. B	36. C
2. B	7. D	12. A	17. A	22. A	27. C	32. A	
3. B	8. B	13. C	18. C	23. A	28. C	33. D	
4. A	9. A	14. C	19. B	24. D	29. C	34. D	
5. D	10. C	15. C	20. B	25. D	30. D	35. C	

Mathematics Achievement

1. B	7. C	13. A	19. C	25. B	31. A	37. C	43. B
2. B	8. C	14. C	20. C	26. A	32. C	38. A	44. A
3. D	9. C	15. C	21. C	27. D	33. D	39. B	45. C
4. D	10. C	16. C	22. C	28. D	34. B	40. A	46. B
5. A	11. C	17. D	23. B	29. B	35. D	41. B	47. C
6. D	12. B	18. C	24. B	30. A	36. B	42. C	

Made in the USA
Las Vegas, NV
23 July 2025

25294323R00131